CHILD MIGRANT VOICES I
MODERN BRITAIN

CHILD MIGRANT VOICES IN MODERN BRITAIN

ORAL HISTORIES 1930s-PRESENT DAY

Eithne Nightingale

BLOOMSBURY ACADEMIC
LONDON • NEW YORK • OXFORD • NEW DELHI • SYDNEY

BLOOMSBURY ACADEMIC
Bloomsbury Publishing Plc
50 Bedford Square, London, WC1B 3DP, UK
1385 Broadway, New York, NY 10018, USA
29 Earlsfort Terrace, Dublin 2, Ireland

BLOOMSBURY, BLOOMSBURY ACADEMIC and the Diana logo
are trademarks of Bloomsbury Publishing Plc

First published in Great Britain 2024

A catalogue record for this book is available from the British Library.

A catalog record for this book is available from the Library of Congress.

ISBN: HB: 978-1-3503-3261-4
        PB: 978-1-3503-3260-7
        ePDF: 978-1-3503-3263-8
        eBook: 978-1-3503-3262-1

Typeset by Integra Software Services Pvt. Ltd.
Printed and bound in Great Britain

To find out more about our authors and books visit www.bloomsbury.com
and sign up for our newsletters.

To Abdul Momen

who set me on this path, and from whom I learnt so much

CONTENTS

List of illustrations   ix
Acknowledgements   x
Biography   xii

Introduction   1

1   **"If then, why not now?"**   17
    Blanca Stern (née Schreiber) and Necha (Natalie) Gluck (née Dux) who
    arrived from Austria, aged eight and ten respectively, in 1938

2   **No man's land**   29
    Duncan Ross who arrived from India, aged eight, in 1956

3   **Precious cargo**   39
    Argun Imamzade who arrived from Cyprus, aged fourteen, in 1964

4   **Following mum to the 'motherland'**   51
    Richard Lue and Roberta who arrived, aged seven and eight respectively,
    from Jamaica in 1964

5   **"I much prefer roasted rat"**   63
    Maurice Nwokeji who arrived, aged nine, from Nigeria, in 1970

6   **The Battle of Brick Lane**   73
    Six young people who arrived from East Pakistan, subsequently
    Bangladesh, aged eleven to sixteen, between 1969 and 1973

7   **A Pakistani Scot with a Mid-Atlantic drawl**   89
    Zohra who arrived from Pakistan in 1975

8   **Out of her depth**   97
    Linh Vu who arrived, aged seven, from Vietnam in 1979

9   **A child soldier who knew too much**   107
    Henry Bran who arrived, aged seventeen, from El Salvador in 1981

Contents

10 "Caught in a flow of water"   117
    Eylem Binboga who arrived, aged twelve, from Turkey in 1987

11 Love of the motherland   125
    Ahmed Ali, originally from Somaliland, who arrived, aged eleven, via
    Djibouti in 2004; Said who arrived, aged sixteen, from Somalia in 2012

12 Girl power – finding a talent and following a dream   135
    Bilqis who arrived from Yemen as a teenager in 2005 and Nimo Jama
    who arrived, aged fifteen, from Somaliland, in 2009

13 On her own   143
    Mariam who arrived, aged sixteen, from Guinea in 2006

14 "Home is where the love is"   151
    Yosef, originally from Eritrea, who arrived aged sixteen, in 2011

15 Seeking sanctuary on a Scottish Island   157
    Syrian children who arrived from Lebanon, aged six to sixteen, on the Isle
    of Bute, Scotland in 2015

16 "We will win"   167
    Mariia who arrived, aged thirteen, from Ukraine in 2022

Conclusion   175
"If I had a magic wand": Final thoughts and insights

Notes   194
Index   223

ILLUSTRATIONS

1   Manuhar and Salam during walking interview on Brick Lane with Eithne, March 2014. Courtesy of *Child Migrant Stories*   9

2   Gershon Dux and Rivkah Dux (née Hacker), parents of Necha (Natalie) Gluck (née Dux). Courtesy of Rabbi Herschel Gluck, OBE   26

3   Duncan, aged eleven, at Northwold Primary School, Hackney, 1959. Courtesy of Duncan Ross   35

4   Argun (right) and brother, Zizi (left) in a photographic studio in Paphos, Cyprus. Courtesy of Argun Imamzade   42

5   Argun showing his photograph album to his wife Hurmus and his grandchildren, Aleyna and Alara. From the film *Life Is a Destiny,* courtesy of *Child Migrant Stories*   47

6   Richard on the day of his confirmation, Stepney, east London. Courtesy of Richard Lue   58

7   Maurice performing songs featured in *Ugwumpiti* at the Being Human Festival Launch, Senate House, University of London, 2016. Courtesy of Maurice Nwokeji and Advanced School of Study, University of London. Copyright © Lloyd Sturdy   72

8   Akikur (left) and Jalal (right), launch of the Bangladesh Youth Movement. Courtesy of Rajonuddin Jalal   84

9   Linh, aged seven, with her father, Thanh Vu, in first refugee camp in Sopley, Hampshire, *c.* 1980. Courtesy of Linh Vu   101

10   Henry with his many guitars in London, *c.* 1984. Courtesy of Alicia Mc Keown, daughter of Henry Bran   111

11   Eylem in her café Brew for Two, May 2014. Courtesy of Eylem Binboga, Copyright © Eithne Nightingale   118

12   Marking the first week as an international household, a week after the arrival of Mariia and Shushik in Horsham in 2022. Courtesy of Riasenko and Barnett families   169

ACKNOWLEDGEMENTS

I am especially indebted to all those who, with great generosity, shared their lived experiences of child migration, co-produced films, participated in public engagement events and actively contributed to this research of whom many, but not all, feature in this book. I would like to thank their families, too, who have participated in several ways, particularly Alicia Mc Keown and Gabriela Bran after the death of their father, Henry Bran and Fazleh Elaahi, son of Abdus Salam, also deceased. I am grateful to those who bridged relationships with those who I interviewed – Thanh Vu, MBE, Ansar Ahmed Ullah, Jama Omar, Abul Azad, Rayah Feldman, Pat Till, Morag Brown, Michael Myers, Nicola Horton, Kate Duffy-Syedi, Cathy Forrester, Errol Forrester, David Barnard, Spitalfields Life and others.

Special thanks go to Professor Alison Blunt and Professor Kiera Vaclavik from Queen Mary University of London and Teresa Hare Duke, formerly of the V&A Museum of Childhood who supervised my AHRC-funded collaborative PhD on child migration; to Dame Diane Lees, DBE, then director at the V&A Museum of Childhood for whom I curated the *World in the East End* gallery, the inspiration for this research; to my writing mentor, Mary-Jane Holmes who helped devise the structure and has been at my side throughout; to John Reeve and Tim Bennett-Goodman who read and commented on the whole manuscript and to those who contributed, and advised on the use of, images. Further thanks go to those who brought specific expertise to individual chapters – Professor Tony Kushner, Ansar Ahmed Ullah, Professor Deborah Swallow, Professor Cathy McIlwaine, Professor Kavita Datta, Professor Alastair Owen, Clare Murphy, Jama Omar, Kazim Altan, Sarah Temple-Smith; members of my writing and reading groups; to those who advised me on key issues including the Nationality and Borders Act – Farhad Mo, Marieke Widman, Wendy Pettifer, Lisa Matthews, Sheila Melzak and Alfred Garwood; for support and advice on contemporary issues of child migration – Safe Passage, The Children's Society, Refugee Council, Baobab Centre for Young Survivors in Exile; Right to Remain; Care4Calais.

A strong feature of this research has been the development of the website, films and public engagement with partner organizations supported by Queen Mary's Centre of Public Engagement, Hassan Aliyu, V&A, Hackney Museum, Migration Museum, Museum of the Home, Ragged School Museum, Autograph ABP, Counterpoint Arts, Refugee Week, Kent Refugee Action Network, Brunei Gallery, Argyle and Bute Council, Hackney Community College, Sidmouth College, Norwich International Youth Project, Rio Cinema, art and refugee festivals in Glasgow, Deal, Oxford and elsewhere.

I am grateful, too for the inspiration and support of fellow writers and mentors at retreats in Spain and France – Casa Ana; Circle of Misse, particularly Wayne Milstead and

Emma Claire Sweeney; La Muse, particularly Artem Mozgovoy; to those who supported my wellbeing throughout – Peter Shoenberg and my neighbours, Helen Carmichael and John Dash who kept me going through COVID-19 and the writing of this publication with regular walks and meals al fresco in our joint garden.

A special thanks to my talented co-creator of *Child Migrant Stories*, Mitchell Harris who I met when he was studying film at Queen Mary and with whom I continue to be creative. And finally a heartfelt thanks to the team at Bloomsbury for believing in this book and for their continued support throughout.

BIOGRAPHY

Dr Eithne Nightingale is a freelance researcher, writer, photographer and film maker. See: eithnenightingale.com.

Eithne has forty years' experience of working on equality, migration and social justice issues in the education, cultural and community sectors in London. As Head of Equality and Diversity at the V&A Museum she co-edited *Museums, Equality and Social Justice*, 2012, and developed the *World in the East End* gallery. This was the inspiration for her AHRC-funded collaborative PhD on child migration, between Queen Mary University of London and the V&A Museum of Childhood, that she completed in 2019. She is the founder of the award-winning films and public engagement programme *Child Migrant Stories*. See: childmigrantstories.com. She is also a photographer and travel writer.

INTRODUCTION

Marie, surrounded by her mother and siblings, pointed to the soiled African cloth displayed in the *World in the East End*[1] gallery at the V&A Museum of Childhood in Bethnal Green. She was talking in Kinyarwanda, a language I recognized from the year I had lived in Central Africa. I didn't need to understand what she was saying. I knew the story and, besides, the label said it all. 'I dared not put down my brother for a second for fear he would be eaten by wild animals.'

Marie was twelve when, for six months during the Rwandan civil war in 1994, she carried her baby brother to the refugee camp in the Democratic Republic of Congo. Six years later, at the age of eighteen, when she worked as a researcher for the museum, she placed the bold green and black cloth, in which she carried her brother, into the 'Journeys' display case.

In 2003, as Head of Equality and Diversity at the V&A, based in South Kensington, I was tasked with ensuring the collections and audiences of the V&A Museum of Childhood in Bethnal Green, reopened as the Young V&A in July 2023, better reflected the lives of local people. The dolls houses, puppets, soft and mechanical toys represented the material culture of upper- and middle-class English childhood rather than that of young people of different ethnic, religious and socio-economic backgrounds living close to the museum. Researchers from Somali, Turkish, Bengali, Caribbean, African, East European, Traveller, East European Jewish and white East End working-class communities were employed to collect oral histories and related objects through their networks in Hackney, Tower Hamlets and Newham – three of the most culturally diverse boroughs in Britain. Eighteen months later the *World in the East End* gallery opened. Visitors of all backgrounds peered into cases at Vietnamese water puppets, a Chinese Barbie doll, a Galatasaray football shirt from Turkey, Jewish menorahs and mezuzahs from when nearly every street in the East End had a synagogue, and a cardboard caravan made by Tracey from the Irish Traveller community. Children rushed up to a girl's blue and silver costume, with matching feather headdress, pram and parasol, made by a Trinidadian carnivalist. They stood on tiptoes to read the Cockney, Cantonese and Kurdish playground rhymes sung by children skipping and whirling hula hoops – the canvas, painted by Dan Jones, a local artist who had collected the rhymes, had been hung too high. Those with longer attention spans listened to audios of bricks thrown through caravan windows by youth shouting, "Stinky Gypo"; of burning rags stuffed through letter boxes of Bangladeshi families and of graffiti scrawled in peoples' doorways, 'Go Home Wogs', 'No Blacks, No Irish, No Dogs'.

Child migration past and present

When the V&A Museum of Childhood collaborated with Queen Mary University of London to apply for three Arts and Humanities Research Council (AHRC) PhD studentships on *The Child in the World*, it was decided one would build on the work of the *World in the East End* gallery. This would focus on migration of children to east London since the 1930s based on people's oral testimonies – it was unlikely that anyone who came before 1930 would be alive to tell their story. As this was a collaborative PhD, a further aim was to share the findings of this research through public engagement at the museum and beyond. I leapt at the chance. The research seemed not only to provide a unique opportunity to draw on, and make sense of, different aspects of my life and work experience but, more importantly, to engage with one of the most pressing challenges worldwide.

By May 2022 the number of displaced people around the world because of conflict, violence, human rights violations or events seriously disturbing public order reached over 100 million for the first time on record. The number of refugees displaced outside their own country had risen to 26.3 million, both figures significantly impacted by the war in Ukraine.[2] Figures have consistently shown that approximately half of those displaced are under eighteen.[3] Brexit and the pandemic have been used to strengthen borders with Europe, leaving children, some with family in the UK, in refugee camps in Greece, Italy and France.[4] Unaccompanied asylum seekers, on arrival on British shores, are now threatened with deportation to Rwanda, if wrongly assessed as adults.[5] Since the government have started to accommodate them in hotels, hundreds have gone missing and are being trafficked across the country.[6] The TV documentary about how Sir Mo Farah, four times Olympic medallist, was trafficked to Britain as a nine-year-old and forced into domestic servitude has highlighted the issue of children as victims of modern slavery.[7] The conflict in Ukraine has caused the largest displacement of people in Europe since the Second World War, with almost 6 million having left by July 2022, many of whom are wounded and traumatized children.[8] The climate crisis too risks displacing millions, making whole regions of the world unhabitable.

The reasons for, and patterns of, migration of children featured in this book are varied. Some arrived with, or followed, adult family members from existing, or former, parts of the British Empire who came to study or fill gaps in the labour market after the Second World War. In the words of the Sri Lankan and British writer, A. Sivanadan, 'We are here because you were there.'[9] Some children arrived as refugees, fleeing war or other forms of discrimination and abuse. Two came on the privately organized child migration scheme, the *Kindertransport*, fleeing Hitler's Europe and leaving their families behind.

The literature, too, on child migration is varied, reflecting the different reasons for, and patterns of, migration although less in volume and scope than literature on adult migration, despite approximately 50 per cent of all migrants being aged under eighteen. Migration studies have often ignored children and childhood studies, ignored migration.[10] But in response to growing awareness that children are central to contemporary migration more recent interdisciplinary anthologies, have covered such wide-ranging topics as legal obstacles to family reunification,[11] transnational family relationships,[12] and society's ambivalence to child migrants from a historical, legal and political perspective.[13]

Studies on family migration, notably from a legal, sociological and psychological perspective, have explored how far children's rights, needs or desires are considered by adults.[14] How far are children consulted over such life-changing decisions and are their views listened to? A particular focus has been on the short- or long-term impact of step-migration when adults leave before their children.[15] Some suggest that this double disruption in emotional bonds, first with parents and then with extended family members who have cared for the children in the parents' absence, has been overstated,[16] ignoring the role of the extended family in caring for children across borders.[17]

Where child migrants do appear in statistics, academic and policy debates and in an increasingly hostile press, it is often as unaccompanied minors or as victims of trafficking.[18] Such studies can subject young people to simplistic binary classifications denying the complexity of their lived experiences. They may be viewed as vulnerable victims or a threat to the state;[19] as passive and needy rather than active agents in their own destinies;[20] as asexual and apolitical rather than sexually and/or politically active.[21] They may focus solely on the children's identity as refugees or migrants or on their experiences of trauma rather than on their resilience and agency.

It is child migration schemes, such as for poor or orphaned children from Britain to the colonies from 1860s to 1970 and to Britain on the *Kindertransport* from Hitler's Europe, that have received most attention by historians. The former scheme has been the subject of considerable controversy for sending children abroad without their parents' knowledge, some of whom were subject to physical and other abuse on farms in Canada or in institutions in Australia.[22] Although many of the 10,000 children who arrived on the *Kindertransport* in 1938 found safety and prospered in Britain, the predicament of the parents who had to let them go and the loss felt by children who never saw their parents again have rarely been confronted. Moreover, the *Kindertransport* scheme has been instrumentalized to show how generosity is integral to the British character, masking the barriers that the British government tried to put in place.[23]

History of migration to Britain, approaches and challenges

For much of the twentieth-century history was the poor relation of migration studies,[24] with refugees allowed only a walk on part, and as subjects rather than actors.[25] Studies of migration were mainly from a sociological or anthropological viewpoint, with the focus on the 'now'. Colin Holmes in *John Bull's Island: Immigration to Britain 1871–1971* (1988) argued that the 'now' of British migration cannot be understood without reference to the 'past'.[26] His work laid the foundation for a significant growth in the historical study of British migration as well as of racism and anti-immigration policies, confronting denial of Britain's colonial legacy and negotiating powerful mythologies about British tolerance and historical homogeneity.

John Bull's Island: Immigration to Britain 1871–1971[27] explored the history of fifty different ethno-religious groups that had migrated to Britain, drawing on novels, art, film, television, museums, memorials and personal testimony. Whilst his focus was on the nation, others have explored migration to the city, or spaces within it, with London considered unique for its interaction of people of different cultures, faiths, languages and immigration status.[28] This 'super-diverse'[29] city has become deeply multicultural despite anti-immigration hostility going back centuries. Such place-based work has laid the groundwork for other studies such as of Leicester's claims of multicultural success drawing on interviews with both immigrant and indigenous populations.[30] But there are undoubted omissions – other cities, towns and rural spaces. As Caroline Bressey writes, 'white imaginaries of the English rural have ignored historical geographies of the black presence.'[31] Neither should place-based studies ignore migrants' 'toing' and 'fro-ing' across borders – single journeys to place of arrival and of settlement in people's increasingly transnational lives are rare, complicating feelings of home.[32]

A major focus for studies of migration, within and outside academia, has been on specific ethnic and religious groupings – Irish, Jews, Black people or Asians, four of the most visible and politically active communities in Britain. Both Peter Fryer in *Staying Power: The History of Black People in Britain* (1984)[33] and David Olusoga in *Black and British: A Forgotten History* (2016)[34] explore Black presence in Britain from Roman Times with Fryer writing that Africans were present in Britain before the English arrived. These have inspired other studies of less represented communities, such as the Polish[35] or Vietnamese,[36] as well as how class, gender or religion and, to a lesser extent, children and youth, have affected people's migratory experiences. Yet an exclusive focus on one ethnic or religious grouping can be constraining. It can neglect interactions between communities and community history, in particular, is susceptible to portraying a sanitized account – highlighting successes and downplaying discrimination.[37] Much important literature on the presence of Black and Asian populations in Britain focuses on second or subsequent generations given that immigration from 'coloured' parts of the British Empire became more restricted from the 1960s.[38]

The East End of London, with its long history of migration, has attracted the interest of researchers, journalists, novelists, community heritage organizations, oral historians and individuals.[39] Some have focused on place, notably Spitalfields settled, over 300 years, by Huguenots, Jews and Bangladeshis, becoming, in turn, Petty France, Little Jerusalem and Banglatown.[40] Others have focused on the history of specific ethnic and religious groups within east London – settlement of West Africans and West Indians in the 1970s,[41] the life and radical politics of Ashkenazi Jews escaping discrimination in Eastern Europe in the late nineteenth and early twentieth centuries,[42] the historic roots of Bangladeshi settlement in east London, from the arrival in the 1600s of Indian lascars (seamen), including Sylhetis from Bengal,[43] to contemporary studies of those who arrived in the twenty-first century covering politics,[44] education,[45] the role of women,[46] housing,[47] class, religion[48] and the complexity of British Islamic identities in the twentieth and twenty-first centuries.[49] There is less research into the history of migration of other communities to east London, for example, from Somalia. If we extend the original borders of the East End to include Hackney and Newham, in addition to Tower Hamlets, there are other communities, such as the Turkish in Hackney or East African Asians in Newham, that have been ignored. Nor do children feature prominently. Existing research, for example on Bangladeshi children in east London, relates to second and third generation migrants.[50] The East End has a long tradition of fighting fascism from when, in the 1930s, Irish and Jews united to drive Oswald Mosley and the fascists out of the East End during the Battle of Cable Street. This is part of our national history but the Battle of Brick Lane in the 1970s, and the involvement of Bangladeshi youth in fighting the National Front, less so.

Except for the child migrant schemes that sent British children to the colonies or organized the migration of children to Britain on the *Kindertransport*, there is a marked absence of child migrants in mainstream British history. Tony Kushner claims, 'We are still in our infancy in studying the inner lives of migrant groups in a British context (and all the global interests they represent) and the wider significance these have in defining that elusive concept of national identity.'[51] Perhaps, in terms of child migration, we are barely out of the cradle.

Oral history with migrants and refugees

'All history was at first oral', commented Samuel Johnson in the eighteenth century[52] but it was British historians in the mid-twentieth century who, in arguing for a history 'from below', laid the groundwork for its growth as a recognized methodology. The *Oral History Society Journal* was launched in 1971 followed by the foundation of the *Oral History Society* in 1973,[53] developments supported by Paul Thompson's *The Voice of the Past: Oral History*.[54] The publication helped oral historians gain scholarly credibility in the face of those who critiqued the 'subjective' nature of people's testimonies. Meanwhile, in the United States, oral historians, who first adopted a 'top down' focus on political, economic and cultural elites, turned their attention to race, class, gender and local communities. Since then, the movement has spread worldwide and now engages researchers, archivists, curators, local historians, educators and others.[55]

Partly in response to a lack of sources in mainstream historical discourse, migration has become one of the most important themes of British oral history. Migrant testimonies contribute both an empirical knowledge and a theoretical understanding of migration experiences, providing insights into everyday life that resonate with broader social and political contexts. They illustrate complex transnational connections, networks and family dynamics and highlight individual and collective experiences impacted by gender, race or class. But it is the 'subjective' nature of oral histories that is their strength as opposed to documents, reports and data – how individual motivations, perceptions and feelings, inform and shape the experience of migration.[56] Migrant testimonies demonstrate resilience even in the most traumatic circumstances, are replete with emotional intensity and human experience with the power to affect and move, making them a potential and significant, political tool.[57] Sylhetis in Tower Hamlets interviewed by Caroline Adams for *Across Seven Seas and Thirteen Rivers: Life Stories of Pioneer Sylheti Settlers in Britain* (1987)[58] were keen to tell their stories as they were 'feeling rather marginalised and neglected by the new generation. They were also very aware of their need to share their history and counter racism'.[59] Since then, new technology has opened up many creative ways for using applied oral history as a tool for empowerment, social or political change – using oral accounts to prosecute for war crimes or to design safer journeys for refugees coming behind.[60]

Questions of reliability of people's testimonies have been replaced by an interest in how memory works as an active process, with people engaged in the process of constructing their own narrative as they evaluate and make sense of their past. It is not a question of recalling past events with an accuracy that can be verified but of reworking and reinterpreting them. They are 'filtered through memory … arguably being reconstructed over time',[61] that along with the affective dimension leads to an enlarged 'notion of truth',[62] helping to form and reshape identity.[63]

Views and guidance about good practice in oral history with migrants and refugees have evolved over time. There are various debates, for example, about the pros and cons of the 'insider' or 'outsider' status and of matching the ethnicity/cultural background of the interviewer with the participant.[64] This has led to considerations about how researchers and community members can participate on equal terms and have a shared authority in the processes and products of historical work. Such issues have continued to concern politically engaged work with migrants and refugees.[65]

An open-ended approach allowing people to actively engage in processing their own narrative and to select what they share has been found to be more appropriate for migrants and refugees who have experienced loss or trauma.[66] Most important of all is to listen as 'If one talks about the trauma without being truly heard or truly listened to, the telling might itself be lived as a return to the trauma – a re-experiencing of the event itself.'[67] Researchers, on the impact of the Holocaust on survivors and their children, claim that while 'empathetic listening can actually be therapeutic' … '"bad listening" … can re-traumatise the witness'. Yet 'those who listen to witness testimony have the capacity to restore the victim's humanity and identity'.[68]

All ethical oral history practice includes securing informed consent on the basis that the participants have understood the aims and nature of the research, that participation is voluntary, anonymity is an option, people can withdraw at any time and personal data will be secure. Where children are involved then good practice is for both the responsible adult and child to be fully informed before both agreeing to participate.[69] Such issues, and the need to weigh up potential harm or benefits for participants, gain heightened significance when working with migrants and child migrants.[70] This is not separate from the nature of the relationship and the trust between interviewer and interviewee.[71]

Researching child migration

A key test, at the start of the research, was finding people willing to share their stories. For the *World in the East End,* I and my colleague, Teresa Hare Duke, were able to draw on the skills, insights and networks of paid, part-time researchers working with, and from, Bangladeshi, Somali, Caribbean, Turkish, Rwandan, East European, Traveller and white working-class East End communities. My only claim to being from a migrant background is that my mother migrated as a teenager from Ireland to London and then to Lancashire where I grew up – hence my Irish name, Eithne, which some mistake for 'ethnic', contributing to the mistaken impression that I am other than white. Given the demand by people of colour and from migrant backgrounds for publishing to be 'by us, not about us' I have tussled long and hard about how to approach the research and share these stories within the public domain.

I have, however, over forty years' experience of living and working in east London so set about reviving old networks. This was not straightforward. Many of the people I knew from working with the Caribbean Elders' Group, Asian Women's Group, Kurdish and Turkish groups in Hackney had long since left. Migrant and refugee organizations were overwhelmed with the number of research students approaching them.[72] Some saw little benefit in participating; others felt protective, wanting their users to look forwards rather than backwards, fearing recall of past events would reawaken past trauma, a fear I shared. There was the issue of trust and how the material would be used, particularly if the user's status in Britain was in question. Hundreds of emails, phone calls and leaflets, distributed to libraries, nail parlours, shops and community organizations, yielded few leads or people prepared to be interviewed.

A launch event at the V&A Museum of Childhood, where I explained the research, invited feedback and screened a short film about Marie, developed for the *World in the East End* gallery, was more successful. A youth worker introduced me to Surma,[73] a group of older Bengali men. They introduced me to the Somali seamen's luncheon group, many of whom were unclear what age they arrived in Britain, but Jama, the group organizer, introduced me to younger, more recent arrivals. Ansar Ahmed Ullah from Swadhinata Trust[74] reconnected me with Bangladeshi activists I knew when working as Director of Tower Hamlets Training Forum, setting up training initiatives with local clothing workers just off Brick Lane in the 1980s. Thanh Vu, whom I had met when the Vietnamese first settled in Hackney in the early 1990s, suggested I interview his daughter Linh who, aged seven, had escaped by boat with him from Vietnam. After the launch I ran into Henry Bran, a musician from El Salvador who had run one of the *My V&A* refugee tours.[75] I grew in confidence and started to recruit more people through local shops and cafes. Of the thirty-six people I interviewed who had come to east London (Hackney, Tower Hamlets and Newham) I knew half; another quarter I contacted through people I knew well. For a different initiative, *Child Migrants Welcome?*[76] I interviewed young migrants, and those who knew or worked with them, in different parts of Britain – on the Isle of Bute in Scotland, in Norwich and Sidmouth. The last people I interviewed, in 2022, were a mother and daughter from Ukraine in Horsham, Sussex, who again I contacted through friends in east London.

Building trust was helped by already knowing some of the interviewees through political activism against the National Front in the 1970s and 1980s and working on issues of equality and diversity in Hackney and at the V&A. I had visited several countries of origin – Bangladesh, India and Rwanda. Showing political support,[77] and knowing about and/or having lived in the place of origin can help build trust but so can having shared similar experiences and/or coming from a similar background,[78] for which I did not qualify. Although already knowing, or having worked and campaigned with, many of the interviewees were clearly reference points there is no doubt that if someone who was more of an 'insider' had carried out the interviews, other narratives and perspectives would have emerged.[79]

Interviews were held in cafes, workplaces, studios, a school, the V&A Museum of Childhood, people's homes, my home, wherever people felt comfortable. I asked open-ended response questions on childhood in the country of birth, departures, journeys, settlement, relationships, impact on adult life and feelings of home, allowing the interviewee to respond without interruption and accommodating unanticipated responses. I gave thought to the ordering of the questions, starting with 'Can you tell me about your life in east London' as opposed to talking about their journey to the UK, where I knew the latter had been harrowing. Given the open response approach, a second interview offered an opportunity to expand on what was said, to follow up on areas not previously covered and to cross-check specific details. For the most part I was led by what people felt important and keen to share, often abandoning the open-ended questions. One exception was with the group of Syrian school children on the Isle of Bute where, for safeguarding purposes and because of their level of English, questions were checked by the education authorities and responses were practised with their English teacher beforehand. On one occasion I used an interpreter, a community worker known to the interviewee, to communicate with a newly arrived sixteen-year-old.

Memories of childhood and of migration, particularly when children have fled wars, been separated from loved ones or faced racism and discrimination in Britain, inevitably bring up feelings of loss and pain. This can be the case even if the child, now an adult, migrated decades previously.[80] Not all interviews awakened traumatic memories, indeed many were full of humour and demonstrated incredible resilience, but some did. Whilst some guidance recommends halting or pausing the interview if people become tearful, I felt this could cut people off too abruptly. I asked one respondent if she would have wanted me to stop the interview and turn off the tape recorder to which she replied "No" saying she would have been unable to resume the interview afterwards. This no doubt depends on the level of stress, and it is crucial to recognize the limited role of the interviewer. On occasion I too shed a few tears – feminist practice does not discourage the interviewer expressing feelings.[81]

I used various methods, in addition to the oral history interview, that I adapted for different ages and abilities.[82] People unearthed and talked about family photographs, although many had been lost.[83] I devised art activities, initially for younger children – drawing a childhood home or of the journey to Britain[84] but some adults, too, responded. The drawings triggered memories, gave insight into everyday lives as well as into traumatic events but they also calmed people once they had overcome concern that they needed to be an artist to complete the task. Walking interviews allowed us to explore links between people and places of childhood significance, with research participants deciding on the route.[85] A walk along Brick Lane in east London, the return to a former refugee camp on the south coast, a visit to people's first home or school in Britain, all worked well. I wrote a diary reflecting on what I felt had worked or what could be improved, incorporating interviewees' own reflections that I gathered at the end of the interview.

I acknowledged and thanked people who had supported the research in different ways. This included returning transcripts for approval and copies of photographs or drawings. But I also found other methods – helping with the publication of a refugee's journey from Vietnam; encouraging a filmmaker to unearth his first film; taking photographs of jewellery for a website; attending a degree ceremony for someone without family in Britain and helping with a funding application for an oral history project with Somali seafarers. I was unable to help with someone's family immigration problems, illustrating the need to avoid raising unrealistic expectations.

Figure 1 Manuhar and Salam during walking interview on Brick Lane with Eithne, March 2014. Courtesy of *Child Migrant Stories*.

Inspired by the success of the film about Marie's experience of the Rwandan civil war I secured funds to develop a website and films based on interviewees' lived experiences and drawing on their literary, musical and artistic skills. For this I enlisted the help of a film student at Queen Mary University of London, Mitchell Harris. Within four years Mitchell and I co-produced, with research participants, a website and over twenty films.[86] The films have been displayed in galleries and incorporated into museum and education programmes. They have been screened widely across the UK and abroad, often followed by discussions with, and performances by, those featured.

One of the prevailing visual narratives of the migrant 'crisis' is of the dramatic, the frightening and the arrival of bodies on European shores.[87] There is sometimes a moment of compassion, for example, with the high-profile use of the image of Aylan Kurdi washed up on a Turkish beach.[88] The experience of *Child Migrant Stories* has confirmed my belief in the need for visual counter narratives to initiate more meaningful change over a sustained period, albeit in limited ways. Narratives that evoke empathy, not a distant pity; highlight agency, individuality[89] and humanize lives reduced to mere numbers and considered a threat to our security.[90]

One of the most interesting aspects of *Child Migrant Stories* was the positive impact not only on those featured in the films and their families but on those with direct experience of the specific issues or conflict represented. This was particularly so where injustices had been highlighted or where subsequent generations felt their parents or grandparents had kept experiences from them. The challenges and responsibilities, however, in developing sensitive, thoughtful portrayals drawn from the words of refugees, should not be underestimated,[91] and can only be achieved through genuine co-production and trust.[92]

I chose not to be the narrator for the films, editing out my questions and foregrounding the voices of child migrants. Eminent oral historians have adopted such an approach in text – using solely verbatim interview material.[93] Influenced by the remarks of John Reeve, previously of the British Museum, that "Oral history is often presented as a sort of sacred text that emerged from nowhere, fully formed" I rejected this approach for the book. Instead, I have inserted myself in the text providing context and some analysis but with a light touch. For many of these stories I have sourced historical material about, or from, countries or origin, including of civil wars, on social justice issues such as female genital mutilation and of relevant, and now historical, anti-racist and equal opportunity policies in Britain.

I have tried to sustain relationships with research participants – writing to thank participants after interviews, to update them on events, film screenings and, for those included from the original research cohort, about the publication of this book. Many have commented on, and contributed to, the chapters and all have given consent. Some have chosen to be anonymous, using a pseudonym; others have chosen to use their first name only. There are two approaches to consent – one focusing on the legal, static, factual and one-way consent and the other on negotiation, process, a two-way exchange, potentially empowering both participant and interviewer. I have chosen the latter.[94]

Key themes

Each chapter focuses on a child, or group of children, from the same country of origin as we progress from the 1930s to the present day. They draw on, illustrate and inform, studies into history, geography, sociology, psychology, law, human rights, education, childhood and migration studies.

Departures

When children migrate with, or to join, family the reasons for migrating are generally linked to why their parents leave – to find work or study; for personal reasons such as divorce or marriage; to escape war, poverty, discrimination, imprisonment or worse, or a combination of the above. Adults who migrate without their children may have no intention of staying in Britain, but sudden war or increasingly restrictive immigration legislation may persuade them to bring over their children. Immigration controls can split families for years meaning the recreation of family life becomes 'an elusive holy grail'.[95]

Children who follow one or both parents to a new country[96] can experience two sets of disruptions in 'affectional bonds'[97] – first when one or both parents leave, and later when the child leaves those who have cared for them in their parents' absence, often a loving aunt or grandmother.[98] Some believe that the effects of such disruptions can be exaggerated and based on a more Western view of what constitutes a family[99] disregarding the role extended families play in caring for children across borders.[100] A child's feelings of loss or abandonment, it is argued, can be mitigated by parents sending presents back, making return visits and effective communication between those who care about, and those who care for, children.[101] The father may leave first, the mother, supported by extended family, providing continuity of care before migrating with her children to join her husband. Or the mother may leave first, perhaps having split from the father and sending for the children later. New technology, over the decades, has revolutionized people's ability to sustain transnational family ties although this never replaces a child's desire to touch, see, hear and smell loved ones.[102]

Previous research into family migration has explored whether the child's needs and interests were a driving force for migration, absorbed into the broader interests of the whole family[103] or considered 'a burden on otherwise mobile adults'.[104] Studies have shown that adults rarely consult, or inform, children about migration,[105] giving them little time to prepare. This would seem to go against one of the four 'Ps' of the United Nations Convention on The Rights of the Child 1989 – 'participation' (in decisions that affect them), the other three being 'protection' (from discrimination, neglect and exploitation), 'provision' (assistance for their basic needs), 'prevention' (from harm).[106] Yet some argue that a 'quality of life' discourse, as opposed to a human rights discourse, can be more respectful of cultures that value collectivism, their elders and people in authority above individualism and autonomy.[107] Also at what age children know enough about the likely consequences of any decision, or the maturity to negotiate their wishes, is difficult to gauge. Children who leave on their own, perhaps, are in a stronger position to exercise agency, albeit often constrained by circumstances[108] and family considerations.

Journeys

Journeys can be life-changing for all migrants[109] but particularly important for children are the sensory aspects – the sounds, sights, tastes and smells of new places. Some children may treat the departure as an adventure, unaware of the danger they are in; for others it can be so traumatic that they block out all memory of it. Migration often involves multiple journeys, 'toing' and 'froing'[110] across cultural and linguistic borders, encountering a 'level of strangeness'.[111] Children can be fascinated or fearful about transport they have never used, food they have never tasted or languages they have never heard. They may face life-threatening situations 'en route', particularly if unaccompanied. Children's 'global imaginings'[112] of their destination, often influenced by media or other migrants' accounts, can affect children differently – from those who imagine streets paved with gold to those who have no idea where they are headed. Whether children travel on their own, with adults or with siblings; whether they have a loving send-off or are welcomed on arrival, can all impact on children's experiences.[113] There is a huge difference, too, between a child of seven and one of seventeen, the latter being the upper age limit defined by the United Nations Convention on the Rights of the Child (UNCRC). Some would argue that 'child' is a misnomer for an older teenager[114] so I have used 'youth' or 'young people' where this seems appropriate but any clear demarcation would seem arbitrary, remembering that concepts of childhood and adulthood and the minimum age to leave school, work, drive, join the military, marry, or be convicted of a crime, differ over time and place, particularly between the Global North and Global South.

Arrival

First impressions, on arrival in a new country, may dash, fulfil or surpass children's expectations. Children may be excited by snow but appalled by the cold, thrilled by the city lights but shocked by graffiti. Those used to rural, wide-open spaces and extended family households might feel constrained by the city environment and cramped accommodation. But it is the impact of migration on family and personal relationships that can be the biggest challenge. Anticipated reunions may be fraught, with children neither recognizing nor remembering the parent who left before them. This may be affected by the child's age, the length of separation and the depth of the child-parent bond before the adult left.[115] Parents and children might have changed in the interim causing rifts in understanding. New family constellations, following a divorce and re-marriage, can be problematic with children having to adapt to a stepparent and new siblings.[116] Joining other adult members of an extended family in a multi-occupational household also poses challenges. Many children adapt over time. Some re-establish strong emotional bonds with parents they have not seen for years, become close to new stepfathers and half-siblings but sometimes it takes years for the family to feel reunited, if it ever does.

Unaccompanied children may have travelled for years through different countries, have been imprisoned or trafficked. In Britain they may know no one of a similar background or who speaks the same language. Many will face intense scrutiny by the Home Office over their identity and age – perhaps being wrongly assessed as adults[117] and be unaware of where to seek advice. Living with strangers in a foster care arrangement or with other young people can bring additional challenges.[118] For such children peer friendships, as well as informed, supportive adults, become crucial.

Many children leave loved ones in the country of origin – grandparents, great aunts, parent/s, siblings and friends. Initially excited or overwhelmed by their new environment some may give little thought about who they have left. Others may be consumed with loss and lose all contact with relatives and friends abroad.[119] Only in later decades has new technology eased communication.

Family households are not static. Parents give birth to new children, return to their country of origin, migrate onwards, die, divorce and/or remarry changing a child's position overnight. There may be no extended family to support the child, and statutory authorities such as social services might be ill-equipped to intervene. Adolescence brings new challenges with possible inter-generational conflict within the family or with the wider community.[120]

Education

Education is an important vehicle for the child to gain social and cultural capital, to achieve their potential and reach their ambitions.[121] Delay in getting a school place, inadequate English language provision,[122] teachers' negative expectations,[123] hostile school environments and a school's reluctance to tackle racism or bullying, can all impact negatively on a young person's future – the nature and target of abuse may have changed over time, depending on the majority and minority make-up of specific schools, but it has not disappeared.[124] But an individual teacher who sees a child's potential, who provides that all important 'social link' which opens doors to opportunity,[125] can change a child's life. English language provision that allows children to participate in the mainstream curriculum and flexible access routes to further and higher education are particularly important for young people who arrive during their teenage years. The age of arrival, specific school or college and encouragement from peers and parents can all make a difference but so too can the child's motivation and determination.

Stepping out

As children settle, they begin to explore other spaces beyond home and school – youth clubs; sport, leisure and cultural venues; religious institutions and workplaces.[126] Such spaces can provide opportunities to make friends, pursue interests, follow religious practices or provide income for their family or themselves. But, depending on the place and year in question, these spaces can be alien, intimidating or hostile – streets where people are racially attacked; social, religious or workplaces that are discriminatory or less than welcoming;[127] cultural venues that do not resonate with young people's heritage or linguistic background.[128] In response, young people may carve out their own spaces along cultural, religious and gender lines – to meet others of a similar background, to explore their identity, as a buffer to racism and discrimination, for safety or political activism.[129] Others may consider cultural, religious or linguistic background irrelevant[130] and search out places that are more diverse, with people who are different.

Child migrants may become financially independent at a young age, often working part-time after school and at week-ends, perhaps sending money back to the country of origin, challenging notions of what are in the best interests of a child – attitudes to child labour may differ in countries from where many children migrate.[131] Just as teachers can play an important role in changing young people's lives so, too, can employers, religious leaders, youth workers, trade unionists or strangers from both migrant and non-migrant backgrounds – influencing career choices, offering housing and employment advice, providing support during a crisis. But children and young people also demonstrate their own resilience and agency.[132]

Impact on adult life

Interviewing people who have arrived since the 1930s – the oldest person I interviewed was eighty-eight – sheds light on how early experiences, such as disruptions in family relationships, exposure to war[133] and challenges of settlement, can impact on adult life. Of particular interest is how relationships, formed in adolescence and then in adulthood, are influenced by those early experiences;[134] whether, for example, they contribute to anti-social behaviour,[135] mental health[136] and intergenerational conflict. Young women caught between two or more cultures[137] may face tensions with parents, extended family and the broader community if they challenge cultural norms around marriage and careers.[138]

Or conversely early experiences of migration and settlement, including disruption in family life, may make child migrants more determined to sustain family unity across borders; to put down roots through marriage and children. This can bring new challenges around the transmission of the culture of origin to the next generation, both within ethnically mixed and non-mixed marriages, and around the potential of secondary traumatization – that is, children experiencing trauma indirectly through hearing details, or witnessing the aftermath, of a parent's trauma.[139] Externalizing trauma, reinforcing cultural identity, highlighting injustice and building resilience through creativity in music, art, poetry and film[140] have healing potential at any stage in life, but particularly where the pain is not expressed, or listened to, as a child.

Child migrants may return to their country of origin at different stages in life and for different reasons. Their experience may depend on the welcome they receive, the memories it evokes, whether dreams of an imagined homeland are realized or unfulfilled; whether it leads to feelings of disorientation or reaffirms feelings of home.[141] Or they may occupy a liminal space – one foot physically, culturally or imaginatively in the village or city of their birth and the other in an area of Britain. They may imagine a different life had they not migrated, where they would have been richer, poorer, happier. They may dream of a home they have left but cannot, or do not wish to, return to. They may have children, grandchildren, even great-grandchildren in Britain but wish to spend longer periods or retire in their country of origin. Or they may consider themselves firmly British or Jamaican, that bears little relationship to their actual citizenship or nationality.

Structure of the book

It is the child migrants' stories, creativity and insights that drive this book as I guide the reader through the decades, interweaving the present with the past. It opens with Blanca and Necha from the Orthodox Jewish communities who, in 1938, arrived on the *Kindertransport* that brought 10,000 children to Britain. The subsequent six chapters feature children from countries that were once part of the British Empire; of Duncan, an Anglo-Indian, caught up in post-partition conflict, who only discovered he was brown after arrival in Britain in 1956 and who still fears, on hearing Farage speak, that he may be sent back to India; of Argun, who rescued his photograph album from his grandfather's bombed-out house in Cyprus in 1964, amused at what his grandchildren said they would rescue in such circumstances; of Roberta and Richard, who arrived in 1964 from Jamaica, as part of the Windrush generation some of whom have been denied their rights, detained and deported. In 1970 Maurice joined his parents in London, having survived bombs and hunger in the Biafra war. Only as an adult, through music and Rastafarianism, did he confront the trauma he experienced as a child. Between 1969 and 1973 six young people, who arrived pre- and post- the War of Liberation that led to the creation of Bangladesh, helped to defeat the fascist National Front spouting 'Make Britain Great Again', a cry adopted by right-wing governments and populists today. And lastly Zohra, who came from Pakistan in 1975, and who creates intricate modernist jewellery inspired by Islamic design that reflects her dual heritage. Most of these children's parents came to the 'motherland' to study or work, sometimes invited by British employers or governments to meet labour shortages. Decisions to bring over their children were often influenced by civil war in the country of origin or, from the 1960s, increasing immigration controls that threatened family reunion.

The following chapters are mostly stories of flight; of Linh, who escaped by boat from Vietnam with her father in 1979, found refuge in art and later studied to be an architect; of Henry, who escaped from El Salvador in 1981 where he was recruited into the army, became a self-taught singer, artist and campaigner for child refugees – he, like Maurice, had seen the impact of civil war on children; of Eylem, whose family as Kurdish Alevis faced discrimination in Turkey, who studied art in Brighton and set up a successful business. Linh, Zohra and Eylem, all talented creatives, went to university and defied their parents' expectations by choosing partners outside their own community. Political conflict, in different parts of the world, drove others from their homes. Ahmed, originally from Somaliland, arrived in Britain via Djibouti in 2004; Bilqis arrived from Yemen in 2005; Nimo from Somaliland in 2009 and Said from war-torn Mogadishu, Somalia, in 2012, all regions that have experienced war and internal conflict for decades. Although most came with, or to join, at least one parent Ahmed found himself in the care of social services after his mother died soon after arrival – his father remained in Somalia. Said, on joining his father in Britain, had to leave his mother and three siblings in Mogadishu under threat from continual bombardment. Yosef, as a twelve-year-old, left Eritrea where mandatory army conscription lasts for decades, travelling on his own across Africa and Europe before he arrived in 2011. Syrian children, having fled war, arrived from Lebanon on the Isle of Bute in 2015 as part of the government's Vulnerable Persons Resettlement Scheme (VPRS). Mariia, aged thirteen, arrived in Horhsam in 2022 with her mother as part of the Homes for Ukraine programme. Mariam's motivation to leave Guinea, as a sixteen-year-old in 2006, was for a more personal reason – to avoid forced marriage and female genital mutilation.

In the concluding chapter I reflect on the core themes that emerge from these testimonies; what they say about how welcoming to child migrants we really are as individuals and as a nation; whether this has changed over time and on the challenges ahead – the hostile environment, government policies, conflict across the world and climate change. Acting as guide, I invite the reader to travel with me into the homes, schools and along the streets where children once played football or fought the fascists, threading together stories of loss and gain, of tragedy and joy.

CHAPTER 1
"IF THEN, WHY NOT NOW?"
Blanca Stern (née Schreiber) and Necha (Natalie) Gluck (née Dux)
who arrived from Austria, aged eight and ten respectively, in 1938

A small boy, holding Paddington Bear on the forecourt of Liverpool Street station in February 2017, lifted his placard, 'Refugees Welcome. Even Bears'. His mother, close behind him, raised her placard, 'Dubs Now: Let the Children In'. Demonstrators handed out leaflets, urging people to join the campaign and write to their MP. Some circled the bronze sculpture by Frank Meisler of five children staring into an uncertain future. An older girl, with plaits to her waist, gripped a battered case; a younger girl clutched a teddy bear; at the feet of a boy wearing a flat cap and dungarees, lay a violin case – belongings the children had packed for their escape on the *Kindertransport* from Germany, Austria, Czechoslovakia and Poland before the outbreak of the Second World War.

Impatient passengers rushed by until Rabbi Herschel Gluck OBE, an impressive figure with a white beard, black coat and crowned hat, broke away from the demonstration. Speaking through a megaphone he addressed the crowd, "My mother, having left her parents in Europe, arrived at this station eighty years ago. She never forgot the kindness of Rabbi Schonfeld who welcomed her off the train and presented her with a two-shilling piece." Curious commuters stopped to listen. "Britain took in 10,000 children under the *Kindertransport* scheme before World War Two. Amongst them was Lord Dubs who has tirelessly campaigned on behalf of child migrants risking their lives on leaking boats or in the back of refrigerated lorries, just to find safety." He paused. "If we took in 10,000 children in the 1930s why not now?"

Two weeks later, I made my way to Rabbi Gluck's house – he had agreed to be interviewed for the film *Child Migrants Welcome?* As I walked past Stoke Newington station, I looked up at the third-floor flat where I first lived when I moved to Hackney forty years ago. The rent was £2.50 a week. When it rained, I placed a wooden plank across the moat that gathered in front of the ground floor entrance so my feet would not get wet. The partition, that separated my flat from those below, was made of hardboard that was easily ripped away. I was often burgled. My greatest loss was of an African wooden frieze made by a craftsman in Burundi from where I had returned after a year's teaching. My salary as a teacher of English as a Second Language to children who had recently arrived in north London and who, to my alarm, were prevented from speaking their mother tongue in the playground gave me no leeway to go upmarket.

Then I had little contact with the Ultra-Orthodox Jewish community who lived, and still live, in the surrounding streets – men in wide-brimmed, circular fur hats with ringlets trailing down their cheeks, long back coats, white tights and black patent shoes; young boys, similarly dressed, chattering in Yiddish behind them; women wearing modest clothes and coiffured wigs – obligatory after marriage – with a toddler or two in tow shopping at the nearby Egg Stores for braided challah and matzoh ball soup. It was twenty years later, when setting up community education classes with such organizations as Agudas Israel and Lubavitch, that I got to know my previous neighbours better.

A small Charedi community has lived in Stamford Hill, Hackney since the end of the nineteenth century when they arrived from Stepney in the East End, its subsequent growth reflected by the establishment of the Union of Orthodox Hebrew Congregations in 1926.[1] They were later joined by those fleeing Nazi persecution – the Holocaust destroyed the Charedi way of life in rural areas of Russia and Eastern Europe as it did other Jewish and secularized communities, although many Jews had already moved to towns and cities. Jewish families, whose houses were bombed or affected by post-war clearances in east London, also settled in Stamford Hill. They were followed, in the 1950s and 1960s, by Jews from India, Burma, Morocco and Aden, now part of Yemen, and those who fled the 1956 Hungarian Uprising, crushed by Soviet tanks. Ultra-Orthodox Jews, particularly from Israel and America, have continued to arrive. There is much to attract them – synagogues, kosher shops, Jewish nurseries, schools, seminaries and spacious Victorian houses, often extended to accommodate large families.[2]

I turned into Cazenove Road, a tree-lined street with handsome Victorian houses on either side. Many have been converted into Jewish and Muslim schools, community venues and places of worship. On Friday, before sunset, men holding the *siddur*, the Jewish prayer book, head towards the synagogue in an old pub with Hebrew signage that advertises its changed use. In the opposite direction Muslims, who arrived from the 1960s, rush towards the minaret towering above the chimneys of a terraced house, answering the *muezzin* call to prayer.

I met Mitch, my fellow filmmaker, outside a large Victorian house in a leafy street off Stoke Newington Common. Rabbi Gluck welcomed us into his living room. Frida, his daughter, made us tea while Mitch set up the iPhone to position the Rabbi in front of rows of hardback books. Then there was a knock at the door. Frida answered and the visitor agreed to call back later. There was a phone call, another knock at the door – a circus of activity. The house reminded me of the northern vicarage where I grew up – a ring on the doorbell advertising the arrival of a bishop or beggar to see my father, a popular parish priest. Another knock on the door. This time it was a radio station asking for a comment from the Rabbi about the road sign put up by an artist suggesting 'No Jews' in the area. Rabbi Gluck is president of *Shomrim*, meaning guardians, that works with the police and others to counter not only antisemitism but hate crime against local Muslims and other communities.[3] Finally, we got down to filming. Rabbi Gluck needed little prompting.

"My mother came over on the first *Kindertransport* train in December 1938 from Vienna to where her family had been exiled from Deutchkreutz (Tzelem) in Burgenland, immediately following the *Anschluss* [annexation of the Federal State of Austria into the

German Reich on 13 March 1938]. But let's not forget over 1 million children who did not get here and ended up in the ovens of Auschwitz and other extermination camps. Over one million children were killed." He cradled his head in his hands. "We sit here and imagine one child being killed, ten children being killed, a hundred children being killed, a thousand children being killed. One million!" he thundered. "It's something we can't even come to grips with and there was an opportunity to save those children." He closed his eyes. "Thank God ten thousand were saved but I think this serves as a lesson that we could have done a lot more."

The Rabbi explained how, to mark the eightieth anniversary since the arrival of the *Kindertransport*, Lord Dubs had laid down a successful amendment to the 2016 Immigration Act (Section 67) requiring the Government to accept unaccompanied refugee children from across Europe – those who had fled war from Afghanistan or Syria, who were adrift, vulnerable to traffickers and living in appalling conditions in makeshift camps in Greece or along the French coast. Rabbi Gluck had visited the camp in Calais, known as the 'Jungle', before October 2016 when it was disbanded[4] and saw first-hand the appalling conditions in which young people were living. But Dubs' initial proposal for the UK to accept 3,000 children was replaced by an unspecified number. By the end of the scheme in 2020, despite local councils across Britain offering up hundreds of places for such children, only 480 children had been accepted.[5]

Rabbi Gluck picked up a framed black-and-white photograph from his sideboard of a middle-aged Jewish couple taken at the beginning of the Second World War. They were dressed in their finest clothes – the woman in a tweed, woollen dress with a trimmed collar that set off her wavy, bobbed wig; the man in a suit, tie and trilby hat, slightly askew, both smiling into the camera. The photograph was of Rabbi Gluck's grandparents who wanted to look their best so their children would have something to remember them by. "My mother felt guilty for abandoning her parents, even though that is an illusion. She felt she came to a safe shore and her parents didn't." Rabbi Gluck's mother was just one of many children who came on the *Kindertransport* who never saw their parents again, affecting not only herself but her son who "always felt in the shadow of her pain." Speaking to camera he urged us "to put ourselves in their shoes, to think what it would be like if, God forbid, we would be refugees; how we would feel and how we would expect others to treat us."

It was a cold, overcast day when I took the 106 past the Egg Stores and the café below my old flat. I got off at Lordship Park, walked under a privet arch, rang the bell of a semi-detached double-fronted Victorian house and waited – I felt nervous about meeting Blanca Stern although staff at Hackney Museum had already ensured she was happy to see me. It was at the museum, from an exhibition about the Orthodox Jewish community,[6] that I learnt Blanca still lived in the same house where she first arrived in Britain, aged eight. But would she trust me enough to tell her story? Would I reawaken past trauma or get upset myself? Would the technology work? The door opened a few inches and a small woman of over eighty, with a reassuring smile and lively eyes, wearing a floral, embroidered sweater, looked up at me.

We sat around an oval, mahogany table where, every weekend, Blanca entertained some of her nine children and many grandchildren. I looked round the room – Victorian coving and cornices still in place, a large marble fireplace and framed portraits of distinguished rabbis on the walls covered in brown damask wallpaper.

"Do you mind if I call my daughter?" asked Blanca. "She asked if she could come." As we waited for Malkie, we sorted out the consent forms we both had to sign.

"Perhaps I won't need glasses after my cataract operation" I confided, as I fumbled in my bag.

"I hope I won't need a cataract operation," laughed Blanca. "I don't want to see my wrinkles." I smiled. This was going to be a good interview. The doorbell rang.

"No need to get up," said Blanca. "She has a key."

"I am here to jog my mother's memory" Malkie explained as she entered the room with a flourish and sat at the far end of the table, a more forceful woman than her gentle, unassuming mother.

"Just in case she can't remember certain details of her childhood." Blanca seemed to have perfect recall – perhaps Malkie was there to protect her mother, in case she got distressed.

Blanca, born in 1930, lived with her father, a diamond cutter, her mother, her older sister and older brother in Vienna. The city was home, at the time, to the largest Jewish community in Europe. On the morning of 15 March 1938 the Nazis arrived, "We suddenly heard lorries and motorbikes. When I looked out the window, I saw masses of Nazi-uniformed soldiers. There was no resistance – people had put up swastika flags to welcome them." Following the annexation of Austria into Nazi Germany, Jews were robbed of their freedoms, blocked from almost all professions, shut out of schools and universities, arrested and terrorized. Events came to a climax on 9 and 10 November 1938 during *Kristallnacht*. "We saw the synagogue go up in flames from our back room; Jewish books flying from windows – Nazis being nasty. We hid in the room furthest away from the front. The doorbell rang, we heard the wood splintering and then nothing. Only hours later did we dare to look. A whole panel of the front door was broken. Anybody could have walked in. For the moment we were safe. For the moment at least." Blanca's home was one of hundreds broken into during *Kristallnacht*. Synagogues were destroyed, shops plundered and, in one night, over 6,000 Jews were arrested, the majority sent to Dachau concentration camp.[7]

When Blanca's parents heard that Dr Schonfeld,[8] whom they had met at a wedding, was organizing a *Kindertransport* for Jewish children to London, they put their children on the list. They assured Blanca and her siblings that they would follow them, via Antwerp where they had relatives. Six weeks later, in the middle of Chanukah, Blanca's father lit five menorah candles before taking his children to the station. Blanca, her brother and sister climbed up on the train, excited and distressed in equal measure. "We had very mixed feelings – we were leaving our parents behind." The children waved goodbye to their father until their arms ached. Their father waved back until his children disappeared under clouds of steam. "Nobody knew at the time how bad it was going to get."

On the sixth night of Chanukah the children gathered in the train corridor to protect themselves from the bitter cold. As one of the older boys lit the sixth candle of his menorah the train screeched to a halt – the rails had frozen over. The children peered through the frosty window at the snow-covered landscape. "We were in the middle of nowhere, thinking *Are we ever going to reach safety?*" They huddled together, drawing comfort from the flickering flame until the train gathered speed. "On and on right through Germany. When we came to the border with Holland, we were very frightened. The German officials could be unpredictable, but they were quite nice. At that time, they were keen to get rid of the Jews."

A reception party in Holland welcomed the children but as soon as they settled down to celebrate the Sabbath, they were told to board the boat for England. Other refugees were arriving. "To travel on the Sabbath was an anathema," sighed Blanca. Dr Schonfeld sent a message, reassuring the children that, in exceptional circumstances, travel was allowed. He warned there might not be another chance, but the children still felt guilty: "When the boat tossed and turned, we thought *This is our punishment.* We didn't know if we'd ever get to the other side."

The crossing from the Hook of Holland took ten hours rather than the anticipated six. Stepping onto dry land was a huge relief. At Harwich the children took the train to Liverpool Street station where Meisler's statue commemorates their arrival eighty years ago. Their first contact with a Londoner, a taxi driver, was encouraging. "He took us free of charge to this house where we were welcomed by Rabbi Schonfeld himself. He had a friend staying with him, an older man who had the same kind of pronunciation as us. We felt very good about that."

I had read that Rabbi Schonfeld, a flamboyant but controversial figure, accommodated some of the children in his mother's house in Lordship Park in Stamford Hill. Vera Fast,[9] an American researcher, questions how forty children could have been housed, albeit temporarily, in a Victorian semi-detached double-fronted house. She had obviously never spoken to Blanca. "About forty of us, aged seven to ten mainly. He sent his mother away on holiday because she was a very proper lady and could never have put up with all those noisy children," laughed Blanca. "There were camp beds in every room." Blanca pointed to the living room door. "I slept in the room opposite. It was fun."

I tried to imagine the house eighty years ago – boisterous children sleeping on camp beds in this room, the next room and upstairs; in a strange land, separated from their parents, and often from their siblings – Blanca's older brother and sister, the eldest, were housed elsewhere. There was support. A group of older girls who had arrived from Germany earlier helped the younger children with their laundry and cooked their meals. Blanca remembers them taking her to Clissold Park and teaching her, 'Here we go gathering nuts in May, nuts in May'. Clissold Park with its lakes hosting wild ducks, geese and swans; its aviary with captive birds; its deer and elegant eighteenth-century villa built by a Quaker philanthropist must have been a welcome distraction for the forty noisy children, a temporary respite from worry about when they would see their parents again.

After several weeks Blanca moved to a nearby hostel in Cazenove Road where she attended a local primary school. War threatened and, although it was the summer holidays, they attended school every day, awaiting orders to evacuate. Blanca asked to join the Jewish school, rather than be sent outside London with her own primary school – she felt she'd be lost without her Jewish connections. Blanca's fourteen-year-old brother, aware that news about the forthcoming declaration of war was censored in Germany, sent a telegram to his parents, 'Grandmother ill, come immediately.' Blanca's parents understood the coded message – there was no grandmother in England. They rushed to the railway station where hundreds of people were clamouring for tickets.

"They were fortunate. Many of my aunts and uncles and whole families were deported."

"What a brilliant brother."

Blanca's father, mother and grandfather arrived in London, eight months after their children, on the eve of war but the promised reunion was short-lived. "It was extraordinary and tragic because on Wednesday my parents arrived. Then on Friday the order came to evacuate." Blanca was one of 500 Jewish children who travelled by train and bus to villages in Bedfordshire, carrying her gas mask and a change of clothes. Whilst many went to Shefford Blanca was billeted to a foster family in Stotfold, five miles away, "Total strangers, it was quite miserable." Villagers, at least initially, were confused by the evacuees' dietary customs and Sabbath observance. The Jewish school, under the leadership of Dr Judith Grunfeld, tried their best to support the children, many of whom could not speak English.[10] It provided schooling, Kosher meals and maintained Jewish traditions in local halls. During Chanukah 1939 children built a six-foot-high menorah out of gold-painted tin cans, the candles flickering behind blackout curtains in a disused cinema hall in Shefford. One night the cinema hall was burnt down but it was a symbol of the villagers' growing empathy for Jewish religious traditions that the fire brigade saved the *Torah* (scrolls of law), the Jewish prayer books and bibles. A move closer to Shefford did not help Blanca. "I was more miserable than ever. I didn't like the girl I was billeted with, another Jewish girl from Germany. We just weren't suited to each other."

Meanwhile in London Blanca's father and grandfather were rounded up by the police and interned on the Isle of Man. When war was declared some 70,000 British resident Germans and Austrians became classed as enemy aliens, with most of the 55,000 Jewish refugees finding themselves in Category C, that is exempt from internment and restrictions. This changed when France fell, and the threat of invasion became imminent. Hysteria, fuelled by fear of traitors whipped up by the media, led to the pronouncement by Churchill's cabinet on 19 May 1940 to, 'Collar the Lot.'[11] Deprived of their status as 'loyal adherents to the Allied cause, [they] were suddenly treated like the Nazis, their persecutors'.[12]

The first 823 prisoners set sail, on 27 May 1940, to the Isle of Man to live alongside Nazi sympathizers in Victorian rooming houses and private hotels ringed with barbed wire. By August 1940 about 14,000 prisoners were held on 10 camps on the island, most of them Jewish refugees. A journalist for *The Jewish Chronicle* wrote in November 1940, 'Today the island has what must be the fullest Jewish life in the world. In ordinary camps on a weekday there are more worshippers than in the Great Synagogue, London, on a Sabbath.'[13] The arrival of talented anti-Nazi and Jewish artists, writers and intellectuals led to a lively cultural programme – an unusual highlight was a German lion tamer who practised his lassoing skills on wildflowers. Despite such cultural richness, many detainees suffered depression. Klaus Hinrichsen, the art historian, wrote, 'all these frantic activities were entered into as a means of distraction from the ever-present anger at the injustice of being interned … the constant worry about wives and children left without a provider and under almost nightly bombardment in London and other towns … from the lack of communication and, of course suffering from the cramped living conditions and the lack of freedom of movement.'[14] Blanca's father and grandfather must have worried about Blanca's mother alone in London during the Blitz and missed the children who had been evacuated. They could only write one letter per week, censored by the authorities, and no more than twenty-four lines long. Perhaps they were reassured by visits of Rabbi Schonfeld who inspected internee camps across the UK on behalf of the British Chief Rabbi's Religious Emergency Council and knew the family. Or indeed by reports of the five teachers at the Jewish School, based in Shefford and surrounding villages, who were also interned.

As camps became full the Home Office began to deport young and unmarried male internees to Canada and Australia with tragic consequences. In July 1940, the *Arandora Star*, transporting British Italian and German nationals, was torpedoed by a German U-boat in the Atlantic, causing the deaths of half the detainees and the British crew.[15] Public sympathy towards the 'enemy aliens', most of whom shared their desire to defeat Hitler, softened. The government performed a U-turn and after the fear of invasion had subsided, started to release detainees. Blanca's grandfather, because of his age, was released first but her father stayed on the Isle of Man for eighteen months. The camp publication, the *Onchan Pioneer* asked: 'Has this country in its terrible struggle no use for the strength of our hearts and the ability of our brains, the might of our work?'[16] After March 1941, internees were offered the chance to enlist, or released to work for the war effort. Once released both Blanca's father and grandfather used their skills in diamond cutting to build aeroplanes. "Diamonds sounds very grand," laughed Blanca. "But we were never well-off." Back in London Blanca's father insisted on paying back the Jewish charity on which his wife, with no family to rely on, had depended.

In the summer of 1941 Blanca found a way to rejoin her parents – many of the other children remained in Shefford and neighbouring villages until the end of war in 1945. "I had to go into London for an eye test and refused to go back." Bombs were falling and food was rationed but Blanca's family, like other Jewish families, adapted, "The English being great tea drinkers, when it came to baking for the Sabbath, we were able to swap tea coupons for eggs, sugar and marge." Wartime experiences were not all negative. "There was very little antisemitism because we were all in it together."

"What kept you going?"

"Being with the family. So many other children I was with were never reunited with their parents."

Most children who came on the *Kindertransport*, including Rabbi Gluck's mother, waited years for news of their parents, only to find out they had died in the Holocaust.[17]

Blanca's biggest regret about wartime is how it disrupted her education. "Terrible to go through that as a 10-year-old" remarked Malkie, reminding her mother of all the schools she had attended in Stotfold, Shefford and Stoke Newington. But aged thirteen, Blanca was allowed to take the equivalent of the eleven-plus examination. She passed and gained a free scholarship to Clapton Secondary School where she developed a love for languages and music. "There were a lot of Jewish girls – not many Orthodox but everybody felt comfortable. It was much more challenging and proper." When she reached sixteen, Blanca went to the Beis Yaakov Seminary in Stamford Hill, a teachers' training college for girls and taught for three years before she got married. "The best years of my youth were in the seminary."

I asked Blanca how she came to be living in the same house as when she arrived in London as an eight-year-old. "We had just a room when we married. Then, in 1952, we heard the old rabbi's wife was selling the house and my husband bought it. I was so happy to be back in my first-ever home in London."

Blanca's voice softened as she talked of her husband.

"He grew up in Czechoslovakia and had been through the camps."

Malkie took up the story.

"My father joined the first group possible that marched out of Auschwitz, first to a different camp and then to three other camps."

In January 1945, nine days before the arrival of the Soviet Red Army, the Nazis force marched some 56,000 prisoners out of Auschwitz concentration camp towards Wodzislaw, thirty-five miles away. The escorting SS guards showed no mercy for those who could not keep up or tried to escape. Fifteen thousand inmates, one in four, were shot or died of cold, hunger and illness along the way. At Wodzislaw, those who had survived were put on freight trains to other camps. The camp where Blanca's husband, then a teenager, lay barely conscious was spared the Death March as it was liberated so suddenly that the Nazis simply abandoned it.[18]

"It was no picnic in any of the camps" sighed Blanca.

"That's an understatement" exclaimed her daughter who described the moment her father was liberated. "Other people stormed houses and ate anything they could lay their hands on, but their shrunken stomachs couldn't take it. That he was unable to move, was a blessing in disguise."

"That was a blessing," Blanca repeated. "He, his father and brother all survived."

"So, he shared his experiences of the Holocaust with you?"

"Yes. In a very positive way," said Blanca.

"We felt proud and grateful," said Malkie. "But he said he never told us the worst."

I found it impressive, if unusual, that Blanca's husband had talked so openly about his life in the camps, even if he had censored the most harrowing experiences. Many children of Holocaust survivors suffer if their parents keep such experiences, in Blanca's words, "locked up."

After the war Blanca's husband studied in Manchester and then moved to Hackney where he ran a zip fastener factory with his father. As a *mohel* he performed the Jewish rite of male circumcision. "He went all over the world," Blanca explained. "He was very skilled and his attitudes to parents, and to everyone, was so beautiful." Blanca brought up a picture of her husband on her mobile phone. A genial looking man with a white beard, wearing the traditional, black-crowned hat and frock coat. He had died nine years previously, at the age of eighty.

"He looks lovely. So cheerful."

Blanca and one of her other daughters came to the first film screening of *Home* at the Museum of the Home in Hackney. Images of swastikas daubed over shop windows in Vienna, synagogues going up in flames and "nasty" Nazis patrolling the streets. Then scenes of a tearful girl leaning out of a train window, leaving her parents and all that she knew; other children, carrying battered cases, disembarking at Harwich dock. Then a close-up of a double-fronted semi-detached house with a privet arch over the front gate. All overlaid with Blanca's clear, soft voice. People were fascinated that Blanca still lived in the same house where she arrived eighty years ago. They were reassured, any shaky beliefs in Britain's reputation of tolerance restored. "Our generation never forgets to be grateful for being able to get here, for being accepted here. And to live a normal life here."

The *Kindertransport* is not always viewed through such a positive lens. As Rabbi Gluck argued, there were far more children who died in the Holocaust than were saved. And it was not the UK government but individuals such as Nicholas Winton, Rabbi Schonfeld and many others, including women, whose contribution has been less acknowledged, who rescued 10,000 children, often circumventing bureaucracy and in the face of opposition.[19] This was a voluntary scheme funded and implemented by the British public – either directly by guaranteeing the children or through refugee organizations set up to administer it that often struggled to support the children. The British government's role was in announcing the scheme and setting the legal parameters. The children were to be sixteen or under and granted transitional visas 'on condition that they would be emigrated when they reach[ed] eighteen'.[20] The government never intended to provide permanent refuge and although many children were loved and cared for others experienced exploitation, abuse or inappropriate care – as privately run schemes there were few safeguards in place.[21] Blanca, in being surrounded by both the Orthodox and non-Orthodox Jewish Community and reunited with her parents, was one of the more fortunate perhaps. There are deeper questions. Why was Britain prepared to accept only children, many of whom lost their parents in the Holocaust? Such loss, as experienced by Rabbi Gluck's mother, could last a lifetime and affect their own children. What of the parents? Was it somehow thought that children, embodying innocence and less of a threat, were more deserving than adults?

When I pass through Liverpool Street station, I look anew at Meisler's sculpture. The young boy, with a violin at his feet, could be six-year-old Alf Dubs; the young girl clutching her teddy bear, eight-year-old Blanca; the older girl, gripping a battered case, Necha, aged eleven. But I think, too, of the grandparents of Rabbi Gluck and of Blanca's extended family who are absent. Louise London challenges the myth that Britain did all it could for Jews between 1933 and 1945. 'We remember the touching photographs and newsreel footage of unaccompanied Jewish children arriving on the *Kindertransport* ... There are no such photographs of the Jewish parents left behind in Nazi Europe ... The Jews excluded from entry to the United Kingdom are not part of the British experience, because Britain never saw them.'[22]

Despite criticisms of the *Kindertransport* there is no doubt that many *kinder* such as Blanca, Necha and Alf found refuge and made a life in Britain. In January 2020 Lord Dubs, still campaigning for the right of unaccompanied children to join family in Britain, wrote, 'When I arrived in Britain as an unaccompanied refugee child, fleeing the Nazis, I never thought I would end up in the Lords. But this country not only allowed me a life and gave me sanctuary, it also gave me opportunity. I never imagined that eighty-one years later, in the same country that gave homes to 10,000 lone refugee children like me, I'd be fighting for just a few hundred to be allowed to find their families here ... The way we treat the most vulnerable people is a test of who we are, what kind of country we hope to live in and what humanity we have.'[23] A few days later, on 23 January 2020, the EU Withdrawal Bill passed into law. Unaccompanied children who found themselves living in refugee camps on Lesbos or on rubbish tips in Dunkirk no longer had the right, previously enshrined in the EU regulation Dublin 111, to apply to join a grandparent, parent, aunt, uncle, cousin or sibling living in Britain.[24] It had taken years for dedicated lawyers and the organization, Safe Passage, to persuade children to follow a safe route

Figure 2 Gershon Dux and Rivkah Dux (née Hacker), parents of Necha (Natalie) Gluck (née Dux). Courtesy of Rabbi Herschel Gluck, OBE.

to join family members in Britain rather than risk their lives. Such a change in the law inevitably means young people will turn to traffickers, travel in refrigerated containers or in unsafe, leaky boats, just to find safety. The most the government committed to was a comprehensive review of safe routes, looking at family reunion for refugees, not just in Europe but globally. The Nationality and Borders Act 2022 and the Illegal Migration Act 2023 do little to advance this.[25]

CHAPTER 2
NO MAN'S LAND
Duncan Ross who arrived from India, aged eight, in 1956

Duncan walked back from St Paul's where he had been vicar for many years, reflecting on what retirement would bring. As he approached the junction of Mile End Road and Grove Road, he noticed a white advan stationed at the traffic lights. Even with his poor eyesight, he could read the words emblazoned on the side. 'In the UK illegally? GO HOME OR FACE ARREST. Text HOME to 78070.' Duncan quaked, as he always did when he saw the words 'GO HOME'. He remembered them from the 1970s, plastered by the far right on billboards and council estates. But these were advans commissioned by the Home Office, whipping up fear with the threat of arrest or deportation. In the top right-hand corner Duncan read '106 ARRESTS LAST WEEK IN YOUR AREA'. Which area? Mile End, Tower Hamlets, some of the most diverse in London? Places where migrants and their descendants have settled for decades? Or was the advan on its way east? This anti-immigration rhetoric might be more acceptable in Barking and Dagenham or further out. Surely not in his parish? Over the years, Duncan had made great strides to bring together white and Black, Christian and Muslim, immigrant and non-immigrant. When local Muslims had lost their mosque, he offered them the use of his church for Friday prayers. It had taken time for the parishioners to accept the idea, but even those who had complained about having a 'Paki' vicar agreed. Duncan peered closely at the blurred images on the side of the advan – what looked like a steel bracelet was in fact handcuffs and was that a border guard's uniform bleeding off to the right?

In the summer of 2013, 'GO HOME' vans were driven around six London boroughs – Barking and Dagenham, Barnet, Brent, Ealing, Hounslow and Redbridge. They became notorious as part of Theresa May's 'hostile environment' when, as Home Secretary, she aimed to crack down on immigration.[1] May, at a later stage, denied she was behind the vans. Krishnan Guru-Murthy, presenting *Channel 4 News*, commented, "It is the use of that phrase 'GO HOME'. Any immigrant or non-white person who grew up in the '60s, '70s and '80s heard that phrase as a term of racist abuse – and the government has put it on a poster!"[2] Diane Abbott, member of parliament for Hackney North, stated that the campaign, "Is akin to scrawling 'Paki go home' on the side of buildings. I don't believe this policy is going to achieve anything besides stoking fear and resentment."[3] Not only did this happen but it was also ineffective. The pilot was disbanded after a month, with only eleven people having left Britain due to Operation Vaken. But it was a reflection as to how far government had adopted the racist rhetoric of the far right.

As Duncan walked towards his new home, he tried to shake off the thought of the advan. Having left the vicarage for the next incumbent, he had rented a house on a

Victorian street near Mile End station. He was unsure whether it would remain his home. 'HOME?' Where was it – in Calcutta, India where he was born or in east London, England where he had arrived aged eight? As he entered the living room, crammed full of unpacked boxes, Duncan turned on the radio. Not again. It was Nigel Farage, leader of UKIP, the United Kingdom Independence Party. Who would be the target this time? People who looked a different colour, spoke a different language, worshipped a different God? "You get all this nonsense that's being spawned about immigration. A slight relief it's not about us brown or Black ones, it's about Eastern Europeans, God help them. The pressure's off."

I visited Duncan, an engaging man with a disarming smile, some months after the advans cruised through east London. As we sat in his front room, he shared his reaction to hearing Farage speak on the radio, "When he starts – there's this horrible feeling they're going to send me back. I'm sixty-six in a couple of weeks. I should be secure by now, but I feel I'm going to be rumbled one day." Although retired, he still wore his cassock and dog collar. "This priest's clothing is the most wonderful barrier. I get respect which I would not see in civvies where I'm clearly just another 'Paki.'" I cringed at the word 'Paki'[4] as I knew it from my Lancashire childhood in the 1960s as a term of abuse for immigrants who had been recruited to save the ailing cotton industry, irrespective of where they came from in South Asia and beyond.

It was only when Duncan arrived in the UK, aged eight in 1956, that he realized he was "the brown sheep of the family." The rest of his Anglo-Indian family were white. "So, way, way back, there was almost certainly an Indian woman. An Indian man would never have dared to take up with an English woman." In the eighteenth century, the British East India Company encouraged employees to marry local women and settle down, but the records of these women are non-existent. "I won't ever find where that Indianness came from," sighed Duncan. In search of his ancestry, he visited Cochin, on the southwest coast of India, where his father was born. Here he learnt that his Scottish sounding surname 'Ross' may be derived from the Portuguese 'Rosario'. Many Portuguese settled around Cochin after the arrival of the explorer, Vasco da Gama, on the Malabar Coast in 1498. Perhaps it was Duncan's Portuguese ancestor who married an Indian woman. "Anglo-Indians weren't just Anglo-Indians, they were Euro-Indians as well. It's this colonial mixing of Portuguese, Dutch, French and British."

Duncan, born in 1948 in what is now known as Kolkata, lived in a first floor flat in the Chowringhee district with his grandmother, parents and older sister. "It wasn't the poorest area … it was middle of the road Calcutta." His father, who had previously worked on the railways, was an accountant and his mother was a secretary for the Calcutta Electricity Supply. Many Anglo-Indians, known as the wheels, cranks and levers of empire, worked for the railways or in administrative roles. Aged two Duncan started school at the prestigious La Martinière College, that his sister also attended. Although his parents were Catholic, Duncan and his sister were brought up in the Church of England. "My dad got divorced in the 1930s. He then married my mum, also a Catholic, which meant his children were born in sin, so he never went to church again – he knew he'd be rejected." His grandmother suggested the Church of England might be more tolerant of his children.

Duncan's family did not mix much with other Anglo-Indians. "They could be quite dodgy as they were ashamed of the Indian and wanting the Anglo bit. We had friends like that. They had houses with grounds, where they'd sip cocktails. My parents didn't quite fit in because they lived in a flat. They were more honest and genuine – not that they ever judged. I put that down to their simplicity of faith, goodness and integrity." Duncan felt this was partly due to his mother's friendship with Mother Teresa, the famous Albanian-Indian Roman Catholic nun and missionary.[5] "She had this extraordinary influence on the rich, rather grand, Anglo-Indian women. My mum wasn't grand or old, but she would give money to the poor."

Duncan's young life centred around school, the church and home. His protective parents did not allow him to play outside or with other children. I asked Duncan if he could draw the flat – I was keen to gain a clearer idea of its layout and surrounding locality. Duncan looked askance – he had drawn nothing since school. "Can I draw a plan?" he asked with typical ingenuity. He chose a lead pencil. "This could take as long as the Sistine Chapel."

Duncan chose the smallest piece of paper, A4. "Anything big means I've got a lot to say." He drew an open-plan living space, with a punka fan in the middle, and a curved balcony overlooking Syed Amir Ali Avenue. He splattered the drawing with words – 'bed' (three); 'cockroaches'; 'cook and ayah'; 'duck'; 'birthday' 'Everest' and 'coronation'. His mother and sister slept in one bed, his father and Duncan slept in another and his grandmother in the third, all in the same space – there seemed to be little privacy. The cook, Boodha Bochi, and Baran Bibi, his wife, who was deaf and mute, were regarded as part of the family. Duncan remembered, "switching the lights on and magically, the work surface in the kitchen would ripple away. It was covered in cockroaches." He was particular about his food. "The cook had to make stews because I wouldn't touch a curry. I hated anything spicy. I don't think it was disdain, I just didn't like spice." He refused to eat Daisy who was a duck that Boodha Bochi bought during Duncan's school holidays to fatten it up. "Daisy pined when I went back to school and waddled towards me when I returned. Duck of supreme character – no one could eat Daisy after that."

Duncan drew a small rectangle representing a large gramophone used by his sister, ten years older, to listen to jazz, popular at that time with Anglo-Indians. One year the family played a record of 'Happy Birthday' to Duncan. "I was terribly embarrassed. I hate fuss being made over me. I'm an introvert, my life goes on inside me." I asked Duncan why the words 'Coronation' and 'Everest' were written so close together. "Blimey, I was a real little Brit," he exclaimed, recalling a day in 1953 when he cut out an image of the Queen's coronation coach from a magazine. As he stuck it to one of his cars his sister, listening to the radio, cried out "They did it." Edmund Hillary's and Tenzing Norgay's arrival at the summit of Mount Everest was announced on the same day as Queen Elizabeth II's coronation – an event celebrated with enthusiasm by many Anglo-Indian families who considered Britain as their 'motherland'.[6]

Duncan scrawled other words along the busy thoroughfare in front of the four-storey block of flats – 'chai shops', 'rickshaws', 'trams', 'buses' and 'floods'. From his balcony Duncan marvelled at the lean rickshaw pullers tottering under heavy loads and the tangle of tram wires overhead. "There was endless hooting and honking, beeping and shouting – and elephants. It sounds exotic but they were working animals." He remembered, too, the clamour of chai sellers.

"Did you visit the chai shops?"

"Excuse me! We weren't Indians, we're Anglo-Indians. Will you please not ask questions like that?" he laughed, mocking the prejudices of Anglo-Indians with whom he did not identify, but pulling himself short, too. "A little bit of that outrage was genuine. Oh, I'm worried about myself now."

Sometimes the family became marooned. "The Hooghly River would flood and there were days when you couldn't get out. Bengal is very watery. If you listen to the music, the poetry, it's very wistful and watery."

Hindu festivals had a big impact on Duncan, not always favourable. "Holi … it scared the wits out of me. A wonderful, colourful, chaotic mess, where people threw coloured water and powder at each other. They would climb into your rickshaw and rub powder into your face and hair. It was anarchy and we were very controlled." As a pious child Duncan disapproved of the timing of the spring festival. "I remember being outraged, saying to my mother, 'How dare they have this festival on St Joseph's'." Duncan was not too keen on Hindu deities either – "they had too many arms." I wondered if Duncan's mother was tempted to rebuke her young son for his disapproval. "My parents never decried or dissed other beliefs. They spoke about Gandhi with an absolute certainty that he'd be in eternity – his favourite hymn was 'Lead Kindly Light'." I looked over at a Hindu deity perched on an unpacked case. Duncan's views had obviously changed. "As a prissy little Christian, I'd be shocked to come in here and see that, but I've learnt that Hinduism has a Trinity as well. It has Shiva, Vishnu, and whoever the third one is [Brahma]. None of us have got a monopoly on it." Festivals that did not clash with the Christian calendar were far more acceptable to young Duncan. "Pujas, where big idols made of earth were carried through the streets, were rather fun. There was drumming, too, as they took them down to Mother Hooghly who bore them away."

I was intrigued by the word 'LEPER' scrawled by the downstairs entrance to the block of flats but also in a fenced off part of the balcony, followed by the word 'almost'. What did 'LEPER almost' mean? Duncan explained. His mother gave money regularly to lepers that graced the steps of their doorway but, inspired by Mother Teresa, she wanted one leper to live on the balcony. "She [mother] even thought of building a little canopy for him to shelter under." But the family set sail for Britain before the leper could move to his elevated pitch.

In 1954, seven years after the partition of India into Muslim dominated Pakistan and Hindu dominated India, riots were still an everyday occurrence in Calcutta and continued to be so until about 1956. Duncan's Anglo-Indian family, on the borderline between the Hindu and Muslim communities, was in a perilous position. "Hindus chasing Muslims and Muslims chasing Hindus. They'd escape up the stairs, get killed outside our front door. The streets were covered in bodies and people with wheelbarrows would demand money to take the rotting bodies away – as a child you don't have the means to deal with this stuff."

As tension increased the Ross family tried to persuade Duncan's mother to stay at home.

"It's riots today, please don't go out."
Duncan's mother refused to listen. She believed the flag on her employer's chauffeur-driven vehicle would provide protection. But rioting youths surrounded the car.

"Stay in the car and you all burn to death. Or get out and we kill you."
The driver slammed his foot on the accelerator and ploughed his way through the mob. Duncan pointed to the 'x' he had drawn between 'RIOTS' and 'FEAR' placed just inside the doorway. "This marks the spot where I was standing when the door opened and this cold, determined, usually timid woman, beyond fear, said 'I've had enough. I'm going. You can come with me, or you can stay.' The whole of my life flipping on that point." Duncan was six at the time.

"This was post-partition India. Hindus and Muslims had got on brilliantly beforehand," Duncan sighed. "Bless you lot, partition happened, Britain withdrew, countries are split. It never did get sorted, really. The strange irony is that, as far as India goes, you guys came for trade. You sidled up sneakily and suddenly were in charge. The next thing we know, we have a Queen Empress ruling the country. Some of us then reversed the trend in coming here, and all hell is let loose." I recalled the words of Ambalavaner Sivanandan, Director of the Institute of Race Relations for forty years. 'We are here because you were there.' The words are as relevant today as when he first coined them in the 1980s.[7]

It took two years for the Ross family to prepare to leave for the 'motherland'. Duncan imagined a "thatched cottage, a garden to play in" – he had seen pastel pictures on the lids of chocolate boxes. In 1956, aged eight, Duncan left Calcutta with his parents and sister – his grandmother had already died. "I remember being a brave little boy, saying goodbye to my dog, Scruffy, and not crying." The family travelled by train to Bombay where they boarded a P&O liner just before the Suez Crisis erupted.[8] "We were the second last ship in the last convoy to go through the Suez Canal. One side was desert, the other side was green and there were men on horseback with guns. It was all terribly exciting. Going to Britain was the peak, the pinnacle." They were amongst many Anglo-Indians to leave. Following partition, and India's subsequent independence in 1947, Anglo-Indians feared that other Indians would identify them with the British. Many left for Canada, Australia, New Zealand, the United States and Britain. Those not able to migrate, often the more impoverished, attempted to find their place in the newly formed nation, uncertain of their status.

When the ship docked in Marseilles, the sight of the gold statue on top of the cathedral seemed to herald a bright future but it was difficult for Duncan to maintain such optimism on arrival in London. "I remember standing on the deck in Tilbury Dock, battling with the cold." As he pressed his face against the taxi window, he bombarded his parents with, "Can I play in the garden when we get there? Will there be smoke coming out of the chimney? Will there be, will there be … ? Silence in the cab. Even on that short journey, I'm thinking I've not got to rock the boat, it's not going to be what you thought. All this processing in my eight-year-old mind."

On arrival in Clapton, Hackney, the family walked up a dark stairwell until they reached their new home with a *mezuzah* on the door – the flat, like many in the area, was owned by a Jewish landlord. It comprised two rooms – one was for 'best' and a kitchen. The family unpacked their metal trunks, thankful that, after such a long journey, their beautiful China tea set and Japanese sake set were intact. "We were wanting to re-establish that way of life but we never drank out of the sake set and we never drank tea. We drank coffee."

The following Tuesday Duncan enrolled at Northwold Primary School. "Solidly Jewish – there weren't any brown people around. Only this ripple of giggles as I walked up the middle, and me being puzzled. But boy, did my education get me through." Other 'puzzling' incidents followed. "As I was ambling across a crossing on Upper Clapton Road, a lorry screeched to a halt and the guy spat at me. The penny dropped. I left one side of the road innocent and reached the other side thinking that's what it's about. It isn't obvious to a kid." Duncan had been shocked, in India, when he heard people talk about 'niggerfied' habits, but he did not think such racism would be directed at him.

Duncan never told his family about the racism he experienced. Perhaps he was unsure whether his 'white' family would understand, or he did not want to worry them. Besides, they were not at home when he returned from school. They were working, his father as an accountant, his mother as a secretary and his sister as personal assistant to a bank manager. Hard work paid off. After five years his sister had done so well that the bank lent her £3,000. The family moved into a house in Cleveleys Road, near Clapton station. Duncan, aged thirteen, had his own bedroom and the garden he had dreamed of where he could put up his six-foot telescope, but it still wasn't a thatched cottage. "I'd grown up a bit by then."

Duncan went onto Hackney Downs Grammar School attended by Michael Caine and Harold Pinter amongst others. "More than half the school was Jewish, bright, Jewish lads. We were East End kids but it didn't mean we had patched, ragged trousers and went 'cor blimey'." Duncan's father was a great support. "He would wake me up at six to do Latin verbs. I appreciate it now but at the time I just wanted to sleep." The school attracted good teachers. "Joe Brearley, who taught us Russian, was an extraordinary man – a total eccentric. He taught us the instrumental case, by getting the whole class walking around Hackney Downs, plonking a musical instrument, with us chanting the endings, som, soi, som, sami." Duncan made good friends, including with Bernard Wiltshire from Domenica, the first Black child in the school who impressed Duncan with quotes from

Figure 3 Duncan, aged eleven, at Northwold Primary School, Hackney, 1959. Courtesy of Duncan Ross.

the Bible and Shakespeare. "We became great mates. Howard, my other friend, became head boy. I gave him religion and he gave me astronomy."

Although Duncan was an enthusiastic member of St Paul's Cathedral congregation in Calcutta, it was some years before he attended church in London. On Christmas Eve he and his sister would attend midnight mass at St John of Hackney, but the church was hardly welcoming. "It wasn't openly racist but clearly we were different." A small act of kindness changed all that. "On this Christmas, when I was fifteen, this lovely churchwarden, Bill Turney, gave such a warm greeting. 'Do come back' he said in a broad northern accent. We went the following Sunday, and I became a server. I wasn't going to be a priest, I was off being a physicist and being paid very nicely for it, thank you. I was ordained at thirty. It was that one man who put me where I am today."

Duncan went to University College, London, to study physics and then later to Cambridge to study theology. His life and work in east London are impressive. Not only has he been a much-loved parish priest, but he has brought up a foster son. "Nicky came to live with me when he was seventeen after being made homeless and stayed for twenty-three years." Duncan has no wish to go to a reunion of the London branch of La Martinière Association. "I've stayed younger and more radical. Doing this job, living in the East End all these years, having brought up a lad from seventeen has kept me young." Duncan loves the diversity of east London. "People like us have been landing in the docks for years whether it's the Jews, the Irish or West Indians, bringing a rich mix of culture, values and language. You don't have to travel … it's on your doorstep. Bless this country, the most favourite meal in Britain is chicken tikka masala, and yet the people who brought it here are not the most favourite."[9]

It has taken Duncan time to integrate different aspects of his life. "There were phases – seven years, twelve years? The first was coming here and wishing to be white. I've always spoken good English. That diverted people's attention and they soon forgot I was Indian. I was pretend white. Then the next phase thinking 'Okay but please don't think of me as too Indian'. Then the last phase, not denying part of who I am. As a priest the bottom line is journeying with other people, so you've got to do it yourself."

Unknowingly, I had been part of that journey. When I first worked at the V&A, I oversaw the touring exhibition *Shamiana, the Mughal Tent*.[10] It was the ground-breaking work of my predecessor, Shireen Akbar. Under her guidance Asian and non-Asian women's groups across the UK and internationally made over fifty silk panels to hang in a vibrant red, travelling tent. The women drew inspiration not only from the V&A's Nehru Gallery of Indian Art but from their own lives. The panels were exquisite. An embroidered elephant with a beaded howdah and gold ringed tusks; a sari-clad woman as the *Tree of Life*, her feet entrapped by entangled roots but with her arms as branches, free and flowering. But there were also embroidered panels of multi-tasking, multi-racial modern women – studying, sewing, working at a computer and enjoying their children.

A friend offered Duncan a free ticket to *Shamiana, the Mughal Tent* at the V&A. "I didn't want to go. But I was going to see him so I thought I'd better visit this blessed exhibition." Duncan entered the magical tent, a tribute to Shireen who had tragically died in her fifties just two months before the exhibition opened, and whom Duncan had known from when she was a community worker in east London. "I spent the next hour weeping. I thought *I'm not just a nuisance. I'm not just an immigrant. I've got a heritage.* Life has all these flicks, like a pinball machine. If I'd faced up to my friend and said, 'I'm sorry I didn't go,' life would not have been the same. Here I was embracing my culture." Duncan was furious, too. He thought no one in east London would go to the V&A in west London, to see *Shamiana*. He contacted the chief curator of the Indian and South-East Asian department, Deborah Swallow. In 1998, Debbie, I and others organized for the panels to be displayed at St Paul's, Bow Common, the modern, brutalist church in Mile End where Duncan was vicar. The panels looked magnificent and the activity programme for local people was a huge success. "I raised £15,000 to get the best silk artists I could. Kids came, all sorts." Duncan was not only reclaiming but sharing his heritage with fellow East Enders.

"I had a dream once, and I was on a glass bicycle. And there was some enormous collision and the bicycle shattered underneath me. I was the boy on the bicycle." It took Duncan forty-seven years, on his first visit back to India, to realize the dream's significance and start to process the flash backs he had been experiencing since he left. He had been prompted to return by his father's death. "It's all about identity, who you are and where you come from. Jackie, my sister, reluctantly came with me. She was older, part of the whole rejecting of India. She really wanted to do the travelling bit to the Taj Mahal."[11] Duncan persuaded his sister to return to Chowringhee, a visit that rekindled Duncan's memory of seeing, from the flat balcony, a boy being pulled off his bicycle and killed. "Whether he was Hindu or Muslim, I don't know, but I remember being pulled back in. My sister said, 'Yes, you sat in the chair, shaking, holding the dog that was shaking too.'"

Duncan revisited India with his foster son, Nicky, who was delighted to be shown his father's childhood haunts. The third time Duncan returned on his own. As the plane landed, he thought, "Where's the bunting? Why is there not a brass band? But I was barged and pushed, I didn't have Nicky to show all these wonders to and I knew no one." He had come 'HOME' as promoted by the UK Home Office advans, as campaigned for by Nigel Farage, only to find it was no longer his 'HOME.' "I just felt so spat out by Calcutta, thinking I never want to come back." Although painful this third visit enabled Duncan to come to terms with having seen the young boy killed.[12] "A left hand, with the whole palm covered in blood still appears occasionally, but it's not haunting or terrorising me." Duncan paused. "It's hard for children who've suffered any kind of trauma. It's dangerous territory. Some of our Somali lads, who first came over, kept themselves to themselves. I had this feeling for them, thinking you guys have seen some awful, awful stuff."

Accepting his 'Indianness', returning to Calcutta and resolving the trauma he experienced have not resolved Duncan's feelings of home. "I've never felt I totally belonged, but I don't belong in India either. This insular mind of some British depresses me. When I go to Rome, I think my goodness, we were on the fringe of that empire so what's Britain up to? It's just a strip of channel that separates us." Duncan's words were prescient. I interviewed him in 2014, the year that UKIP, headed by Farage, won the most votes in the European Parliamentary elections. The result contributed to the decision of Cameron, leader of the Conservative Party, to commit to a referendum about Britain's membership of the European Union.

It is the conflicts and divisions in Duncan's life story that have made him who he is. "In every bit of my life there were sides – Catholic/Protestant, Hindu/Muslim, Christian/non-Christian. Post-partition moulded my mindset, making me realise what happens when people are divided against each other. Growing up along all these fault lines, there was a determination in me that never, ever would I do anything to foster division."

At the end of the interview Duncan brought out photographs that he had found whilst helping his sister move into a care home. Grainy black-and-white images of him with his dog Scruffy and the cook Boodha Bochi; grand Anglo Asian women, in full skirts on bicycles and the decaying grandeur of Calcutta. There were more recent colour images, too, of the flats in Chowringhee and the landing where Hindus and Muslims were massacred, photographed on his return to Calcutta. As I thanked Duncan for sharing his story he confided, "No one has ever asked me about that period of my life before." Had some assumed he was just another 'Paki', the specificity and individuality of his life ignored?

On my way home I strolled through Victoria Park, reflecting on the impact of racist rhetoric on Duncan's life and his sense of belonging, I remembered the Rock Against Racism concert held in the park in 1978.[13] Then I lay on the grass with friends and colleagues; danced to the music of The Clash, Steel Pulse and the Tom Robinson Band. We were young, naïve and a little foolish, optimistic too, marching with our banners, 'Black and White, Unite and Fight', thinking that, through music and activism, we could defeat right-wing movements such as the National Front. We never imagined that such slogans as 'GO HOME', forty years later, would be co-opted by government and plastered on the side of vans that skirted the park, passing within yards of Duncan's 'home'.

CHAPTER 3
PRECIOUS CARGO
Argun Imamzade who arrived from Cyprus, aged fourteen, in 1964

Mitch and I sat with Argun in the garden of his half-timbered Tudor-style home on a leafy avenue in a north London suburb whilst Hurmus, his wife, assisted by her son and daughter, prepared the barbecue. The setting was quintessentially English – a sweeping lawn, fringed with lupins and lavender, hosta and hollyhocks, sheltered by a towering wood. Argun had moved up in the world since 1974 when he brought over his wife to live in a rented room costing £6 a week. "My landlady got jealous and cut off my gas so we couldn't cook or wash. I broke her window and turned the gas on." Two weeks later he rented a self-contained flat and the newlywed couple settled down to married life.

Argun, owner of Argun Printers and Stationers in Hackney, has become a successful entrepreneur. Business is in his blood. Even as a young boy, he rode on his bicycle to remote parts of Cyprus delivering goods from his stepbrother's stationery shop. Both Duncan, a Church of England Anglo-Indian, and Argun, a Muslim Turkish Cypriot, were born under British rule but, unlike Duncan, Argun is clear where he belongs. "I've made a life here, I'm totally British. My home was Limassol and Paphos but today London is my home."

Argun had agreed to be filmed talking about the photograph album he had rescued from his bombed-out grandfather's house. It was the only thing he brought with him when he arrived in Britain from Cyprus, aged fourteen, in 1964. Argun first showed me the album on a visit to his shop where I have been buying stationery for years. "This is my treasure. This is my life," said Argun, patting his album with the cover of an English country garden.

Argun Printers and Stationers, located under Hackney Central railway arches, was busy the day I interviewed Argun in the back of his shop. People browsed through shelves stocked high with a maze of essentials – paper and envelopes of every size and colour but luxury items too – fine art materials and moleskin notebooks. Trains rumbled overhead and a Xerox machine was going full pelt, printing booklets to be flown to Turkey that night. Other printing jobs were waiting to be collected – menus for a local Vietnamese restaurant and service sheets for a Caribbean wake. Hurmus was at the counter, calling out to her assistants. "Sylvie, show this customer the address books." "Abdul, how much for the printing of Adjei's wedding invitations?" Hurmus, efficient and charming, wished the bridegroom well as she gave him his receipt – years ago Hurmus had given up a job in banking to support her husband's business. Employment of family members has been an important ingredient of business success for migrant communities.[1]

When the shop got quieter, Hurmus peered into the back office. She was intrigued as to what Argun and I were up to – although this was my third visit to interview Argun it was the first time he had shown me his album. At six o'clock she left to look after her grandchildren, Abdul switched off the printing machines and pulled down the lime green shutters. Now only the screech of trains braking, as they entered Hackney Central station, interrupted Argun's story.

"During the fighting in Paphos in 1963 we were forced to leave our homes and even though we were running for our lives I did not want to lose my photos. I hid this behind a metal cupboard in case the house got burgled or burnt down. We started living in tents in a graveyard but, one day, both parties agreed a truce to let people pick up their possessions. People had ransacked the house, but they didn't see this."

Argun opened the album to reveal a sepia photograph of three distinguished men, two in suits and striped ties, the other in a military-style suit, all with impressive moustaches, short back and sides tucked under flat-topped conical black hats.

"They look fantastic. Who are they?"

"My grandfather and his two brothers," Argun explained, swelling with pride at his Ottoman heritage.

"They're very modern with shirt and tie but still wearing fezzes."

The Ottomans ruled Cyprus from 1571, after defeating the Venetians, but in 1878, as the Ottoman Empire disintegrated, Britain took control over the island as a protectorate.[2] This was ostensibly to support the Ottomans against an ever-expanding Russia, but it was also to defend Britain's interests in the Suez Canal and the sea route to India. When Turkey sided with Germany in the First World War Britain formally annexed Cyprus into the British Empire, albeit under a unilaterally annexed military occupation. In 1925, following the dissolution of the Ottoman Empire, Cyprus became a crown colony and remained under British control until independence in 1960.[3]

The years leading up to independence saw an increase in intercommunal violence.[4] EOKA, Ethnikí Orgánosis Kipriakoú Agónos, was an underground Greek Cypriot nationalist organization dedicated to independence from British rule and eventual *enosis,* unification with Greece. Its armed campaign under Colonel Georgios Grivas, an officer in the Greek army, reached its climax in 1956, the year that Makarios III, Orthodox archbishop of Cyprus, was deported by the British to the Seychelles for his suspected support of EOKA.[5] In 1957 the Turkish Cypriot community spawned their own resistance movement, the TMT, the Türk Mukavemet Teşkilatı. Fearing they would be forced to leave the island, as had happened in Crete, the TMT worked with British forces in resisting *enosis* but later supported *taksim,* division of the island.[6]

At the time of independence, Cypriots were given a choice as to where their loyalty lay. "In 1960, after independence, people who didn't want to take out Cypriot nationality kept their British passports, that's what our parents did." In fact, Argun's parents were already settled in Britain. "We Cypriots are truly British. We've been in the colony and have more in common with British people than we have with people in Turkey."

Argun turned to a sepia image of a young soldier in uniform with an impressive moustache. "Uncle Saleh. He was in the British army – defending democracy, against

Mussolini, Hitler." Uncle Saleh, seated at a bureau, fountain pen in hand, seemed to be searching for inspiration as to what to write to his family. His father, mother and siblings looked on – waiting anxiously to hear from Saleh fighting at the front. It was a dreamy, soft-focus montage produced long before the invention of Photoshop. It celebrated, even romanticized, the role that Uncle Saleh played alongside 30,000 Cypriots who served in the British forces during the Second World War.[7]

Argun, born in 1949, smiled as he turned the page. "My first photo of me at seven months and eight days." A baby boy, with penetrating dark eyes and a shock of black hair, dressed in a long-sleeved smock and knitted bootees, stared up at me from a large armchair. There was no mistake. It was the face of the man who had been printing my business cards for over twenty years.

"Gorgeous," I said. "You look very chubby."

"Chubby," he chuckled. "I've always been chubby. I used to like my food."

"Don't we all," I laughed.

"Sweets, baclava, Turkish delight, Cadbury's chocolate."

On the opposite page, Argun, still dwarfed by the armchair, was surrounded by his family. Zizi, his older brother, also dressed in a smock, stood beside him on the seat. His mother, wearing a wide brimmed hat and stylish white coat, perched on the chair's left arm with her hand on Argun to keep him still. His father, in a dapper suit and tie, sat on the right arm. The image was badly creased with blue ink splattered across their faces as if signalling that all was not well with this elegant, prosperous family.

"Is that you dressed as a girl?" I asked pointing at a charming image of two children standing in front of mock Greek pillars in a photographic studio.

"Yes," Argun laughed. "And that's Zizi beside me."

Zizi, on the left, was dressed in trousers and T-shirt but Argun, on the right, wore a white brocade two piece with a gathered skirt. Both wore fine strap-leather sandals.

"Why are you wearing a dress?"

"I'm the fifth son of my mother. She wanted a daughter."

"What did you think of being dressed as a girl?"

"What choice did I have?" laughed Argun. "I was only two years old. My mother was a very modern lady. First marriage she had three boys; second marriage, Zizi and myself; eventually, third marriage, she had a daughter."

Not even the ear-splitting cry of police sirens along Mare Street could stop Argun talking about his parents' divorce, a tale he must have been told, perhaps by his older brother, as he would have been too young to understand its significance. "You're not going to believe this. We were all watching a black and white movie with the actor, Errol Flynn – my mother liked him, you know, as an idol. When we came out of the cinema a man was passing by on a bike. 'Look, Errol Flynn' my mother shouted. It wasn't Errol Flynn. He was a Cypriot who lived there, just someone who looked like him. That was it, my father's marriage was over."

When Argun was three, in 1953, Argun's mother left for England with her Errol Flynn look-alike. Argun's father, who after the divorce had shut down his shoe factory in Limassol, had left for London a year earlier. "People who have committed a crime

Figure 4 Argun (right) and brother, Zizi (left) in a photographic studio in Paphos, Cyprus. Courtesy of Argun Imamzade.

or have marriage problems, need to get away." Argun and Zizi went to live with their maternal grandparents and three stepbrothers from their mother's first marriage.

Argun turned to a photograph of him and Zizi in cowboy costumes, gun holsters at their hips, book ending their three stepbrothers in formal suits and ties. "You've got stepbrothers, they're not as good as your real brother, are they? When you say, 'Step, step, step', it's not a 100%." Argun loved his grandparents, but they could not replace his parents. "My grandfather brought me up when my mother left me. He and my grandma took care of us. But it's not like mum and dad, is it?" Argun's grandfather was a headmaster and the Mayor of Paphos who owned properties and vineyards. Argun pointed to a small, grainy black-and-white image of his grandfather, in trousers, jacket and a trilby hat, a cigarette hanging from his lips. He leant on a walking stick, surveying his land with Argun and Zizi, potential inheritors of his wealth, crouched either side of him. "War kills everything," sighed Argun.

Argun's first direct experience of war was at a school assembly in Paphos in December 1963 – he had moved from his grandparents' village, Aydin, to go to the lycée. "Greek police officers were shooting above our heads, so our teacher said, 'Everyone run for your lives, go home.' No one got killed that day, but they scared us badly. That was the last time we went to school." As the conflict intensified, Turkish Cypriots were pushed into a smaller area of Paphos, confined to their homes and surrounded. "We had to form a kind of army, for self-defence. Who's in the army? Fathers and sons, just ordinary people. We had about four or five guns. We didn't have any organisation to send us arms. My brothers got injured and lots of friends and people I knew got killed – the shop owner, postman, teachers. We didn't know whether we were going to live or die."

Argun believed it was the failure of the constitutional power-sharing agreements at independence from Britain in 1960 that led to war. "There was a seventy per cent [Greek], thirty per cent [Turkish] agreement but government positions and funds were unfairly distributed. The Greeks had control of the roads, the water, electricity and food supplies. My village of Aydin, with 2000 people, had just a telephone. All the surrounding Greek villages of 150, 200 or 300 people, had running water, electricity, asphalt roads. We didn't have that. Instead of making a Cypriot state, a good life for everyone, equally shared, they tried to take over." Tension came to a head, when, in December 1963, Greek Cypriot police stopped a Turkish Cypriot couple. A hostile crowd gathered, shots were fired, and two Turkish Cypriots were killed. Argun was at pains to emphasize his friendship with his Greek Cypriot neighbours and resented those who fostered division. "They were Christians, we were Muslims. They spoke Greek and we spoke Turkish. Every other thing we did was the same – same food, we lived in same way, we did the same things. They think they're Greek but they're not. They're mixed."

Argun's grandfather sat Argun and Zizi down for a serious talk.

"After this war, you will have no future here. There will be no school for a long time. Go to your parents in London. You'll have a better chance in life."

Argun did not want to leave Cyprus, despite the war. His parents were strangers, having only returned once to visit him and Zizi during their ten-year absence. There was no arguing with his grandfather. "My parents paid £30 for the fare and sent me £12 pocket money but I gave £10 of this to my granddad – he needed it more than me." Argun left Cyprus, taking only a carrier bag containing his photograph album and with only the clothes he stood up in.

"You must have had shoes?"

"Just flipflops. When they ransacked the house, they took everything."

Gone were the beautiful strap-leather sandals designed by his father, captured in the photograph of the boys standing against the mock Greek pillars.

On the day of departure Argun and Zizi boarded an Israeli-owned cruise ship in Limassol harbour. Argun was excited despite feeling sad at leaving his beloved grandparents and the island for the first time. The only other refugees on the ship were a mother and five children each carrying a huge watermelon – "Don't ask me why," laughed Argun. The refugees were given tickets for shared accommodation on the lower deck, far away from tourists but Argun found another man sleeping in his bunk bed. The crew member, no longer able to turf Argun off the boat as they had left the port, was forced to issue Argun with another ticket. "I started walking back down but he said, 'No, up.' I was on my own in a room with just two beds."

"Were you in first class?"

"Yes," Argun laughed. "My brother had to get up at eight to get his breakfast or he would miss it, but I just waited for a knock on the door. 'Come in,' and they served me in bed!"

During the five-day crossing to Marseilles, the Israeli crew organized a singing competition. Argun chose a Turkish song that, unbeknown to him, was familiar to many Israelis on board. The passengers joined in; the clapping machine soared. As a prize Argun was handed a bundle of Italian records and a £7 coupon exchangeable at a bank. On arrival in Marseilles Argun, Zizi and the other refugees took the overnight train to Paris. After twelve hours in the waiting room at the Gare du Nord, where they were instructed to stay, Argun, Zizi and the refugee family, who had eaten their watermelons long ago, were famished. "I'm going out to find food," said Argun who, on exiting the station, was forced to give up his ticket. He found a bank where he exchanged the £7 coupon and, in a nearby shop, filled up five bags with French baguettes, cheese and tomatoes. Triumphant, he headed back to the station but, without his ticket, the guard refused him re-entry. Undeterred Argun walked into a travel agency backing onto the station, asked to go to the toilet, climbed onto the cistern, opened a top window through which he squeezed himself, his five bags of food as well as his photograph album. To Zizi's relief he caught the train but with just seconds to spare. They were all grateful for the food.

Argun's father picked up his sons from Victoria Station. He drove Argun, aged fourteen, to the house in north London of his ex-wife, now married to her Errol Flynn look-alike. Zizi went to live with his father and new wife in west London where he had a shoe repair shop. It was not a happy arrangement for either of the boys, but particularly for Argun. "At the first house in Grosvenor Road my mother had three beds upstairs empty, but she kept me sleeping on the couch for six months – she wanted me to pay rent. After that my grandfather sent her £3,000 to buy a house in Palmers Green. It had seven bedrooms, but she still made me sleep on the couch in the kitchen until I paid her £1.50 for a room."

Argun started to work after school, seven nights a week, for Mr Sheps, a Jewish man who opened a Wimpy bar in Palmers Green. "I had to eat and pay my rent. If I didn't do washing up, I would have starved." The first photo of Argun in London, in black and white, was of him wearing a chef's cocked white hat and a white buttoned up overall. "That's me in the Wimpy bar." Argun stood between two young white waitresses, one with an impressive beehive hair style, against a backdrop of Coca Cola signs and milk shake machines. The first colour photograph was of Argun in his bedroom, for which he paid his mother £1.50 a week, wearing a 1960s green flowery shirt and bright blue tie. He had done his best to cheer up the room by hanging a Chinese restaurant calendar embossed in red and gold and a map of the world on the walls decorated in brown wallpaper.

Argun's mother held parties to sell Avon cosmetics, his stepfather was a mechanic who drove recovery vehicles. They were clearly not wealthy, but I was surprised to hear that Argun not only paid his mother rent but gave her a shilling for every shirt she washed. He ate at school during the day and at his workplace in the evening, rather than at home where the atmosphere was tense. "Once when my brother visited, he brought a chicken and gave it to mum, saying, 'I fancy this with macaroni'. She left half of it for her husband but when he came home, he picked up a piece and said, 'Where has this come from?' When told it was from Zizi he spat it out. How do you feel? You just don't want to be there. There's no family atmosphere, no harmony. Stepfathers and stepmothers don't treat you like mum and dad, do they? You're not wanted so either side you get a poke in the eye." Argun missed his grandparents.

Because of his lack of English Argun left school, aged fifteen, just over a year after he had arrived in London with poor exam grades. Little regard was paid to his previous education record or continuing need for education. "The careers officer advised me to go to this screw making factory – such a noisy environment, oil, water, steam coming out of machines. I got paid half a crown an hour." Argun decided to go into catering and soon progressed from washing up to waiting. "I thought, double my money, I can do the chef's job." He started to work for a Greek Cypriot who had arrived in 1922, one of the first Greek Cypriots to settle in England.

Argun enjoyed his work and started to make plans. "I met my wife in 1972 when I visited one of my stepbrothers in Paphos. I was hooked very badly. I thought *This is the girl of my dreams.*" Over the next year Hurmus and Argun wrote to each other. "Everything was letters, there was no email, no Facebook, no telephone." A year later they married in Limassol. "I was so happy because I'm finding a home. Can you imagine? To me it was the happiest thing that could ever happen."

We leafed through the black-and-white wedding photos – of Hurmus with flowing dark hair, her gauze veil billowing out from a sculpted headdress that framed her delicate face, the soft pleats of her white dress, decorated with embroidered trails of entwined leaves, cascading to the floor. Of Argun, at her side, with long, thick Ottoman hair, wearing a flamboyant black bow tie and lacy shirt, a white handkerchief tucked into his top pocket. They danced cheek to cheek and walked hand in hand through Limassol, money pinned to their clothes by their guests – a Greek tradition of contributing to the wedding expenses so the couple would not start out in debt.

In 1974, after a honeymoon in Cyprus, Argun and Hurmus were held up at the airport on their way back to London. The military junta in Greece had backed a coup of Greek nationalists against Makarios, elected president in 1959, replacing him with pro-enosis Nikos Sampson – many Greek Cypriots still desired *enosis* (unification with Greece) while some Turkish Cypriots wanted Cyprus to come under the jurisdiction of Turkey. Within days Turkey landed troops in Northern Cyprus, having failed to gain the support of Britain and Greece, the other guarantors of the Republic of Cyprus. Greek Cypriots fled their homes, the coup collapsed and President Makarios fled. Turkish forces occupied a third of the island and enforced a partition between north and south roughly along the 'Green Line', the line drawn up by UN forces as part of the ceasefire in 1963. About 165,000 Greek Cypriots fled, or were driven from, the Turkish-occupied north; about 45,000 Turkish Cypriots left the south for the north, Argun's grandparents amongst them. Thousands died on both sides with missing persons still being identified. The UN Security Council passed a resolution calling on Turkey to withdraw its troops. Turkey refused, despite repeated UN Security Council resolutions making the same demand over the following decades.[8]

During this time Argun was running one of the London restaurants owned by his Greek Cypriot employer who, impressed by Argun's hard work, was planning to offer him a partnership. This was not to be. "His children came running to England, 'Dad, we've got no house, no work'. I was getting good money, £200 a week, but the atmosphere was terrible." Argun had to find alternative employment. "I don't know why I became a printer, it's not an easy job and, in those days, it was a closed shop. You had to have an uncle, dad or somebody to get in." This did not deter Argun who went on numerous training courses. A black-and-white photo of Argun shows him turning the wheel of a printing machine from a bygone era, his sleeves rolled up, his hair trailing over his collar. "I worked and worked and then about 1980 I joined Isracards, a Jewish printers' in Upper Clapton Road. They did letterpress and I did litho. It was hard at the beginning. I saw the signs. 'No Blacks, No Irish, No Dogs'. If you're not English, you're a foreigner. Then you were treated far better in south London than in north London, but it's levelled up. It's much better now." He and Hurmus have run the stationers and printers under the railway arches in Hackney, a busy hub of the community, for over twenty-five years. They have been married for fifty years.

After the war in 1974, Argun returned to his grandfather's land in Aydin, south of the Green Line. "I cried like a baby. All the houses were in ruins, no one was living there. They did not just kill Turkish Cypriots, they killed the culture of Cyprus, both Greek and Turkish." In 1983 the Turkish Cypriot leader declared the northern area as the Turkish Republic of Northern Cyprus but only Turkey recognizes it as an independent country. Cyprus is still separated by a UN monitored buffer zone although border restrictions are more relaxed than previously and negotiations over reunification resurface from time to time.[9]

"He was right," said Argun, referring to his grandfather's insistence that he and Zizi leave Cyprus, sad as it had been to leave their beloved grandparents, and painful as it had been to feel so unwelcomed by their parents and new spouses. "It's good they [parents] brought us here, but they didn't take care of us, they didn't help to educate us further. They just dropped us like a parachute on London and left us to our destiny."

After a delicious barbecue of kebabs and kofta Hurmus, and her daughter's two children, Aleyna, aged thirteen, and Alara, aged eleven, gathered round Argun on the terrace. Mitch set up the camera as Argun leafed through his album. An image of him as a chubby baby who loved his food; dressed as a girl in one image and a cowboy in another; of his beloved grandfather surveying his vineyards with Argun and Zizi at his feet, land that he lost in 1974. Of the room in his mother's house in London for which Argun had to pay rent; dressed in a green flowery shirt that his mother washed but for a price. "I think we are all proud of Grandpa," said Hurmus, surprised at Argun's revelations of how he had been treated when he first arrived in London. "People who've suffered so much often become harsh and unhappy but for Argun to go through all that and to be so positive and to always help people I think is amazing." Hurmus, tears slipping down her cheeks, tried to compose herself. Aleyna and Alara each grasped a hand to comfort her. "He never feels angry with anyone. Not many people can achieve that."

Argun, humbled, turned towards me.

"I was telling my wife this morning 'Look at my mother, if she did not get divorced and marry my dad I would not be here. I would not have my son, my daughter, my grandchildren. Life is a destiny. You take it as it comes."

Argun turned the page to photographs of the marriage ceremony.

"I was so young, so naïve," exclaimed Hurmus, looking just as elegant as she did fifty years ago.

"Your dress and veil are lovely," exclaimed Aleyna, the same age as Argun when he rescued his album from his grandfather's bombed-out house.

"What would you take if you had to leave your home in a hurry?" I asked Aleyna.

"I would take my phone and my charger," she replied, stroking her plaits.

Figure 5 Argun showing his photograph album to his wife Hurmus and his grandchildren, Aleyna and Alara. From the film *Life Is a Destiny,* courtesy of *Child Migrant Stories.*

"In my experience, when you have an emergency," laughed Hurmus "You don't care about phones. All you care about is your life and your family's life. You just want to be safe."

"No," said Aleyna standing her ground. "They would most likely take you to a house and most houses have plugs, then I would charge my phone and keep in contact with all my family to make sure they were OK."

Hurmus and Argun looked unconvinced.

"I know it sounds bad" Aleyna continued. "But I would not care about social media and stuff."

"In my childhood, we did not have phones. If I didn't take this," Argun explained, patting his album, "I would not have my childhood photos. Pictures were very important to me."

"But I would have childhood photos on my phone," Aleyna continued.

Aleyna had a point. Mobile phones can not only store more photographs than Argun's album ever could but are a lifeline for today's refugees. "Our phones and power banks are more important for our journey than anything, even more important than food," claimed Wael, a Syrian refugee.[10] Phones help refugees plan routes, trace lost friends and family, translate, access money and research key information. They even store evidence in support of asylum claims and can be used in emergencies. Refugees crossing the Mediterranean or the English Channel on rickety boats can send out SOS messages with an exact GPS position if they get lost or in trouble, hoping, often tragically in vain, that they will be rescued.

"What would you take with you?" I asked Alara, the youngest granddaughter.

"I would make sure I had all my family with me. And Alfie too."

"Ahhhh, Alfie," they chorused. Alfie was the dog.

On this, at least, grandparents and grandchildren could agree.

Several months later, after checking the final edit with Argun, Mitch and I returned to Argun's house to screen *Life Is a Destiny*. Local politicians and members of the Council of Turkish Cypriot Associations seated themselves in the living room overlooking the garden. After the film ended there was silence, then applause except from a trio of people in the back of the room. They disputed the text at the end of the film that Turkey 'invaded' Cyprus in 1974. On the contrary, they argued, Turkey, as one of the guarantors of the power sharing-arrangements of the Republic of Cyprus and following the refusal of the other guarantors to act, had, justifiably, intervened on behalf of the Turkish Cypriot community.

Despite this, Mitch and I were commissioned by the Council of Turkish Cypriot Associations (CTCA) to produce a further film about 100 years of Turkish Cypriot migration to the UK. I interviewed ten people who had migrated since 1930, some of whom came over when Cyprus was still part of the British Empire, others who came later during, or following, the conflicts of 1963/4 and 1974, who had seen harmonious relationships between Greek and Turkish Cypriots torn apart. All those interviewed had made a life in Britain, had children and grandchildren. But they differed in whether their hearts lay in Finchley or Famagusta.

In December 2017 I waited anxiously at the back of a full lecture theatre of the V&A Museum for Mitch to bring the film *My Heart Belongs to … 100 Years of Turkish Cypriot Migration to the UK*.[11] I left desperate messages on his mobile.

"Mitch, where are you? There are 300 people waiting."

All turned out well. The audience, mainly Turkish Cypriots, laughed and cried in equal measure. Most moving of all was when young people in the audience, the same age as Alara and Aleyna, put up their hands, eager to get answers from the post-screening panel. "We hear our parents and grandparents whispering in secret about these events. Why do they never talk to us about them? We need to know."[12]

CHAPTER 4
FOLLOWING MUM TO THE 'MOTHERLAND'
Richard Lue and Roberta who arrived, aged seven and eight respectively, from Jamaica in 1964

I tossed and turned, unable to sleep during a cold winter night in January 2020. The deportation flight to Jamaica was scheduled to leave in the early hours. I picked up my phone to follow Right to Remain and Detention Action on Twitter. One minute the deportation flight of fifty people was going ahead. An hour later, the Court of Appeal ordered the Home Office to halt the flight – some detainees had been unable to access legal advice because of no internet or telephone signal. The Home Office appealed and threatened to go ahead with the flight anyway. Distraught detainees, unaware of what was happening, were shipped from pillar to post in the dark. Children asked where their fathers were; families were going out of their minds. Then the plane took off with seventeen people detained in a centre not affected by the network breakdown. Thirty-three people had escaped deportation. For the moment, at least.

David Lammy, the member of parliament for Tottenham, north London, and a son of Guyanese parents, tweeted, 'The government is deporting people who arrived in the UK as young as two, often for one-time drug offences'. He wrote, 'The lessons from Windrush have not been learned. Lives are being ruined because we don't remember our history'.[1] The Windrush scandal, named after the ship, the *Empire Windrush* that brought one of the first groups of West Indian migrants to Britain in 1948, broke in 2018. For two weeks *Guardian* newspaper headlines highlighted cases of people of pensionable age who had come from the Caribbean as children with, or to join, their parents who had responded to Britain's call for labour after the Second World War. People who had gone to school in Britain, worked hard and could barely remember the place they were born, had been deported, detained, lost their jobs or homes. They had been denied benefits or medical care to which they were entitled. Some were refused re-entry to Britain after a visit abroad. They were treated as illegal immigrants even though, if their parents had arrived prior to 1 January 1973 when the Immigration Act 1971 came into force and had remained in Britain ever since, they were in the UK legally. In their minds they were British. What had changed, in the intervening years, were the procedures put in place under the 'hostile environment' policy whereby people had to prove their legal status through supplying multiple papers for each year of residence. Landlords, employers, the NHS, charities, banks, acting as arms of the Home Office, were liable to fines of up to £10,000 if clients, tenants or employees were unable to prove legal residence in Britain. Hard data is difficult to come by, but it is estimated that up to 57,000 people may have been affected.[2]

Amelia Gentleman, a *Guardian* journalist, featured several of these injustices.[3] Vernon Vanriel, a professional boxer, who arrived in Britain aged six, was refused re-entry to Britain after a holiday in Jamaica. He was stranded homeless on the island for thirteen years, having lived in the UK for over four decades. Paulette Wilson came to Britain in 1968 when she was ten or eleven but was detained and only narrowly escaped deportation having worked in the House of Commons canteen. She died in July 2020, aged sixty-four, after years of campaigning. Renford McIntrye lost his job as a driver for the NHS, was not allowed to work or claim benefits, and became homeless after fifty years in the UK.

There was uproar. These were people who had worked hard, paid taxes, brought up children and grandchildren. Heads rolled. Amber Rudd, Home Secretary resigned after claiming that the Home Office did not have targets for removal, something later established to be untrue. Sajid Javid was appointed and changed the name, but not the direction, from the 'hostile' to the 'compliant' environment; people's cases were fast tracked; a compensation scheme was established; deportation flights to the Caribbean were suspended and an independent review set up. But few of those who have applied have received compensation[4] and by the time the government resumed deportations to Jamaica in February 2020, the Windrush Lessons Learned Review had still not been published.

'These are all foreign national offenders – they have all received custodial sentences of twelve months or more. They are responsible for crimes like manslaughter, rape, dealing in class-A drugs', Javid told *BBC Radio 5 Live*.[5] But some of those who the Home Office wished to deport had only minor drug or driving offences from years ago and often in their youth. Many had partners, children and grandchildren in Britain.

A leak from the delayed Windrush Lessons Learned report[6] suggested the government should 'review its policy and approach to FNOs [foreign national offenders], if necessary, through primary legislation'. These included considering 'ending all deportation of FNOs where they arrived in the UK as children' and only using deportation in 'the most severe cases'. As Amelia Gentleman wrote, 'In apologizing for their mistakes, ministers cast those affected as deserving migrants who had laboured hard in the NHS and on the buses, had paid their taxes and behaved impeccably ... So, what did that mean for people whose records were less immaculate? Immigration lawyers argued that a pre-1973 arrival meant a right to remain in the UK, regardless of convictions, but the government seemed at pains to wash its hands of anyone with a criminal record.'[7]

David Lammy saw the roots of such injustices in our history. 'Much of this is because it still fails to confront the legacy of empire. The UK and Caribbean are entwined because the British Empire enslaved Black Africans and brought them there in shackles on slave ships.'[8] The link to Britain, for those of Caribbean background in the UK, is not only through slavery but as colonial subjects when they considered themselves British. This was before the different Caribbean islands secured their independence during the second half of the twentieth century while, nevertheless, remaining Commonwealth members.

The *Pathé* newsreel of the arrival of passengers on the *Empire Windrush* in 1948 features dapper young Black men listening to Lord Kitchener, the Trinidadian calypsonian, singing 'London Is the Place for Me.'[9] One newspaper headline struck a different tone to what we have become, unfortunately, used to. 'The Evening Standard greets the 400 Sons of Empire.'[10] The subsequent article notes that many of the new arrivals knew Britain for serving in the armed forces during the Second World War. There is no mention of the sixty-five women who travelled on the *Windrush*, all of whom paid double the fare as only the upper deck cabin car was considered suitable for females. There were no headlines about the 'Daughters of Empire' who had responded to recruitment adverts in the 1950s and 1960s; who had no doubt read the book *Going to Britain*; and who had often left partners and children behind, the latter in the care of extended family. Charlie Brinkhurst-Cuff in *Mother Country – Real Stories of the Windrush Children* showed that as many, if not more, women than men came over from the Caribbean in the 1950s and 1960s.[11] Among these pioneers were the mothers of Roberta and Richard. Their children were of similar ages – Roberta aged eight and Richard seven – when they followed their mothers to the UK, travelling by air from Jamaica in 1964. But their experiences of arrival, reunion and settling in Britain, and the impact on their adult lives, differed in significant ways.

Roberta who arrived from Jamaica aged eight at Heathrow, London, in 1964

"I was always told that my mother was gone, but that she would send for me."

Roberta's grandmother, who cared for Roberta during her mother's absence, always assured Roberta that her mother still loved her, that she had not abandoned her – Roberta often received parcels from her mother in London, with dolls and bits and pieces inside. Roberta retained vivid memories of her mother – she still had the crinoline dresses that her mother had bought for her and that she insisted on wearing when going with her mother to church. She still remembered how she used to climb a tree to watch her mother selling shaved ice and of how her mother used to warn Roberta's two brothers not to put her into the canal. "If they did, I'd scream, 'I'm going to tell mummy!'" Then Roberta would sit on the canal bank to protect her brothers' clothes and watch out for the patrol man – it was forbidden to swim in the canal. So, it was no great surprise when Roberta heard, aged eight, that her mother had saved enough money to pay for her, and one of her older brothers, to fly to London.

Roberta was one of the first people who agreed to be interviewed. As a mature PhD student, she knew it was difficult to find volunteers. We sat in the living room of her Victorian terraced home drinking tea. She and I went back a long way. In the 1980s and 1990s we had worked together setting up adult education courses in Hackney – in literacy, art, saz, dog training, women's assertion, African drumming and cake decorating, the most popular class with Caribbean women. We established classes for mental health service users in Homerton Hospital; for recently arrived refugees in Kurdish community centres and for Irish Travellers on Hackney Marshes – that is, before the Travellers were moved to make way for the Olympic Games in 2012. I had spent a holiday with Roberta in Spain and photographed her entering British women's weightlifting championships, doing the 'snatch' and 'clean and jerk', that she invariably won. I had never listened to her story of migrating as an eight-year-old from the countryside in Jamaica.

Roberta's mother was one of the many pioneers who, in responding to the motherland's request for labour, left her children in the care of extended family.[12] "I admire my mother so much – she left my father because she said he was lazy. She packed me and my first brother to live with my grandmother, left my second brother with our dad and flew to England." Roberta was excited at joining her mother in Britain, that is until idle gossip made her anxious. "Everybody said, 'You're going to turn white when you go there'. It's ironic because most of my time has been spent in a white world. I've had white partners and my friends are mostly white." Roberta smiled. "Don't you remember the school keeper at the door of Clapton School who used to say, 'A white, you white'?' whenever I asked for something like an umbrella if it was raining." We laughed, remembering the eccentric Black school keeper who worked on the evening shift for the adult evening classes.

Roberta could not remember leaving her grandmother who had looked after her for three years as a child. It was as if she had blocked out all memory of it. "I don't remember any sadness. I don't remember any joy." She remembered travelling on the coach to Kingston. "Seeing blue sea and tangerines on the trees. I still dream of it" – her mother had always taken Roberta and her brothers to the beach. Although Roberta did not remember leaving Jamaica, she did recall arriving in London. "I remember mum coming to collect us at the airport. I was eight." She recalled, too, that immigration officers in London did not believe it was her signature in cursive writing on the passport – Roberta's mother had paid for her education. "No one writes like that at your age," huffed the officer. It was to be the first time, but not the last, that she felt undermined by white authority figures. "It's almost like people never believe in who you are."

Roberta's mother took her children to the one room she rented in a large multi-occupational Victorian house in Tottenham, north London – her brother, who was in his teens, disappeared soon after. It was the first of several, similar houses in north and east London where Roberta lived with her mother over the next ten years, all with a shared bathroom, a shared kitchen, a crocheted doily over the back of an old settee and the obligatory calor-gas stove. "Horrible places really." Sometimes Roberta mistrusted the other residents, particularly when her mother was out, something that may have prompted moving so frequently. Roberta learnt to be practical and house proud. "Silly me one day I said, 'Shall I help you?' So, after school, I did the cooking before my mother would get in. I was what they call a latchkey kid." To this day Roberta's house is always immaculate.

In those first few months Roberta missed Caribbean food – ackee, saltfish and callaloo. Like many children confronted with strange tastes she reacted. "I spat out Irish potato as I was used to sweet potato." One day, the Indian family upstairs invited Roberta up to dinner and "I took a mouthful and nearly died. People think you're racist, I wasn't. I just never went back in case they gave me food. I used to eat a lot of sweet stuff. I loved condensed milk on bread." It was not easy for Roberta to make friends. The parents of one white girl living next door never let Roberta cross their threshold. Instead, Roberta played with the girl from an upstairs window – inventing new clapping games and using her doll as a puppet. One day the girl disappeared – her parents had stopped her seeing Roberta. "I didn't ever think it was my colour. I always thought I was ugly."

Nor was school a welcoming place. Roberta, the only Black child in class in her first school in Tottenham, took time to speak up. When she did, the other children dissolved into giggles. "I had a thick Caribbean accent, so I had to lose that quick. I picked up this Cockney accent which I now regret because when I hear a Caribbean accent, I think there's a lovely twang to it." In those early days Roberta and her mother socialized with people of their own colour. "If we went out it would be to relatives' or friends' places, Black friends, that are having some sort of get together." But Roberta's mother also socialized with people of all backgrounds. "Hence the Indian family, Jewish people and even Greek. She went to Greece with the hope of living there. Thank goodness she decided against it."

I asked Roberta if she would draw her house in the Caribbean. She tried and then gave up. "You should have given me notice." Instead, we drove to one of the primary schools Roberta attended as a child – moving from house to house meant moving schools. We parked the car near London Fields and strolled under the huge plane trees, until Roberta's old school came into view. As she looked up at the tall windows on the third floor of the imposing, red-brick Victorian building, she stiffened, "No particular friend, no particular teacher, no particular anything. It's like you just exist." Roberta was often the butt of racist insults. "I got called, 'Rubber lips' and then I remembered Mick Jagger and I thought, whoopee, he's got big lips." Her laughter subsided as she remembered what happened to one Black boy at her school. "I remember people saying he scrubbed himself white with bleach, and I thought how odd. But then I began to understand why I was being called names. I think he died."

Secondary school teachers often singled Roberta out as a troublemaker. "I don't remember making a noise but, because I was at the front, I'd get chucked out." The art room became her refuge. Roberta entered the British education system in 1971, the year Coard published *How the West Indian Child Is Made Educationally Sub-normal in the British School System*.[13] I knew Coard's work from when, in Camden in the 1970s, I was involved in campaigning against the number of Black children being excluded from school for being 'troublemakers'. Roberta, like many other Black children, felt teachers failed to recognize her potential. "Looking back, I'm angry because nobody wanted me to learn. I was just the wrong colour, wrong accent, wrong everything." It was Angela Davis, the Black woman activist with the enormous Afro, a key figure in the Civil Rights movement in the United States, who kept Roberta's aspirations alight. "When I was ten or eleven, at the time of the Black Power movement, I had my hair out like Angela Davis and wore white plimsolls with 'POWER' written on them. I used to wear these John

Lennon type glasses and come home from the library with books under my arm. I've always had this intellectual side. People must have been laughing at me as there was no glass in the frame."

After leaving school Roberta worked in an accountant's office and then moved to different companies just as she had moved between different schools and homes. Later she became a qualified teacher through the Keep Fit Association and started to teach in adult education. I watched as she progressed through the ranks of women's weightlifting – as many times British women's weightlifting champion, first in the EEC (European Economic Community) and sixth in the world; as she travelled internationally as captain of the British women's team, senior coach and strong advocate of women's weightlifting. The intellectual spark lit by Angela Davis and other feminists, both Black and white, never completely died. When her university lecturer said she should publish her master's degree focusing on psychiatric inpatients at Homerton Hospital, Roberta laughed, "I don't get things published" to which he replied, "One day you ought to do a PhD." Years later she recalled his advice, choosing as her subject the educational and social experiences of lone parent students in higher education. Roberta told me about her graduation ceremony. "The whole hall cheered and clapped." Perhaps they knew, or related to, the discrimination, racism and challenges that people with Roberta's life experiences and background often face when pursuing their ambitions.

When I worked with Roberta, in the 1980s and 1990s, I often wondered why she was so resistant to returning to Jamaica where she still had family. She explained. "When I left Jamaica, I never made contact with anybody again. I regret that so much. It's about survival. I had to survive here, and I never thought about there. My grandmother died at 103 and I hated myself for never going back. I thought, *You silly woman*." It was Roberta's current partner who persuaded her to return, almost forty years after she left. "We were going to Florida to compete in a weightlifting event, and he says, 'It's near Jamaica, aren't you going to see your family?'" Roberta arrived too late to see her grandmother but in time to see her father. "He couldn't believe his daughter was there – but seeing a small, frail man was not what I expected. I remembered a taller, more powerful man." Roberta stayed with her older brother, a cricketer for the West Indies who had been prevented from joining his mother and siblings in Britain because of immigration restrictions. Several people recognized Roberta. "I felt a bit like Lady Diana Spencer – they all looked at me as if I was royalty." She wanted to see the tourist sites, so her brother took her by car to the White River Hotel in Ocho Rios and along the river by boat, passing Black people fishing along the riverbanks. When they reached the open sea and sand, Roberta noticed only white people on the beaches. "I thought, *Are we in South Africa?* That, and the sad state of the infrastructure, are the reasons I haven't returned."

Roberta's father died soon after, leaving Roberta land she has never claimed. "I regret that but I'm not bitter. It served me right." What haunts Roberta most is that she never went back to see her grandmother. Roberta's struggle to survive in London left little room for her to acknowledge, or deal with, feelings of loss. There was no WhatsApp or Skype to keep the relationship going. Not that these are a child's substitute, as the Home

Office sometimes maintains when they separate families, for the touch, sound, feel and smell of a loved one. Roberta's return to Jamaica, after having lived in London for forty years, disorientated her. Rejecting Jamaica has not resolved Roberta's views about where she belongs. "I feel comfortable living in the East End, but I still feel as though I don't quite belong."

Richard Lue who arrived from Jamaica, aged seven, at Heathrow, London in 1964

I took the lift to the thirteenth floor of a tower block in Bow, east London. Richard, a tall man with long dreadlocks and a light brown complexion, answered the door and welcomed me into his living room. I had met Richard through his friend, Errol, who had migrated from Jamaica aged thirteen. I was keen to interview Richard as there were interesting parallels with Roberta's experience.

As I looked over the docks through his front window, Richard fetched a large cardboard box from under his bed. We chatted side by side on his sofa, as he pulled out photographs. Colour and black-and-white images of his great aunt of Jewish and Indian descent and of her husband, Papa David; of his Chinese paternal grandfather and of his father of mixed Jamaican and Chinese descent and of Richard as a teenager with shorter dreadlocks.

"Perhaps such mixed ancestry contributed to your good looks."

"I was always one for the girls," he chuckled.

Richard had fond memories of his early childhood. During the week he lived with his great aunt, Papa David and twelve other children in a large colonial house in Kingston, furnished and fitted in fine mahogany. Richard was his great aunt's favourite child. "I had the first bath in the sink tub of a Sunday." Much to the anger of his siblings and cousins, he was chosen to accompany his great aunt to the Jamaican independence celebrations in 1963. "My great aunt was close to the political leader of the PNP [People's National Party] so she got VIP passes. All these posh people and royal family and little old me with my aunty! The whole island was partying. It was rocking!" At the weekend his rich Chinese grandfather would take Richard to stay with his Chinese wife and children in Portland. "I was doted on as the first grandchild." The Chinese grandmother welcomed this grandson from her husband's affair with the family's Jamaican maid. Richard rejected any use of the term 'step' or 'half' sibling or cousin. "We don't believe in 'half' brothers and sisters, everybody's one," asserted Richard, challenging more Western assumptions of who makes up a family.

Richard, unlike Roberta, never expected to leave Jamaica and had little time to prepare. "My grand aunt, my grandmother's sister, told me I'd be flying to England in the morning to be with my mother. It didn't register until I got on the plane. I was crying. I didn't want to come." Perhaps his great aunt thought it would be less painful for Richard to be told of his departure at the last minute. Or perhaps, in pain herself, she could not bear to see his sorrow. Richard arrived at Heathrow airport in midwinter, dressed in his school uniform of cotton khaki shorts and shirt. He was met by his maternal grandparents whom he had never met, and his mother whom he didn't recognize. She had left when Richard was a toddler. "They were strangers to me. It was like they took all my childhood away and sent me off to this freezer."

Richard moved into a flat with his mother and grandparents in a large, rambling house on Cazenove Road in Stoke Newington, popular with the Orthodox Jewish community. What shocked Richard most was the cold. "1964 was the wickedest winter in memory. I was trembling. I remember the horse-hair blankets, I had thirteen of them over me." Soon after, Richard moved with his mother, a nurse, to south London. Two years later Richard's mother moved abroad, and Richard went back to live with his grandparents in Cazenove Road. "She went to Australia first, then to Canada, then to America where it was better pay." Richard was philosophic about his mother's decision to leave him. "I didn't want her to go but I had to accept it. We always kept in communication. I was her closest child towards the end."

Figure 6 Richard on the day of his confirmation, Stepney, east London. Courtesy of Richard Lue.

Richard's grandparents wanted Richard to become a Catholic, even though they themselves never attended church. His grandmother practised her faith at home. "I think because she didn't like the cold weather. Her church was in her bedroom with her altar, rosary and holy water. She used to pray every night." Richard became an altar boy and at the age of eight took confirmation, but with no family present. "My grandmother didn't turn up. In Jamaica everyone would have been there." The photograph of a smiling Richard in his confirmation clothes shows no trace of the loss of his extended family at this important rite of passage.

Richard pointed through the window to where his maternal grandfather, a seaman of mixed German and Jamaican heritage, took him as a child to greet his old boat. "He was a cook on *The Producer and the Planter*. The old Jamaicans in London were there – drinking, laughing, playing dominoes – you could smell the white rum before you walked on the boat. And then we used to go down the gambling house in Cable Street with pockets full of money because that's where the seamen's café was – African seamen. I was eight or nine at the time. Everyone in east London was on the drink, especially on a Friday night. I remember the cocktail bar where my grandparents used to have the glasses and ice buckets. VP wine, that's what they used to drink. It used to send them doolally. Crazy arguments started and when they ran out, they sent me over the off-licence to get another bottle." His grandfather was a disciplinarian, different from his grandmother who was "the most beautiful lady you could imagine, so kind, so loving, she'd do anything for me."

In his first primary school Richard, like Roberta, was the only Black child in class but, unlike Roberta, never felt subjected to racism. "Even in my secondary school I never suffered racism. And this is east London." Unlike Roberta, who was ostracized by her white friends' parents, Richard was accepted. "I used to be in their house every minute. Their parents loved me and there was no malice." It was unclear why Richard experienced less racism than Roberta. Was it just different schools or different neighbourhoods, because of gender or Richard's lighter skin? Colourism, a phrase coined in 1982 by Alice Walker, the American author, to describe skin-based tone prejudice, is now more openly acknowledged as a form of discrimination.[14]

Richard enjoyed exploring east London with his friends. Perhaps, as a boy, he did not take on the same responsibility for housework as Roberta. Or perhaps he had more freedom. "We was just doing what kids do, exploring old bomb sites, building our own camp and fires." In his teenage years things became more difficult. His white and mixed-race African friends "didn't like Black Jamaican guys, so we used to have a lot of fights." Richard began to follow Jamaican music, particularly reggae and especially Bob Marley. Bob was important to Richard for other reasons. "He was mixed, his dad was Scottish. We've got so many mixed-race down there it's unbelievable." Along with his friend Errol he visited Four Aces music club in Dalston, Hackney until the early hours. Richard also went to the Roaring 20s club in Carnaby Street, Soho. "It was a Jamaican club, but Rod Stewart used to go there and Mick Jagger – to let their hair down, smoke their draw, drink their liquor." Richard preferred shebeens to clubs as fights in private houses were less likely.[15] "You used to pay an entrance, fifty pence in them days. It used to kick off about twelve o'clock and stay there until about seven, eight o'clock in the morning – that's what you call partying. Every room used to be packed – 500 to 1,000 people in a big house in Hackney. Sometimes, but not often, the police would raid it." In response to being excluded from pubs and dance halls Caribbean people, as early as the 1950s, had created their own private entertainment spaces but these were often targeted by police.[16]

Richard and I laughed when we realized we could have been at the same shebeen on Cazenove Road in the 1970s, just round the corner from my first flat in Stoke Newington. I remember the smell of rum, of rice and peas and goat curry; hovering on the edge as elegant Black women shuffled to the music in the centre of the room whilst young men, with long riffs, looked on; my feet twitching to music, not daring to join in.

Richard, too, like Roberta, left school at fifteen but unlike Roberta has not returned to education. "I wish I went to uni. I was bright but it wasn't encouraged like it is today." Richard worked in the fur and other industries until he trained to be a carpenter, something he enjoys. He shared how he went to prison for three years for robbery, even showing me letters he received from his father in Jamaica whilst inside. "There's no one else to blame. But you can be influenced and there were a lot of problems from police. I couldn't walk the streets without being stopped."

Richard's experience at the hands of the police was not unique. The disproportionate use of Stop and Search against Black youth, what came to be known as the 'sus law', contributed to huge resentment within the Black community, fuelling the race riots of 1981. It led to the Scrap Sus campaign, supported, amongst others, by race relations organizations including the Camden Committee for Community Relations where I worked in the late 1970s.[17] Although the law was repealed in August 1981 it was replaced by new stop and search powers in 1984 under the Police and Criminal Evidence Act (PACE). In 2019 the UK government extended Stop and Search powers, making it easier, under Section 60 of the Criminal Justice and Public Order Act 1994 than under PACE, for police to stop and search anyone without the usual legal requirement for "reasonable suspicion".[18] Figures published by the UK government in May 2022 show that seven times as many Black people are stopped and searched than white people.[19] David Lammy's review into the treatment of Black people by the criminal justice system, commissioned by Downing Street, showed that while Black people are four times more likely to be in prison than white people, the incarceration rate rises to nine times more likely for those aged under eighteen.[20] In 2020, 32 per cent of children in prison were Black despite Black prisoners accounting for only 13 per cent of the entire prison population.[21]

Richard's grandparents stood by him when he went to prison and took care of his children at the weekends. On his return home his grandmother determined to get rid of the dreadlocks he had grown in custody. "At night-time I used to feel like someone was pulling my hair. What you supposed to do when someone's laughing at you at four o'clock in the morning?" Richard cared for both his grandparents until they died in the flat where he now lives and has not removed his grandmother's altar from her old bedroom. When, at the age of seventeen, Richard got into trouble with the law and started to feel homesick, his father came to collect him, but his grandparents refused to let him leave. He sometimes regrets this decision and imagines how different his life would be had he returned. "I would have been better off in Jamaica, career wise, money wise. Then again, my brother turned out the opposite because he ended up being a gun man for one of the political parties down there. He got involved with politricks and gangs, all them things."

When Richard first returned to Jamaica for a holiday, he had less difficulty than Roberta reconnecting with the places and people of his childhood. "The breadfruit tree's still there and the guinep tree's still at the front … it was like I'd never been away. You think you'd forget tings, but you don't. And then I'm hearing someone call my name. 'You're Ricky from Tower Street … You don't change'. I replied, 'I left here when I was seven!'"Richard considered himself to be a Jamaican although he considered himself a British citizen too but for practical reasons he held a Jamaican, not a British passport. This allowed him to visit his mother in the United States for periods of six months rather than three although later restrictions, due to his conviction, prevented him from obtaining an American visa to see his mother before she died or to attend her funeral.

As the Windrush scandal broke I worried about Richard and his lack of a British passport. His right to live in Britain should not be in question given he came to join his mother before 1973 when the 1971 Immigration Law came into place, restricting the entry of Commonwealth citizens. But others in a similar position, with a criminal offence, no matter how minor, have been detained, deported or not allowed back into the UK. A recommendation from the Windrush Lessons Learned report that the government should consider 'ending all deportation of FNOs [foreign national offenders] where they arrived in the UK as children' and only using deportation in 'the most severe cases' has not been implemented. Indeed, the government has rowed back on several of the report's recommendations.[22] Richard clearly loved Jamaica and after his youngest son, still at home, had gone off to university, wanted to spend more time there. But a forced removal or refused return would separate him not only from his children but his three beloved grandchildren. "They're perfect. They're my joy."

I rang Richard but there was no reply. Errol had sadly died so I could no longer contact Richard through his friend. I worried, remembering Amelia Gentleman's words that 'the government seemed at pains to wash its hands of anyone with a criminal record'.[23] I thought of Lammy's powerful speeches saying that those deportees who were British citizens had already served a sentence appropriate to their offence. To be detained and deported compounded such punishments and could be a death sentence. *The Guardian* revealed that at least five people had been killed after being deported to Jamaica.[24] I reflected on how experiences of separation, reunion, relocation and racism, such as those experienced by Roberta and Richard, could contribute to transgressive behaviour; to acting above and beyond the law. I kept an eye on the reports of aeroplanes, full of deportees, to Jamaica and, sometimes at night, lay awake, following my Twitter account.

Two and a half years after the postponed flight to Jamaica I was able to contact Richard. We met at the house of Cathy, Errol's widow. It was clear that my fears had been well founded. Unable to provide a British passport at work, Richard had been sacked. "It was my son who saved me." If Richard had not been the sole carer for his youngest son, a minor at the time, the Home Office could well have detained Richard or deported him to Jamaica. For two years he was unable to work, claim benefits to which he was entitled or leave Britain. He acquired huge debts and suffered serious depression but, after submitting all his employment, tax, national insurance and other records going back decades, and with the support of his member of parliament, Richard was granted indefinite leave to remain – due to his early conviction, he cannot apply for citizenship. He successfully applied to the Windrush Compensation Scheme. Richard was clear that this did not make up for what he had been through.[25] "This country is not for Black people," he sighed.

CHAPTER 5
"I MUCH PREFER ROASTED RAT"
Maurice Nwokeji who arrived, aged nine, from Nigeria, in 1970

I checked my watch as I listened to a talk about trauma in the lecture theatre of the School of Oriental and African Studies in London. I texted Maurice, 'Where are you? The film starts in 10 minutes.' I texted again at eight minutes, six minutes, four minutes, two minutes. Just as well the session was running over. I kept an eye on the door, hoping to see Maurice walk in, guitar in hand, his dreadlocks swinging. Maurice was no rigid timekeeper, but it was unusual for him to be this late. I wrote one last text. 'You're going to miss the film.' Then I looked down at the conference programme – an impressive list of events to mark the fiftieth anniversary since the outbreak of the war in Biafra. Oh no! I was in the wrong place. The film was being screened in another room.

By the time I arrived at Room 202, *Ugwumpiti*[1] had already been screened. The atmosphere was electric – Maurice, in his blue tunic embroidered with gold African lions, was answering questions. A young woman stood up. "I too am a victim as my parents never talked about the war." Others followed, some in tears. "We dared not talk about it, dared not mention Biafra." *Ugwumpiti*, narrated from the perspective of a child, had encouraged people to talk. The film was later installed in the exhibition *Legacies of Biafra*[2] in the Brunei Gallery and has subsequently toured. But such is the sensitivity around the subject that neither the film nor the exhibition can tour Nigeria.

Maurice had already explained why there was a taboo about discussing the conflict that killed 2 million citizens. "After the war we had a military government so, if you said, 'Biafra,' you'd be shot. So, because we lost, we weren't allowed to grieve. It's only recently that our people are becoming vocal about what happened. We're traumatised, the Igbos." The Republic of Biafra, established in eastern Nigeria in June 1967, after the genocide of 30–50,000 Igbos in northern Nigeria, finally surrendered in January 1970. At one stage, during the war, 1,000 children a day died of starvation.[3]

I first met Maurice, a tall, charismatic Igbo man – he would never call himself a Nigerian – on the terrace of the South Bank overlooking the Thames. He had just played to audiences in the Festival Hall to celebrate the opening of an exhibition by the Migration Museum in which he featured.[4] He had donated a keepsake – a book of Igbo nursery rhymes that he remembers his grandmother, who died of starvation in front of him, had taught him. During his reggae performance, inspired by his childhood experiences of civil war, Maurice let drop that he had migrated to Hackney when he was nine. I approached him as he relaxed with a cool beer on a stifling hot day.

"I am doing research into … " I stumbled … "into child migration to east London."

"I would love to. I've always wanted to tell my story."

I did not expect a stranger to trust me so quickly. We exchanged contact information. I left him to finish his drink.

A few days later Maurice arrived at my Hackney home. It did not take long for the interview to get going – Maurice is a natural storyteller. The only interruption was a phone call to a friend who was mending his guitar. Maurice returned a fortnight later, instrument in hand. I was surprised to hear he had not learnt to play the guitar until his late thirties – he was now in his fifties. At a low time in Maurice's life – after his partner, with his first daughter, had left him – he picked up a friend's guitar. Twenty-four hours later, unable to wrench it from Maurice's hands, the friend loaned him the instrument. "I wonder if someone had given me a guitar, say when I was twenty-one, whether life would have been different. It gave me a place to go with my frustration. There's an outlet – the aggression has gone." Maurice smiled. "Even what we're doing now is an outlet. It's like being constipated for a long time and suddenly … " Maurice clapped his hand and we burst out laughing.

It is easy to mistake Maurice, who plays reggae and has dreadlocks, as a Jamaican rather than an Igbo but, since arriving in London, Maurice has always been attracted to Rastafarianism.[5] "I saw people with locks, and I was interested. Plus, red, gold and green are the colours of Biafra. Besides, Jamaicans are from Nigeria. When the slave masters went to sleep, they all talked Igbo." Maurice met Jamarcus, a Jamaican Rastafarian from north London, in his teens. Together they operated clubs in squats around Hackney, setting up a sound system until the police shut them down. Jamarcus had a profound influence on Maurice. "My parents taught me that, because we lived in mud huts, we were not civilised. Then this Rastaman said to me, 'You're a prince. You're an African, walk your head high.'" It was in his late thirties that Maurice became a Rastafarian. "As I played the guitar, I saw signs and felt I was being called. Then I found out it was Jah. That gave me peace."

Maurice was born in the village of Akuma in eastern Nigeria. His father had joined the British army when Nigeria was part of the British Empire and came to study in London. His mother, a teacher, joined him, leaving two-year-old Maurice and his six-month-old brother, in the care of extended family. Maurice understands why his father needed his mother's support. Posters across London saying 'No Blacks, No Irish, No Dogs' in the Swinging Sixties made clear that people like his father were unwelcome. The boys went to live with an uncle in Benin but when war broke out the children fled back to Biafra. "There were loads of Igbos moving east, road jams everywhere. It must have taken us days to get home." In Akuma, Maurice and his younger brother were looked after by their two grandmothers who adored the boys and fought over the right to look after them. "That used to make us feel special."

As the war progressed, food became scarce. "My whole day was about catching lizards with my catapult, which was hit and miss. I caught rats and killed a few snakes. They're fairly tasty when you're hungry." Maurice picked up his guitar to sing 'Nne, Nne' dedicated to his grandmother. "I shut down for over thirty, forty years. Then, about ten years ago, I would write one line, cry for a week, be depressed and then write another.

But I was determined for people to know my grandma, my mum's mum." Maurice rarely performs this song in public. "She was a beautiful woman and there was nothing wrong with her. She just needed food." Maurice put down his guitar. "Her death made me unhinged. Aged seven I started crawling again. My brother, without understanding why, followed me on his hands and knees." Maurice has no memory of this event – it is his younger brother who reminds him. "When we meet up, we talk about it, which we didn't for years."

The death of his grandmother frightened Maurice. "I realised we were going to die, so I started to thieve. Then people would beat the shit out of me." A local teacher told the Red Cross the boys were orphans, even though their paternal grandmother was alive, and the boys' parents were in England. This entitled Maurice and his brother to one life-saving meal a day. "There would be thousands of us and when kids died in the line you just pushed that kid away and moved up one. Without the Red Cross we would have died, for sure."

I remembered the newspaper images in the 1970s. Children with eyes staring out of hollow skulls, skeletal limbs staggering under the weight of bloated bellies. There was outrage – John Lennon took up the cause as did politicians like Jack Straw. Britain's role in supporting the Nigerian government, that was withholding emergency supplies from Biafra, was kept under wraps.[6] There were demonstrations too. It seemed incredible that Maurice was one of these pot-bellied, sunken-eyed children queuing up with an empty bowl, sharing his story in my living room with such generosity and humour. "*Ugwumpiti* was cornmeal mixed with powdered milk and water in a big oil drum and stirred with a big stick. Nothing has ever tasted as beautiful as that. For me, even now, it's the food of the angels."

At the end of each day the Red Cross would hold a singing competition and, as a prize, the winner would lick out the oil drum. Maurice picked up his guitar, his voice quickening with excitement as he remembered singing, 'Sabo, Sabo'. The song, with its marching, jaunty rhythm, urged children to inform their leader, Ojukwu, of anyone suspected of being a traitor, a saboteur. Maurice won and shared his prize with his brother, just as he shared the food he scavenged. "Me and my brother were inside this big oil drum, cause it's bigger than us, and we were licking the whole thing for hours." Maurice has a natural musical talent – it seemed a shame it took so long to take root.

When the bombing started Maurice and his brother dived for fox holes, emerging hours later to see destruction and bodies all around. The incessant attacks disturbed Maurice's paternal grandmother. First, she stopped talking. When she refused to eat for a week the priest gave her the last rites. Maurice and his brother, with no one to look after them, lined up to go to neighbouring Gabon. They were promised food, shelter and school but the boys' grandmother, suddenly coherent, rushed to retrieve them.

"They're not orphans," she screamed. "Their parents are in England." Maurice and his brother were disappointed. "I couldn't understand why my grandma, who couldn't afford to send me to school, was objecting and I was angry. But now, as an adult, I've learnt that out of 250,000 children that went to Gabon only 5,000 returned."[7]

Maurice, as a child, was keen to support the Biafran cause. "Ojukwu used to broadcast to children at seven o'clock every evening. There would be one radio in the village. We'd all gather round, and he'd tell us to be strong." Maurice was disappointed he was too young to join the Boys Brigade. He liked the idea of pretending to be an orphan and getting lost in the bush. The enemy soldiers would feel sorry for such boys, take them in and feed them. Then, at night, the boys would slip back to inform Biafran soldiers where the enemy was hiding. But Nigerians soon realized they were being duped and started to kill the children.

Moses, Maurice's twelve-year-old cousin, was recruited as a child soldier. "My biggest ambition was to be like him, to go and kill many men. When he came to the village the old men were frightened because he had a Kalashnikov and drank whisky all day – no one could tell him off." When boys, such as Moses, were old enough they would be kidnapped, given a gun and two days' training, then sent to fight. "He died on the last day of the war, on his way home. He was only a boy – he must have got drunk and talked rubbish in front of the enemy soldiers and they shot him. It's from him that I learnt the army drill. To this day, I can still assemble a Kalashnikov." Maurice clicked his phantom weapon, ready to shoot. "We were very militant children. We weren't brought up on nursery rhymes, but on songs like 'Kill the Enemy, We Are the Biafran Freedom Fighters.'" The odds were stacked against the Biafrans. "It was a shambolic war. We had no planes, no jeeps, no tanks."

When the Biafrans were defeated, Maurice and his brother were sent as servants to different households in other parts of the country. Their grandmother was too ill to look after them. "That was horrendous because I didn't have my mum and dad and now, I didn't have my brother or grandma." Maurice stayed with an aunt whose husband maltreated her. "I wasn't beaten, but my auntie was badly abused. I slept on the floor with the pig. In the morning, I would take it into the bush. That pig was the only family's asset so, when it ran off, I thought *This is the end of my life.*"

Fearing to go back without the pig, Maurice stayed outside in the rain. He was found unconscious, suffering from malaria, and taken to a children's sick bay set up during the war. He dreamt of being carried away by a white bird towards a great ball of orange light. "The nearer we got the better I felt, the warmer I felt, the happier I felt. Then I woke up." Nurses were beating on his chest and his aunt was throwing herself on the floor.

"Oh God, please take me, don't let this child die. How am I going to tell Matthias that his first son is dead?"

Days later Maurice overheard her aunt telling a friend,

"Maurice died and then he got up. I've never seen anything like it."

In the aftermath of war, when Nigerian soldiers were rooting out Biafran soldiers, women, like Maurice's aunt, were particularly vulnerable. "I saw my uncle and his children sitting in front of his house crying and a long line of soldiers. I was too young to know what rape was, but I knew they were hurting my auntie. All my aunties were raped."[8] Maurice longed for his parents. "I wanted my mum and prayed every day. When other boys bullied me, I went, 'One day my dad's going to come and deal with you.' Then they'd beat me up more because they saw me as some flash kid telling stories."

The boys got their comeuppance. "One minute I was herding a pig in the middle of a bush, with no shoes or clothes on, with a load of other kids bullying me. The next minute we saw this guy in suit and tie coming towards us. I was always in trouble because I was stealing food and getting caught."

The man approached the boys.

"Is there anybody here called Maurice Nwokeji?"

Maurice started to back out.

"That's him," said the biggest bully of the group.

"Don't run. I'm not here to harm you. I've been sent by your father. You're going to England."

"What?" screamed Maurice.

"Yes, come with me."

Maurice moved towards the man, wary but hopeful.

"Don't you forget us in England," shouted the bully.

"You? I'll never forget you. My father will come back and kill you."

Maurice's faith that his father would rescue him, a belief that sustained him throughout, had come true at last.

Maurice went back to Akuma to say goodbye to his grandma. From there he travelled by cattle truck to Ibi where he met his brother for the first time in a year. "It was like Heidi, running as soon as he saw me. We never used to get on but we both knew we were the only family we had. We slept the night together, then went in a cattle truck with a load of goats. It took three days to get to Lagos. I remember seeing rows of dead bodies, covered with brown leaves and birds feeding off them. I've never seen so many vultures in my life."

In Lagos they stayed with their uncle who helped organize papers for the boys to leave. With time on their hands the kids explored the neighbourhood. "Now it looks bad kids playing in the rubbish, but that's when I tasted cornflakes. We didn't know it was for breakfast. It was only when we came to England and I went, 'Oh, I've had this.'" Maurice had no regrets about leaving. "How could it be worse than where I was coming from. We were going to have food, to meet our parents. No, it's great."

At the airport Maurice's uncle took his nephew aside.

"When you need to go to the toilet you say, 'I want to go and urinate.'"

Maurice took a deep breath.

"I want to go and … … ur … in … ate."

"Good. Don't forget it."

Maurice took his brother's hand as he waved his uncle goodbye.

"I can speak English," Maurice boasted as he fumbled with his seat belt and helped his brother strap himself in. It was the first time the brothers had been on a plane.

"Get away," said his brother.

"I can," Maurice insisted. "You'll see."

As they rose into blue skies, leaving Lagos behind, Maurice raised his hand.

"Yes?" asked the air hostess, keen to help her young charges.

"I want to go and … ur … in … ate."

The air hostess led Maurice to the back of the plane where he stood outside the cloakroom for what he considered a convincing amount of time. Then he returned to his seat.

"Wow," said his younger brother, impressed by his brother's new-found skill.

Maurice repeated the antic.

"I want to go and URINATE."

He was on a roll now. Other passengers smiled at seeing a skinny nine-year-old speaking the Queen's English with an Igbo accent, hovering outside the cloakroom door but hesitating to go in. It took Maurice several performances, strolling up and down the aisle, before he discovered the magic of flushing loos.

As the boys wiped the sleep from their eyes, they looked down to see a wide river curling between tall buildings and rows of terraced houses. They had arrived in London. A hostess escorted the boys off the plane and through immigration. As they looked around the arrival lounge, wearing their new shorts, sandals and socks, they recognized no one. People melted away until there was a small group of Black adults left. Even then it was difficult for Maurice to work out who was who. His mother looked different – she had put on weight.

Now it was Maurice's turn to be impressed. He could never have imagined his father would own a car, and an Anglia at that. Maurice chatted non-stop as they drove to their new home in Hackney. About how, after the war, he was sent to work as a servant; how he slept on the floor with a pig and, at dawn, took the pig into the bush; about how, one day, the pig ran off. The words tumbled out in quick succession – there was so much to tell but his parents didn't seem to be listening. Maurice wondered what else he would have to keep to himself, to pretend had never happened.

When I approached Maurice with the idea of making a film about his childhood, he jumped at the chance. He was an obvious candidate – a musician and performer with an extraordinary story to tell. At a pre-arranged time, Mitch and I waited for Maurice outside a terraced house on Rectory Road, his first home in Hackney. As soon as he arrived, he flung back his dreadlocks and stretched out his arms to almost the entire width of the ground floor. Mitch, acting as cameraman, had barely time to get out his iPhone. "This is my roots in this country, this is my England. If I had enough money, I would buy this house." Maurice pointed up to the first floor where he had shared a bedroom with his brother. "We'd never had a room before." To welcome their sons Maurice's parents had decorated the boys' bedroom with Sooty and Sweep wallpaper. The boys, thinking the TV puppets were demons, scratched out their eyes so they would not look at them in the dark. Maurice laughed. "It was funny coming from a war, killing snakes and then being spooked by Sooty and Sweep."

On the first morning in their new home, awakened by a child's cries, Maurice's brother asked,

"Whose is that baby?"

"Don't you know?" his mother exclaimed.

"I take my hat off to her," said Maurice. "Watching all that on the tele. Not knowing if we were alive." A doctor thought the cure for his mother's distress was to have another child. Maurice felt for his mother. "Having no children to suddenly having three in one year – a baby and two war-traumatized boys."

The boys went for regular appointments to Hackney Hospital. Their growth was stunted from lack of food, they had parasites living under their feet and their stomachs protruded. "We had to be dewormed and I had one of those big bellybuttons that had to be put inside because all the kids were playing with it." A speech therapist, who helped Maurice get rid of his stammer, found a pebble, from the bombings, in Maurice's ear. "Wow, I could hear."

Even in the 1970s, Rectory Road was busy. Cars and double decker buses, that Maurice still loves, hurtled round the one-way system – down from Stamford Hill, the Jewish area; past Ridley Road Market, where Maurice's mother bought African vegetables and down to the City of London. But the boys were not used to busy roads. In Biafra they ran straight out of their hut to play. The inevitable happened. In the first week the boys were knocked down by a black taxi and went straight to hospital.

"These boys have survived the war" screamed Maurice's mother. "And as soon as I get them back, they're going to die right here."

Maurice and I crossed the road where the boys were run over, with Mitch running ahead to catch us on camera. We walked past the newsagent where Maurice's father had bought his sons a treat. The boys had never tasted chocolate before. "It's nice," said the children stuffing it down the back of the seat of their father's Anglia, pretending to chew. They hated the chocolate. They found it so sweet it made their minds go numb. "The only thing worse than chocolate was cheese. We forced ourselves to like it. We wanted to be like other children, to fit in. I would have much preferred roasted rat."

In those first few weeks, the boys stole down to the kitchen during the night, took what they fancied and stuffed it under their mattresses. "We didn't understand there would be food tomorrow." In the morning Maurice's mother would come downstairs to find the fridge empty. It took time for her to understand her sons' behaviour. But the hardest thing for the boys was missing their grandma. "She really was our parent."

We walked down the road to Benthal Primary, Maurice's first school. His greatest ambition was to get an education, something denied him in Biafra, but he was nine and had never been to school. One sunny day, in the playground, he took off his shoes, socks, T-shirt, short trousers and underwear. It was hot. Children giggled and looked away.

Horrified teachers urged Maurice to cover up. "For me, clothes were decoration. I didn't understand it was a moral issue." Another day a clown, with ruby red lips, baggy checked trousers and huge shoes, entered the school grounds. He held a placard, 'Apples are good for you.' Maurice hid behind his teacher's skirt. The clown reminded him of the voodoo men whom he would find in the bush back home.

Only in London did Maurice become conscious of his colour. "Where I come from, everyone's Black, so you're not Black, you're just normal. And then I came here and discovered I was Black, so I thought okay, let me seek out other Blacks. But I found out some were Nigerians." Nigerians had bombed his village, caused the death of his grandmother, cousin and other members of his family. They were the enemy. Yinka, a Nigerian girl in Maurice's class, became the butt of his hatred. "I remember plotting to kill her. I used to dream about killing someone every night and sometimes I ate people. I think I had those twisted dreams until I was in my late twenties. It's not the Nigerians' fault because most Nigerians are not politicians or soldiers."

Neither were Jamaicans his natural allies. "They used to call me 'African bitch'. I didn't know what that meant but I knew it was derogatory. And they spat at me. But I'd been farming since I was five and been in a war so trying to fight me wasn't a good idea." Maurice's mother, who taught her son to say "He hit me first," was frequently called into school. It took Maurice two years before he started to understand English. Then he realized his so-called friends had been abusing him too. "I had to beat up all the boys who'd been calling me names, especially the white boys. I'd go home and say, 'Mummy, I'm a 'nig-nog'. One day I discovered what 'sambo' was, so I beat up my friend Noel."

It was during the second interview in my home in Hackney that Maurice spoke of his troubled teenage years, his twenties and thirties – before he found music, before he became a Rastafarian. "I was a damaged child. I felt I was coming from the war, that I was the one that was let down. But I was being told I was letting everyone else down. My parents were strangers and my father, being an army man, felt I needed a good clip. He gave me more than a clip. In Africa, I would have gone to an uncle. I couldn't go to social services because they might have arrested my dad. Even though corporal punishment was allowed at that time, I felt it was a bit excessive."

Maurice felt he had no choice but to leave home. "I lived on the streets at King's Cross for a couple of years and got into being thiefy although I was never really a thief. Then prostitutes started to buy me food and I became their angel." Defending the girls angered the pimps who got together and paid someone to deal with Maurice. "I was playing pool in the Play It Again, Sam arcade in Pentonville Road when I was struck in the back of the head three times with a crowbar. I tried to stand up but was struck again on the forehead and the hook made a hole in my skull which made blood flow into my eyes, so I could not see my attacker. I wiped the blood from my face but as he went to hit me again, I leapt on him and bit his nose off." Maurice was stitched up at University College Hospital nearby but still has a scar on his forehead. His attacker lost half his nose. "After that no one wanted to fight me. The legend of Angel was born and whilst many people loved Angel, I hated him. He was a survival tactic that got out of hand." Maurice became addicted to drugs. "I was looking for a less painful way to die and crack seemed a good choice." After the attack in the arcade the probation service sent Maurice on an anger management course. Over time he found the love of a good woman, learnt the guitar and discovered Jah. "Instead of crack and heroin, music was my new addiction and still is to this day. I've done five albums, written about 200 songs and travelled all over Europe. I'm not surprised I ended up being violent and aggressive because I see now where it all came from."

Having survived, Maurice feels a responsibility to communicate the effect of war on children. "That's why I was spared, so I can do what we're doing now. I want to show what war is from the point of view of a six-year-old." War affects children differently. "I have cousins who will never form relationships, then some who were not so badly affected – their parents were there. They didn't get much food but they weren't going to die. But there's a scar that goes through all my people. Even my children born in England, it's in their DNA."

We first launched *Ugwumpiti* at the Floating Cinema, a converted barge on the River Lea in the summer of 2016. Maurice had provided the music, chosen the title and approved the latest cut. He stood at the back of the barge, silent and nervous. After the screening, he came forward and played his guitar, calling out the names of those he had lost – his grandmother, cousin, Moses and many more. "I keep on calling and after a while I feel they're there." An older man, as he climbed back onto the towpath, urged us to contact the organizers of the annual conference about Biafra. "They would love this film."

Ugwumpiti has been shown in many different settings – at the Rio cinema in Hackney, attended by all of Maurice's five children, the eldest, in her twenties, cradling Joy, his youngest; at KPMG in Canary Wharf and in Glasgow where the film was shown alongside *Seeking Sanctuary on a Scottish Island* about Syrian children on the Isle of Bute. Maurice feels for other children who have experienced war. When *Ugwumpiti* was nominated as Research Film of the Year 2017 Maurice, his wife Sharon, Mitch and I attended a glittering evening at BAFTA. We were disappointed not to win but it was exciting to be nominated, to pose for photographs next to BAFTA's iconic tragicomic mask.

Maurice, Mitch and I have cried and laughed together as we have toured *Ugwumpiti*. Perhaps it is partly Maurice's humour that has sustained him. Another child survivor of the war in Biafra wrote, 'Your story-telling ability – your factual realness and ability to still laugh has created the possibility for revisiting subliminal traumas … I was nine in 1967 and my heart still aches for children all over who are forced to go through what we went through.'[9]

In January 2020, to commemorate the fiftieth anniversary of the end of the Biafra civil war, the journalist and novelist, Frederick Forsyth, wrote, 'Buried for 50 Years: Britain's shameful role in Biafra.'[10] He pulled no punches. 'British covert interference had become huge. Weapons and ammunition poured in quietly as Whitehall and the

Figure 7 Maurice performing songs featured in *Ugwumpiti* at the Being Human Festival Launch, Senate House, University of London, 2016. Courtesy of Maurice Nwokeji and Advanced School of Study, University of London. Copyright © Lloyd Sturdy.

Harold Wilson government lied and denied it all.' He explained that the food that saved lives, transported into Biafra by Joint Church Aid, was the 'world's only *illegal* mercy air bridge'. Forsyth's time in Biafra haunted him still. 'As for me,' he wrote, 'sometimes in the wee small hours I see the stick-like children and hear their wails of hunger and their low moans as they died.' How much worse must it be, in the 'wee small hours', for those, like Maurice, who was one of those 'stick-like children' who survived.

CHAPTER 6
THE BATTLE OF BRICK LANE
*Six young people who arrived from East Pakistan, subsequently
Bangladesh, aged eleven to sixteen, between 1969 and 1973*

I shuddered to hear Boris Johnson vow, in his first speech as Britain's prime minister in July 2019, to make Britain the "greatest place on earth."[1] It echoed Donald Trump's right-wing rhetoric, during his presidential election campaign in 2016, to "make America great again." The roots of my fear of nationalism go back much further to when, in the 1970s and 1980s, I read similar slogans scrawled on tower blocks in east London and on placards held up by right-wing National Front members, marching down Brick Lane. The Battle of Brick Lane in 1978[2] signified the moment when young Bangladeshi activists, supported by trade unionists, anti-racists and socialists, confronted the National Front after years of intimidation, physical attacks and murder on the streets of east London, including of Altab Ali, a 25-year-old man of Bengali origin.[3] Altab Ali was fatally stabbed by three teenagers, on his way home from his work as a machinist in Hanbury Street, just off Brick Lane, solely on the grounds of being a 'Paki' in May 1978. He had arrived as a fourteen-year-old from what was then East Pakistan and, in 1975, went back to Sylhet, in what had become Bangladesh after the war with West Pakistan in 1971, to get married. When Altab returned to London his bride stayed with his parents, hoping to join him later. She never arrived.

Manuhar, Salam and I stood in what is now Altab Ali Park, at the bottom of Brick Lane, just yards away from where Altab Ali was murdered over thirty years ago. Manuhar, who arrived in Spitalfields from Sylhet, on his own, aged sixteen, knew Altab well – they came from the same area of Sylhet and met up in London, every weekend. "I was horrified and thought *This could happen to me*," Manuhar sighed. "I thought *This cannot go unchallenged.*" Salam, who arrived in Spitalfields, aged thirteen, with his mother and brother to join his father, agreed. "We thought if the police won't help us, if politicians aren't interested, then we must help ourselves." At the time, Manuhar and Salam were members of the Progressive Youth Organisation.

Ten days after the murder of Altab Ali 10,000 Bengalis, supported by anti-racist organizations, trade unions, the Anti-Nazi League and the Socialist Workers Party, marched silently behind Altab Ali's coffin, first to Downing Street where they presented a petition and then to Hyde Park. Demonstrators held placards, 'Self-defence is no offence', 'Here to stay, here to fight'.[4] It was the biggest Bengali-led demonstration in British history. Jalal, then secretary of the Bangladesh Youth Movement, remembers the day well. He had arrived in Birmingham, aged twelve, but three years later came to east London, with his brother when his parents returned to Sylhet. "I was 16 and the only young person allowed to speak. My English wasn't good, but I think it was powerful. You had big names like Tariq Ali and Darcus Howe but many people, even today, say, 'Remember that speech you made.' That's the first time the Bengali community reached a one-column article in *The Times*."

I joined that demonstration with Abdul Momen, each of us holding one pole of our banner, 'Bengali Workers Action Group Against Racism'. We both worked for Camden Committee for Community Relations, funded by the local borough to further race equality. Momen worked as a community worker with the Bangladeshi community and I as the education officer. Momen battled with the Home Office over migration matters when single men, fearful of pending restrictive immigration laws, tried to bring over families. He lobbied the housing department over cramped, squalid housing conditions in which Bangladeshis lived, particularly after women and children arrived, and liaised with the police, health and social services over the many issues that affected families. He established restaurant co-operatives and set up the Bengali Workers Action Group[5] – Bengali men settled in central London to be near the restaurants where they worked as chefs, kitchen porters or waiters until the early hours. I battled with ILEA (Inner London Education Authority) over the refusal of schools to accept newly arrived children from Bangladesh and teachers' unwillingness to deal with racist thugs who attacked the children within and beyond school gates.

Racist attacks were even more common in east London, where many found work in the clothing industry. In the first four months of 1978 Gulam Mustafa, Altab Ali's employer and secretary of Brick Lane mosque, recorded thirty-three racist incidents.[6] Bangladeshis were attacked with hammers and knives, beaten with bricks and sticks and knocked unconscious in broad daylight. They had their faces slashed and lungs punctured. Lighted rags were pushed through household letter boxes with women and children inside when men were at work. Bengali victims, rather than being supported by police, found themselves being charged with carrying offensive weapons and subject to immigration checks.

Young activists started to learn self-defence and set up vigilante groups to protect themselves and others. Salam, a judo enthusiast, took on what he thought was a skinhead amongst a group of racist thugs but was, in fact, a plain-clothed policeman. Only representation by a good lawyer prevented Salam from being convicted. Ruhul came to London, aged thirteen, with his family. He had heard about the racism that friends had experienced at school so, on his first day, aged fifteen and after a two-year wait, he gathered friends around him and fought a group of skinheads. That was the end of his schooling. "Everybody said, 'Don't go back, your life is under threat.'"

In a provocative move, just four months after Altab Ali's murder, the National Front moved their national headquarters to near the top of Brick Lane. On Sunday mornings they would hold rallies, sell newspapers and smash the windows of Asian businesses, such as the popular Taj Stores. Young Bangladeshi activists started to camp out the night before, blocking their entry to Brick Lane, to be joined, in the morning, by other activists and supporters, myself and Momen amongst them. We marched in thousands along the narrow street; past the mosque, a Huguenot chapel and synagogue in earlier decades, holding placards and shouting, 'Self Defence Is No Offence.' At the top of Brick Lane fights broke out between the activists and close cropped, shaven fascists wearing hobnail boots and sixteen-hole Doc Martins. Jalal, who can be seen in old photographs at the head of demonstrations, remembered the feeling of victory. "We were able to defeat the National Front as they had to relocate."

Pola watched these Sunday morning confrontations from her flat. She had first lived in Newham when she arrived from Bangladesh in 1972, aged thirteen, with her mother and siblings, to join her father. On her marriage, in 1976, aged sixteen, she moved to Bethnal Green, directly opposite Brick Lane. Pola felt not only lonely but trapped as her husband, who worked long hours in the leather garment industry, had warned her not to venture out on a Sunday. But Pola, now Baroness Uddin of Bethnal Green, watched Labour Party members standing around Belle Harris's Co-operative stall, from her window. She had heard they tried to protect the shopkeepers. "I was so impressed that individuals would put themselves in harm's way for us that I had to explore this forbidden space." It was to be the start of a lifetime involvement with the Labour Party.

The victory over Brick Lane did not signal the end of attacks – two years later Waris Ali, from Sylhet, was also murdered. In response Ayub, a member of the Progressive Youth Organisation with Manuhar and Salam, spoke at a demonstration of 400 people in what is now Altab Ali Park.[7] "I was quoted in *The Independent* when I talked about why the racist always picked on the Bangladeshi community. My answer was that they went for the most vulnerable. When a Bengali family called the police, they pursued the victim. If you are a perpetrator that's an ideal situation. The police are on your side."

In 1979 I moved from my job in Camden to take up the post of Director of Tower Hamlets Training Forum, located in a Huguenot weavers' cottage, just off Brick Lane. My first task was to set up a training workshop to upgrade the clothing and English language skills of garment workers, the majority of whom were of Bengali origin. We ran special machining courses for men who worked in local sweat shops and for women homeworkers, living on nearby estates – most Bangladeshi clothing workers were employed to sew up only the shell of the garment. We also taught pattern cutting, the best paid and most respected skill in the trade, but rarely carried out by Bangladeshis. The initiative, backed by the Trades Council, The Tailor and Garment Workers' Union and others, was set up before the demise of the clothing industry in east London.

Several of the young activists were involved with the Forum. Manuhar was employed as the Forum's outreach worker, Salam was on the management committee as was Ayub who was also a trainer, having been a machinist since the age of thirteen. Ruhul would pop in to talk about his latest film project. Jalal would drop by, too. Most worked in the clothing industry on a full- or part-time basis, or had done so in the past, often combining this with political activism or further education. Pola was then a youth and community worker at Avenues Unlimited along Brick Lane. They had all arrived in Britain under eighteen, between 1969 and 1973 from East Pakistan or what became Bangladesh in 1971.

As Jalal explained, not everyone in the community supported their activism. "The older generation said, 'It's not our country, we have to go back, don't get involved.'" But the youth were determined to forge a future for themselves in Britain. Pola, one of the few female activists at the time, set out the reasons why. "Our generation did not regard Tower Hamlets as a place of transition but home for always. I was not prepared to be uprooted for a second time so, as a collective force, we challenged discriminatory practices and actively engaged with institutions to improve the quality of education, gain equal access to housing and health care, and enhance people's lives."

Manuhar, Salam, Jalal, Ruhul and Ayub all came from the mainly rural district of Sylhet in the northeast whereas Pola came from Rajshahi, a university town in the northwest, near the Indian border. Many of her mother's family were lecturers and professors in higher education and her mother's older sister was the first principal of Rajshahi Women's College. "There was never a question that each girl and boy in the family would graduate. I had always been interested in medicine and took care of sick animals so I was expected to become a doctor." Pola's paternal grandfather was a successful businessman and her treasured mentor and guide. As a reminder of her beloved *Daada* [grandfather] Pola still searches for jasmine, her favourite perfume amongst his large store of imported Attar oils, wherever she travels.

Pola did not want to leave Bangladesh and protested in every way she knew how. She was devastated at leaving her grandparents, aunts, especially her *Khala* [mother's older sister], uncles as well as her cousins and friends, so much so that she has blocked out certain memories of her final departure. "I have no recollection of our air travel to UK. I felt utterly hopeless and lost, having left behind all that I loved and all those who loved me. But I clearly recall a grey and freezing London, rainy East Ham and being dumped by our father in this small, terraced house, the five of us having to live in one room. We stayed in those horrendous circumstances for months."

Plashet Park opposite was a lifesaver, but it was no match for the Padma River where Pola used to walk with her *Nana*, her maternal grandfather, a lawyer. In Rajshahi Pola, her mother and four younger siblings had lived in large, extended, households owned by Pola's two grandfathers – just a five-minute rickshaw ride from each other. One overlooked a circular courtyard with mango, coconut and pomegranate trees, overflowing with vegetables and flowers tended by her mother's green fingers. "I was often angry with my mother for not allowing me to remain in Bangladesh, but it was difficult to share my grief with anyone. We felt betrayed by our father who had come to study law in London and whom we had not seen for years. In Rajshahi my mother worked as a teacher, looked after us as well as my grandparents' household. She also had health issues – I cannot imagine the suffering she endured. But during the Liberation War she was our main source of strength and courage, my grandfather adored her and was completely unforgiving of his son whom he thought irresponsible. As Bangladesh began its journey to a new nation *Daada* insisted our father arrange for us to join him in London so that we could secure an education but, as soon as we arrived, he more or less abandoned us. As a single mother with five children my mother had to find work, organise alternative housing, negotiate a new life without support from her husband, family or friends."

Pola, her mother and siblings moved to a flat on an all-white estate in Canning Town. "It's hard to depict the bare-knuckle racism of being shouted at, spat at, told you smell and chased by thugs. Luckily, we were blessed with good neighbours, an English woman, married to a Moroccan who became part of our family. We were also friends with other white families." School, too, was a challenge. "Asian girls were mostly bullied by white girls although, sadly, a small group of Black girls joined in. My English, although not good, was sufficient to show I would not tolerate bullying. I would say, 'Look, my family fought wars. Do you think I'm going to let you bully me and my friend?' Or something stupid to that effect. The best friend in my class was Aisha who had also just arrived from Pakistan. No one came for us much after that."

Joining secondary school, in the middle of her GCSEs, with little spoken English put Pola at a significant disadvantage. "I had the ugliest time with my chemistry and maths teacher who thought I could not speak English and was therefore a brainless, Asian girl. As someone who was outstanding in science and maths prior to coming to Britain, it was difficult to swallow. Some teachers were so brazen. I was informed I could never become a doctor and, after a good set of GCSE results, told not to bother with A levels. A careers teacher who assumed that all Asian girls were doomed to early marriage and factory work, remarked, 'At sixteen you will just have an arranged marriage and five kids.' 'What's wrong with that?' I replied. 'My mum had five kids.'" Pola's English teacher, Nicole Freni, with whom Pola is still in touch, was one of the few exceptions. She encouraged Pola to take part in different aspects of school life including drama, music and the literature society. "Nicole still says, 'there was this formidable glint in your eye.'"

Pola leant back into one of the high backed, velvet upholstered wooden chairs in a lobby in the House of Lords and laughed. "As it happens, I did get married at the age of 16 and have five kids." By her own choice, Pola married a young man, originally from Sylhet, with whom she shared a love of music. They had similar journeys from Bangladesh and Pola liked him as a person. "I'm reluctant to say you can fall in love at the age of 16. I believe, if the concept exists, that it grows over time." Her father's disapproval did not worry her, but she desperately wanted her mother's blessings. "My mother wanted me to marry someone from a similar background and was displeased he did not have a university education. I felt I had let down my mother and left her to manage alone. I kept in touch with my family although the relationship was strained for a while. It eased over time as my children came along."

Partly because of pressure from Pola's father to leave her husband the couple moved to Manchester where Pola's husband found a new job and where two of their sons were born. They moved back to London when Pola got a job as a youth worker at Avenues Unlimited in Brick Lane, about the same time as I moved to Tower Hamlets Training Forum. Here she became immersed in community work, local politics and led numerous projects to empower women such as the Jagonari Women's Centre in Whitechapel where the courtyard is based on the one in Rajshahi where Pola spent her childhood.

Ruhul, although a member of the Progressive Youth Organisation, knew his way of expressing injustice was not just through political activism. As a child Ruhul lived in Sylhet Town that boasted three cinemas showing anything from Japanese Godzilla films, dubbed in English, to epic Hollywood films like *Ben Hur*. As a reward for doing his homework Ruhul spent Saturday mornings, absorbing "spectacular, colourful and frightening" images of America and Britain. "I had this idea that these people are always fighting," laughed Ruhul. He fell in love, too, with black-and-white, arty Bengali films, such as by the filmmaker, Satyajit Ray.

Everyday Lokkhi, one of the pretty young tea workers from the famous tea gardens in Sylhet, delivered milk to Ruhul's house but would stay outside and wait.

"Why does Lokkhi sit under the sun for forty-five minutes?" Ruhul asked his mother. "Why doesn't she come inside and deliver milk to the kitchen?"

His mother laughed.

"Ruhul has fallen in love with Lokkhi."

"Can I go to the tea garden and see how these people live?"

"What's there to see? It's just forest?"

Ruhul loved Lokkhi's village of thatched mud houses with a neat courtyard full of beautiful flowers. He had been told that the tea workers were dirty so was amazed to find the huts clean and organized. He ate their delicious food too. When seven-year-old Ruhul returned from the forest he asked his family, "Why do you call them coolies? They're beautiful and much cleaner than us. I'm going to become a filmmaker and tell the story of Lokkhi."

People laughed.

"Where are you going to learn filmmaking?"

Ruhul's father was a dreamer who wrote poems and short stories. As the war between West and East Pakistan approached, his father, who had sold off much of the land he inherited from his grandfather, decided to try his luck in London, taking his family with him. Ruhul, aged thirteen, resisted. He had heard, through his father who helped migrants with their paperwork, that many ended up washing dishes. Ruhul feared this might happen to him. Then he calculated that migrating might be his only chance of pursuing his ambition. There was no way, without the right connections, that he could become a filmmaker in what was then Pakistan.

Ruhul's first impressions of England differed from the images he had seen in films in Sylhet Town. "It was wintertime, the whole sky was dark and there were no leaves on the trees. I thought *There must have been a fire. They're all burnt.*" His father rented rooms in a multi-occupational, run-down Huguenot weavers' cottages in Princelet Street that stank of paraffin. "We had big houses and a garden in Sylhet Town, so it was a total contrast to where we came from. But I was determined to stay and become a filmmaker."

Ruhul got bored waiting for a school place, so his father suggested he go to the cinema – the Naz on Brick Lane or the Palaeseum on Commercial Road. When Ruhul tried to persuade his new-found friends, living in the same house, to go with him they were reluctant.

"You only came six days ago. How do you know about cinemas?"

"My father told me."

Ruhul's friends, most of whom were from villages and had not had the same access to cinemas in Sylhet, weren't allowed to go to the Naz or Palaeseum. Adults, but not children, could watch Hindi films; English or American films were out of the question because of the sex scenes. But his friends followed Ruhul into the Naz, checking first whether any of their relatives were lurking in the back rows. It was a shock for Ruhul to discover that, for them, going to the cinema was forbidden for religious reasons. His family, all keen film buffs, were practising Muslims. Ruhul shocked his new friends further by asking where he could buy a movie camera.

"This guy must be crazy. We don't make films."

Ruhul got a tip-off that you could buy second-hand cameras at what was then the Dog Market. This was a legacy of the French Huguenots who kept canaries and various singing birds. As time progressed dogs and other animals were also sold, even a pet lion, but, eventually, it was closed under pressure from animal rights groups.[8] Ruhul scoured the stalls, shutting his ears to the cacophony of barks, yelps and screeches until he came across an elderly Jewish stallholder selling cameras.

"How much?"

"£5."

In 1971, £5 was a lot of money.

Ruhul went back the next week with more questions – how to load the film, focus, press the shutter. Finally, Ruhul handed over his £5 and, on the stallholder's advice, went to a chemist to buy a roll of film for yet another £5.

"Bring it back and we'll get it processed," said the chemist. "It's included in the price."

Ruhul bought a second hand Super 8 projector for a further £7 to show his first film but nothing appeared against the stained white wall in Heneage Street. It was only after several visits to the elderly Jewish stallholder for advice that, when adjusting the lens to screen his fourth film, Ruhul saw something move. "My God, what's this?" he screamed. Standing on a table, he adjusted the focus to get an even clearer picture. "I jumped up, banging my head on the light and ran into the street, with blood pouring from my scalp, 'Come and see my movie'. My friends loved the film. 'Now we're going to make a movie together.' They put on their best clothes and started punching each other like in Hindi movies. Someone's lip got scarred, someone else's nose bled. 'No', I shouted. 'Just pretend.' It was amazing. But soon after we moved to a house in Deal Street, someone broke in and everything was stolen – the projector, the camera, everything."

After a few weeks, Ruhul's father gave up his work as a presser – he felt pain all over his body. He found another job but every night he returned home saying,

"When the war stops, let's go back."

His mother agreed – she hated queueing for the public baths in Cheshire Street – but it was more difficult persuading their son.

When the war ended Ruhul's father arranged for his son to live with a man he knew on a housing estate in Poplar – at that time, a no-go area for Bangladeshis. Ruhul's father did not know that the man, a heavy gambler, used to vanish for days leaving his wife with little to feed even her two daughters. Ruhul, who was constantly hungry, decided to go to the shops with some of the money his father had sent from Bangladesh.

"Don't go out, you'll be attacked," warned the woman.

Gangs of boys on every corner, shouting 'Paki', glared at Ruhul. He reached the shop, bought bread and butter, rushed home and stored them in his bedroom. After a week the man returned with a bag of shopping. On hearing the row in the couple's bedroom, Ruhul thought *This is no place for me.*

Ruhul went to live with other young Sylhetis in a shared household in Princelet Street in Spitalfields – Salam, whose family had also returned to Sylhet, was amongst them. Ruhul told his friends, "I can clean the house, chop vegetables and you can teach me how to cook, but I can't wash dishes." As he needed money to pay for food and £3 a week rent, he found a job in the rag trade, earning £7 a week initially, and then £14, but he never bought scissors.

"Why don't you buy your own," asked his friends when Ruhul asked to borrow theirs.

"That means I'm stuck. I want to become a filmmaker."

Ruhul joined the National Film Theatre and sought out international films at the Academy Cinema in Oxford Street or at La Continentale Cinema in Tottenham Court Road. "Once I took these friends to watch *Pather Panchali*, one of Satyajit Ray's masterpieces. As a kid I'd heard his name – my father loved film. My friends came out half-way, telling others, 'Keep away from Ruhul. He'll ask you to see one of those boring films.'"

Ruhul joined a film making class at Bethnal Green Adult Education Institute where elderly students showed holiday footage of the Alhambra in Spain and the beaches of Yugoslavia. They welcomed Ruhul but he soon realized he needed more. John Newbigin, a youth worker at Avenues Unlimited, told Ruhul about Four Corners in Bethnal Green where Ruhul learnt how to use a 16mm camera. He was encouraged to put in a grant application to Tower Hamlets Arts Committee. *Purbo London* (meaning East London) *a Day in the Life of a Bengali Kid*, produced in 1979, was Ruhul's first film. "I shot everything and edited it myself." The central and only character of this fifteen-minute film was Ayub.

"Have you still got a copy?" I asked Ruhul, as he looked through the kitchen window at his back garden in Newham.

"Buried under rubbish in the shed. I need to retrieve it one day."

Some months later I sat at home watching a DVD transferred from the original video of *Purbo London*. It was Ayub as I remembered him. Handsome, well turned out, walking the streets of Spitalfields in the early morning light, crouched over a sewing machine in a dimly lit sweat shop, meeting up with friends before returning to his room to cook his evening meal; all the while talking about his hopes, for a different life. It was a lyrical, beautifully shot piece that told an important part of Ayub's story. Ayub had come to Britain from Sylhet, aged eleven, to live with his uncle in Birmingham but two years later moved to east London to live with his cousins. From the age of thirteen, after school hours and at weekends, he worked as a machinist in Whitechapel. Within two years, he was left in charge of the workshop when the manager went back to Pakistan. Ayub enjoyed the work – it gave him independence and allowed him to pay his way living with his cousins in Stepney. It was also a release from the racism he experienced at Stepney Green School. "I used to look forward to work rather than staying at school, because I was with my mates, and we listened to music." Ayub desperately wanted to get out of the rag trade and knew that, but for the racism and his lack of English, he would have done far better at school.

Ayub experienced a different childhood from Ruhul in Sylhet. He was born in Chhatak, half an hour's drive from Sylhet Town. His father, a farmer, owned land, chickens and cows. Ayub, the youngest of five, loved the countryside. In the dry season he would play marbles and football on the parched paddy fields. In the monsoon season he would build rafts from banana stems and paddle along the canals to reach *bubi* and *boroi*, his favourite berries. The water was never more than waist deep so there was no danger of him drowning if, trying to catch fish, he fell off his raft. Ayub was a good student at his school, the top of his class.

During the war with West Pakistan, he fled with his family to a more remote village – Ayub's family was a target as his cousins were freedom fighters. When the war was over Ayub remembered watching the Bangladeshi Mukti Bahini army shouting 'Joy Bangla' as they marched towards Sylhet Town. He remembered, too, collecting empty shells as toys.

His mother's brother always visited his sister when he returned from Birmingham to Sylhet for a holiday.

"Take Ayub soon," Ayub's mother would say.

"When the right time comes."

Initially Ayub was excited. "People who went to Britain had nice clothes and money; their houses were different, and they would eat differently so I knew that the way to go up in the world was by coming to London." Ayub was only eleven when he left his family and travelled, on his own, to Britain. "I remember having sleepless nights and crying on the day. I cried for a year – I was very attached to my mum. My uncle was having second thoughts – maybe we should have left it a few years." Birmingham was not the smart, clean city Ayub imagined. "Sparkbrook, an inner-city immigrant area, with rubbish housing, was not what I expected. Relatives and my uncle's friends were living three or four people to a room, going out to work, using the same kitchen to cook. Friday, payday, people would be happy. But Monday, Tuesday, it was miserable. It showed on their faces. These were young men missing their family, working twelve hours a day, in appalling conditions."

Within two years Ayub had moved to London to live with his cousins in Stepney, a no-go area for Asians. Unlike Ruhul, Ayub persisted with his education, gaining some qualifications, whilst still working in the clothing industry. He, like Manuhar, Salam and Ruhul, was a member of the Progressive Youth Organisation based at the Montefiore Centre just yards from the Tower Hamlets Training Forum. "In the late '70s, early '80s this used to be the only community centre in Tower Hamlets where members of the Bangladeshi community could network, socialise, and work. It acted as the cradle of Bangladeshi political activism – a safe environment for us to come together. You could meet other people who would reinforce what you were doing. You didn't get much of that if you were a Bengali because you were seen as a victim, and other people wanted to help you."

Ruhul continued to take an interest in his friends' activism, but his dream of becoming a filmmaker never left him. One day, he stumbled across a camera crew filming around Brick Lane.

"Can I look through the viewfinder?" he asked Peter, the cameraman.

Ruhul loved the perspective and depth of field that only a professional camera can capture. He approached Simon Heavens, the director.

"May I stay around and watch what you do?"

"You can be our guide."

Simon was about to film a series of documentaries on multicultural Britain for *Channel 4* and asked Ruhul if he would find premises where the crew could edit. Ruhul found the ideal place in Heneage Street. Once again Ruhul asked Simon if he could help.

"By all means," replied Simon. "But I can't pay you."

Simon gave Ruhul the keys to the premises so, at night, after the day's filming, Ruhul could log the rushes and sync the film footage before joining the shoot the following morning – he was a quick learner. With Peter's support Ruhul got a union card and started to get paid the full union rate, despite Ruhul's protestations.

Ruhul's friends used to knock on the office door in Heneage Street and ask, "Is Ruhul there?" Ruhul feared they might spread rumours that he had a job serving tea to a white man. But Ruhul need not have feared.

"You don't have to make tea for me" Peter said. "Only if you're making one for yourself."

Ruhul showed *Purbo London* to Sue Woodford, a commissioning editor for *Channel 4*, who he met through Simon. Surprised to hear that Ruhul had never been to film school, Sue asked him to send her proposals for other films. She agreed to three half-hour documentaries developed with the Bangladeshi youth organizations, but with Simon as the nominal producer. It was not easy for Ruhul to reach agreement with the young activists. "It was chaos so I said, 'You're welcome to come up with ideas about women and young people and Simon will direct you but let me just make one film on culture, without interference.'" *Flame in My Heart*, produced in 1982, was Ruhul's first film for television.[9] "We'd never had an Asian filmmaker before," Ruhul said with pride.

Channel 4 then commissioned Ruhul to make a feature film, *A Kind of English*.[10] Critics, who wrote in *The Guardian* and *The Times*, compared it to the early films of Satyajit Ray and of the Italian filmmaker, De Sica, renowned for *The Bicycle Thief*. After that Ruhul worked for five years for various *Channel 4* productions as an assistant and film editor. "Altogether I made about thirteen independent films for *BBC* and *Channel 4*, mostly documentaries and experimental drama."

Ruhul was not always comfortable working with colleagues. "I became friendly with a lot of middle class, but I couldn't relate to English humour. They said, 'Ruhul, come to pub,' but whenever I spoke with a strange accent, I felt embarrassed. So, after a glass of orange juice or Coke, I ran out. They invited me to their house parties, too, all Oxbridge people, talking so sophisticated." I was lucky to catch up with Ruhul between film shoots in Bangladesh and India for his film about a legendary Sylheti folk poet. It had long been his ambition to honour Hason Raja,[11] but he had found it difficult to get financial backing about a film based outside Britain. "You've lived all your life here. What is this idea about Bangladesh?"

I was lucky, too, to catch Ayub – he now spends more than half the year in Sylhet. Ayub first went back to Bangladesh, in a professional capacity, with Lord Ennals to see how the British Government's charitable contribution of 11 million towards the Campaign for Disaster Prevention in Bangladesh was being spent. "I was on the front page of lots of daily prominent newspapers. That gave me a buzz. I realised I felt much more valued there and at home." In 2000 Ayub was appointed by Tower Hamlets Council to work for the Sylhet Corporation on urban management initiatives, funded by the European Union.

As we strolled through Spitalfields, past the old premises of the Tower Hamlets Training Forum where we first met, Ayub explained his decision to live more than half the year in Sylhet, even though his wife and children are in London. He enthused about how he had set up a school in the village of his birth, his plans to establish a hospital and care home for returnees but above all his desire to enter parliament. "In Bangladesh it's a blank canvas so the prospect of doing something meaningful at a bigger scale, excited me." After gaining a degree, a qualification in social work at Ruskin College, Oxford and an MA at Brunel University whilst working for local authorities Ayub had served as a Labour councillor in both Tower Hamlets and in Newham but, at some level, was disappointed at what he had been unable to achieve in Britain.

In Sylhet, Ayub is able to reconnect with the landscape he loved as a child, the paddy fields where he played football in the dry season; which flooded during the wet season allowing him to forage for his favourite berries. "When I worked in this open plan office in Tower Hamlets Council, there were hundreds of people looking at these bloody computers," he laughed. "Now I sit in my office overlooking the paddy fields, with my laptop, my iPhone, receiving emails and reading *The Guardian*."

Ayub reflected on the dilemma of people like Jalal and himself who aspired to be politicians in Britain. "The non-Bengali community didn't have confidence that we would be able to represent them because of our lack of education and familiarity with systems but also because of our divided loyalties, one minute here, the next minute there. Whereas this third and fourth generation they don't have that problem, they were born here, they went to school here."

Jalal, who brought together the different youth organizations under the Federation of Bangladeshi Youth Organisations, was one of the most promising young men of his generation. "From 1978 to 1990 I was a key reference point for the Bengali community, it was a twenty-four-hour job." He became the first Bangladeshi councillor in Tower Hamlets but the prediction that he would become the first Bangladeshi to be elected as a member of parliament was never realized. Jalal had a different view from Ayub as to the reason. "My teacher told me if you are going to progress in this country you have to be certified by white people. The fact I challenged people in the Labour Party meant the establishment decided I wasn't safe. I wasn't obedient. I speak my mind. I have no regrets. I have done what I believe in."

Manzila Pola Uddin is the only person of this group of Bangladeshi activists to have made a full-time career in mainstream British politics. She became the first ever Bengali women to be elected a local councillor when she became a Labour councillor in Tower Hamlets in 1990 and the youngest and only Muslim and Asian woman to sit on the benches when she became Baroness Uddin of Bethnal Green in 1998. Pola believes that her family's experience of contributing to the Liberation movement and fighting for an independent Bangladesh shaped her thinking and activism. "Such early exposure to war and conflict often helps individuals mature; to gain understanding about fundamental rights as well as the self-confidence to stand and say, 'We're not going to take it'. I believe the essentials ingredients that drove the movement for justice in the '80s, early '90s in this country, specifically within the Bangladeshi community, is because we believed this was our home. We would not tolerate bullying by people on the streets or discrimination by institutions that provided poor public services to our families."

During the Bangladesh Liberation War Pola and her brother would run through the alleyways to avoid Pakistani military, to take food for her families and cousins some of whom were freedom fighters and later died. "Look I am shivering as I speak of it even now 40 years after the event." Under a shower of bullets and a roar of tanks, she and her siblings would duck under tables and beds while her mother would tend to Pola's

Figure 8 Akikur (left) and Jalal (right), launch of the Bangladesh Youth Movement. Courtesy of Rajonuddin Jalal.

grandparents. Her mother had a hidden radio and the family would listen to *Swadhin Bangla Betar Kendro* station, the radio broadcasting centre of Bengali nationalist forces and an important source of information. Pola paused, and softly, so as not to disturb her fellow peers, sang one of the freedom songs, from a forbidden radio station, that she, her siblings and mother would sing along to. During the night Pola's "warrior mother" spent months making a flag for the new country, stitching together her red, green and yellow silk saris. The family took the flag onto the streets the day independence was declared. "We were told that on the last day the Pakistani army murdered 3,000 eminent doctors, scientists, educationalists and engineers in Rajshahi. This was a deliberate act of barbarism, a war crime, to jeopardise the rebuilding of the new nation, Bangladesh. I can't imagine what it's like to be in Gaza or in Iraq or Syria right now. I can still feel the pain and wonder what would have happened to our family if the army had had access to today's modern weapons."

Jalal's family, too, were active supporters of a free Bangladesh. "During the night freedom fighters would come to our house and ask for food and my mum would provide that. My uncle was a freedom fighter – he was shot by the Pakistani armed forces and supported a lot of Hindus in our neighbourhood to cross the border to India, so they burnt down our house. On one occasion my brother and my cousin were blindfolded and taken to the camp where the Pakistani army killed people suspected of supporting the freedom fighters. They were saved only because a Muslim League supporter happened to be a relative and saved them. Even I got beaten up by the Pakistani armed forces and their Bengali collaborators. We wanted the right to speak Bengali, promote our own culture and choose our own destiny."

Jalal, like Pola, recognized that his experience during the war, as well as in east London, influenced his activism. "What happened in Bangladesh and in Tower Hamlets made me stronger. It inspires you to fight for freedom and equality. For other people it's different. In your case it will be your enlightened middle-class background." I was not sure it was that simple.

That early commitment to forge a life in Britain has not dimmed Pola's or Jalal's memories of, or affection towards, the country of their birth. "For years I missed everything – the scent, the colour of flowers, the music, the sound of the River Padma or the call to prayer, *adhan*," Pola explained. "When I go back, my first act is to take off my shoes, I feel at ease and free." Jalal returns regularly. "We meet friends, family because all of us have a connection with our roots. We always feel that, don't we? Wherever you were born, that pulls you back. Even when you die that pulls you."

Pola speaks for all the young activists when she sums up their contribution to the development of east London. "There was only a handful of us willing, or able, to stand up so that today we can walk on the streets and be safe, so that housing allocation is less biased, so that our kids can go to university and are treated equally in the workplace. I could be blasé and say that the place we live in today is the creation of the activists of 1980s and without us Tower Hamlets would have remained a no-go area. I shall not. I will say we were the lucky generation that were afforded the opportunity to shape and change an entire community for all its people and make it a better home."

Pola is unsure whether today's generation has the same resilience and determination. "Our children's generation, who take so much for granted, seem less willing to protest against cuts, demand equal access to health care and occupy town halls in support of homeless families as we did. I think their strengths lie in their certainty that this home belongs to them as much as anyone. Although the numbers of British Bangladeshis in public office remain unacceptably low, I take enormous pride that the number of graduates in every household is growing, with many in leading positions. This is promising integration although time will tell if we have left a worthy legacy of activism which can inspire another revolution, if one is ever needed."

It was Jalal who contacted me to write an obituary[12] for my colleague and friend, Abdul Momen, in January 2020 – it was Momen who had organized the occupation of Camden Town Hall, that Pola referred to, after a woman and her two children, living in sub-standard homeless accommodation, died from a fire. Momen's death revived many memories – not only of making the banner to take to anti-racist demonstrations but also of sharing an office opposite Kings Cross station. When I arrived at work, bleary eyed, Momen, with his goofy smile and laughing eyes, would entertain me with his favourite selections from William Blake's poetry. That was the subject of his PhD at Leeds University before his sponsorship from the Pakistani government dried up because of the War of Liberation in 1971. He would lean back in his chair, prop his feet on the desk and between puffs of his Players' cigarette, quote *The Divine Image* from *Songs of Innocence.*

"For Mercy has a human heart
Pity, a human face:
And Love, the human form divine,
And Peace, the human dress."

After a stiff coffee, we got down to business. If we were despairing at yet another racist attack or the Home Office's insistence that someone was lying about their marriage, he would quote Rabindranath Tagore, the Bengali writer, poet, composer, philosopher and painter.

"You can't cross the sea merely by standing and staring at the water."

Momen went onto teaching youth and community work in higher education, inspiring future generations. He never had time to finish his PhD. I had kept contact with him over the years, acting as one of his best women for his second marriage and had visited him in his care home before his death.

As I wrote the obituary for *The Guardian* and local newspapers, that Jalal translated for the Bengali newspapers, I reflected on my discussion with Jalal on the various influences on our respective lives. In my case it was not just my background as the child in a vicarage household in a Lancashire cotton town, but the people I have learnt from, and got close to along the way. To Momen I owe a huge debt of gratitude. Without his influence and friendship and the work we did together, I would not have moved to the Tower Hamlets Training Forum; met Ayub, Jalal, Manuhar, Salam, Ruhul and Pola; and indeed, in all probability, done this research. I felt some relief that not only did Momen die, in his care home, before the coronavirus pandemic but that he was probably too affected by Alzheimer's to hear Johnson and others clamouring to make Britain great again.

Salam died, too, of COVID-19 that has disproportionately affected the Bangladeshi community. Not all battles for equality have been won. It was hard, but a privilege, to say goodbye to Salam, full of fun and one of the earliest and leading young activists, over Zoom, with prayers conducted by a local imam.

CHAPTER 7
A PAKISTANI SCOT WITH A MID-ATLANTIC DRAWL
Zohra who arrived from Pakistan in 1975

Zohra posed against a backdrop of hammers suspended by their metal heads in neat rows behind her. She picked up a saw frame and set to work. I photographed her chiselling a piece of silver, her long jet-black hair falling over the bench. Then I zoomed in on the jewellery – a silver ring, pair of earrings and bracelet, decorated with delicate, geometric designs. They reminded me of the arabesque patterns and tessellations in the Jameel Gallery of Middle Eastern Islamic Art at the V&A Museum. Zohra and I had done a deal – I would take photographs of her jewellery in her workshop for her website; she would agree to be interviewed about migrating to Britain as a child.

I met Zohra when she was South Asian Education Officer and I was Head of Equality and Diversity at the V&A. We shared many memories – travelling to gurdwaras across the country to encourage the Sikh community to visit *The Arts of the Sikh Kingdoms*;[1] feeling proud to see the exhibition crowded with Sikh families and enjoying the education programme Zohra had organized. We watched with horror, during a performance of *gatka*, a Sikh martial art, as a turbaned warrior sliced open a melon balanced on another warrior's head. We stared open-mouthed when, during *bhangra*, a Punjabi folk dance, Sikh men climbed on each other's shoulders to make a human pyramid, swaying to the rhythm of *dhol*, the double headed drum. There were calmer moments. During Diwali, young girls wearing saris and scarlet bindis on their foreheads, a tealight in each hand, danced before Hindu deities; when sari-clad women made circular, rangoli patterns, out of powders, ground rice and scented petals, of Ganesh, the Hindu god, on the floor of the Nehru Gallery of Indian Art. Zohra ran workshops too, often in jewellery, the subject she studied at Glasgow School of Art and the Royal College of Art in London.

Zohra's parents had moved as children from central India during partition between India and Pakistan in 1947. "Both families had property and were quite wealthy, but they were forced to leave with what they were standing up in." Partition, an arbitrary line separating India and Pakistan drawn by the British authorities, caused the deaths of a million people, the displacement of 13 million, the destruction of properties worth billions of rupees and the escalation of communal hatred between Muslims and Hindus. 'No greater indictment of the failures of British rule in India can be found than the tragic manner of its ending,' wrote Shashi Tharoor, introducing his book *Inglorious Empire*.[2]

Zohra had a huge extended family in Karachi with grandparents, aunts, uncles and cousins living within the house or nearby. She was the middle of five children, having both a younger and older brother and sister. "It wasn't like living in one house with a nuclear family, in the Western sense. There was always something going on." Like Pola from Bangladesh Zohra had a father who came to England to train to be a barrister but there was a difference – Zohra's father visited his family regularly during the years, 1968–74. Indeed, her youngest brother was conceived and born during this period.

Zohra believed, from a young age, that she would join her father in England. One of her favourite games, with siblings and cousins, was elaborate neighbourhood weddings, acted out with Indian dolls. They would make colourful garlands and clothes for the bride and bridegroom; perform *mehndi*, decorating the bride's hand with henna, followed by the *baraat* – the groom's procession to the bride's house for the ceremony. But Zohra's view of her own wedding was different. "Because my dad was living in London, I am told, I would wander around boasting, 'I'm going to London and will marry an Englishman.'" We both laughed, knowing that Zohra's childhood fantasy had become a reality. "It was not even a Scotsman, which is what you might imagine, having been brought up in Glasgow."

Zohra reflected on how the British Empire had impacted on her childhood. "Things like spinning tops, stick games and hopscotch." The railways, often quoted as Britain's gift to India but were, in fact, conceived by the East India Company, provided more entertainment. "There was a railway track in front of our house, and we used to take nails and put them on the lines. When the train flattened them, they became like swords, so we used to fight with them."

Zohra was brought up to pray and read the Quran at home – girls and women tended not to go to the mosque. Everyone joined in *Eid ul-Fitr*, the highpoint of the religious year. "It was such a special day. In the morning, you'd put on new clothes and have *seviyan* – vermicelli cooked in milk with pistachios, almonds, raisins and rose water. It was delicious. We'd get money from our elders to buy cumin biscuits and simple things. I remember we ran down to the shops to buy this hideous, kids' kind of lipstick in this plastic container, but we loved it. Everyone wore perfume and greeted each other in the street, 'Peace on earth, and joy to all mankind'. It was exciting and beautiful."

As the date of departure approached, the extended household was abuzz with talk. Seven-year-old Zohra listened in to the gossip, conjuring up images of amazing riches and wonderful toys in London. "There are dolls as tall as you," she was told. Like Pola, she seems to have blocked out memories of saying goodbye to her grandparents, her numerous aunts, uncles and cousins but she had clear memories of arriving. "I was utterly overwhelmed, not so much scared, but just feeling as if I was in a very strange place. Obviously, the streets weren't paved with gold, but I don't remember being disappointed. I remember massive dolls in the shop windows and thinking, 'My God, it's true. These dolls are as big as me.'"

In May 1975 Zohra, her mother and siblings moved with their father to Canning Town, a working-class area near the docks in east London that was heavily bombed during the Blitz. Soon after, Zohra attended school – she had only attended school in Karachi for a few months as education did not start in Pakistan until the age of seven. "On my first day the teacher asked me my name, but as she was talking in English, I didn't know what she was talking about. After she repeated it a few times, I worked out that 'name' must mean *nam* in Urdu. I caught up quickly. My older brother and sister, who were nine and eleven, always struggled, but, at seven, I didn't. Maybe a year or two later it would have been too late."

By this time Zohra's father had taken on several jobs including at Ford Dagenham, the car factory, and on busy market stalls. "Dad had given up law as he couldn't work, study and support his family. I think he was disillusioned – originally the idea was that he would practise in Pakistan, but he felt there was too much corruption, and in terms of practising here, he would have thought, there's no way I will be accepted – it's a very elitist world. His dad encouraged him to study law, so maybe that's the only reason he did it." Zohra's uncle suggested his brother help run his corner shop in Glasgow, so after six months the whole family moved to Scotland. "My dad still regrets it to this day," laughed Zohra. Soon after Zohra's father set up his own corner shop in Rutherglen, in south-east Glasgow.

As a child Zohra considered that her father, who had come to Britain to train to be a barrister, was too intelligent to be running a shop. "I'd be mortified thinking he shouldn't be doing this but my dad's take on it was that he'd rather be working for himself." Zohra hated working in the newsagent. "My younger sister helped every weekend for years and my older brother practically ran the shop with my dad. My other two siblings helped as well, but I didn't want to. It was such a chore, freezing cold and you had to get up at five thirty am or six o' clock." But Zohra would be protective towards her father. On one occasion, when a customer hurled racist abuse fourteen-year-old Zohra was so horrified she gave chase. "Are you completely mad?" her father shouted. Another day it was her brother who was the target. "Take anything you want," said Zohra's father, as a man held a knife to his son's throat. "That was the most, dramatic thing that happened. The police would never do anything about it. We lived in one of those tenement houses in London Road. It was very tough and working class with only a handful of South Asian families living nearby. There were few Urdu-speaking families in Glasgow – the larger population was Punjabi so again, for us kids, it was isolating as we didn't speak Punjabi. People of my parents' generation could switch, but we couldn't."

Zohra's family moved out to a four-bedroom new house on a council estate when she was ten and when the tenement buildings were being demolished. "My dad bought the council out quickly as, like many South Asian people of his generation, he didn't like debt. Class is a funny thing in Glasgow – as a child we were often considered well off because my dad had a business, owned his own house and two cars but they were simply a tool for our livelihood – you needed cars depending on how many adults were working in the newsagent, to go to the cash and carry, to open and close the shop."

Education, as for many immigrant families, was important to Zohra's parents. "My mum and dad really instilled education in us – we never felt we were less than anyone else. In fact, I often felt quite superior. I don't know if that's a bit of armour I built to survive," Zohra laughed. "There wasn't a huge amount of racism, but it was there. At primary school, we would learn Scottish dance and each year there would be a dance where we would put what we had learned into practice. Often, I would not be asked to dance by the boys because I was different, Pakistani. I would be mortified but then I'd think *I don't want to dance with those hideous, white boys.*" It was only at the language school, that Zohra attended initially one day a week, where she met students from different backgrounds. "The Italians came first to Glasgow, then it was the Chinese and then Pakistanis. So, I remember these three communities from growing up."

Secondary schools in the east end of Glasgow could be particularly challenging. "There were a lot of deprived kids shipped to our school." Though this made studying disruptive it did not deter Zohra. "The teachers were amazing and could focus on someone who wanted to learn. My favourite subjects were English and art. At one time I fancied myself as a writer. My all-time favourite book was *Wuthering Heights.*" Zohra harassed her teacher, again and again.

"Can you give me another book like *Wuthering Heights*?"

"There's no other book like that in the English language," her teacher insisted.

"Eventually she recommended *Cider with Rosie* by Laurie Lee, so I realised I didn't have to stop at *Wuthering Heights.*" Zohra enjoyed German as well as sciences and was good at maths but her ambition to be an architect was stalled as she failed her higher exams, having done well in her O Grades. Zohra stayed on at school to re-sit and get her folio together for art school.

Attending school in a rough part of Glasgow toughened Zohra's resilience. "When I was sixteen, a girl said some horrible racist comment. I just slapped her. My art teacher was watching from the window, and when I went back up to class, he said, 'That was amazing'. I thought he was going to tell me off." On her first day, registering for a diploma in art at Cardonald College, a man muttered under his breath, "Go back to where you came from." Zohra froze thinking *My God! This is going to follow me.* "I usually gave back as good as I got but I remember being struck silent because I thought I'd left all that behind." Despite this Zohra flourished at Cardonald College. She discovered her passion for jewellery and, persuaded, by her lecturers, stayed on at college for a second year to complete the course, before applying for the four-year degree course at Glasgow School of Art.

Zohra's parents, particularly her father, supported their children's education. "After dad had made sure we'd done our homework we'd do English dictation. He used to read out from one of the broadsheets, like *The Guardian* – the stuff we got wrong we'd have to write out ten times. Even to this day I think I'm great at spelling because of that." Her father was more prepared than some Asian families to compromise over school uniform. "I remember one Asian girl had to wear trousers under her skirt whereas my dad said, 'Of course you must wear the school uniform' but, when we got home, we had to change into our *salwar kameez.*" Her parents also did not limit, or influence, their children's choices. "They were completely happy with whatever we wanted to study. And, because we didn't live in a community, I didn't get that from other people, so I wasn't held back." Other people's prejudice still affected Zohra. After her degree at Glasgow School of Art, she went on to study an MA at the Royal College of Art in London. "When I did the MA

I would worry that people would say, 'Oh yes, but it was art', so when I did my Museum Studies MA I thought *Actually, I've done a proper academic MA.*"

Zohra's parents, whilst keen that their children flourished in Britain, were concerned they did not forget their roots. "At the weekends we'd do lessons in Urdu and read the Quran – a lot of children were sent to mosques, but there wasn't one near us and, although my siblings and I spoke English to each other, we spoke Urdu to our parents. Even in my twenties, when I visited home, I would wear *salwar kameez* out of respect for my mum and dad." The family's social life was limited. "We just didn't have any cultural kind of references." Occasionally they socialized with Asian friends of Zohra's parents and, at one point, cinemas in Glasgow started screening Indian films. "The whole community would turn out, dressed up to the nines." It was when Zohra went to art school that her social life expanded, causing arguments with her parents.

There is no sense of regret in Zohra about her upbringing. "I am grateful for my childhood. I've never felt hard done by, in want of anything or less of a person. My mum and dad, who had a very close relationship, grounded us. Probably just surviving and working alongside each other for such a long time brought them together, but they're very different." Zohra believes one of the reasons she was closest to her mum is because her dad was mainly absent for the first seven years of her life but there were other reasons too. "I remember him as a disciplinarian – we came from a very traditional family and I can be quite rebellious, so I would have hated being told what to do. It's not just a gender thing or because I'm his daughter. It's personalities as well. In my family, I think I'm most like him. He was always very straight and principled and I'm very much like that."

When Zohra returned to Pakistan with her family, aged fourteen, seven years after she left, she was confronted with how different she had become. "My cousins would think we were from a totally different planet because we'd had such a strict upbringing and were quiet. They had boyfriends and we didn't, and they thought that was hilarious," she laughed. "This is what happens with immigrant communities. When the adults move, they take their upbringing with them, whereas in the country of origin it's evolving. So even in a Western country where you're open to loads of influences, you're stuck in a time frame, like in the '60s or the '70s, and Pakistan had moved on to the '90s."

Pakistan was not so liberal when it came to Zohra being treated the same as her brother. "There's certainly a division of the sexes – you'd get attention from men and that was all quite strange. Also, you couldn't have a serious conversation or hang out on the street like my brother. He could play cricket with cousins and friends. We'd be indoors in case a particularly strict uncle would say, 'Why were you hanging out on the veranda?' whereas in Glasgow there was no one to watch you." Being treated differently because of her gender was not all negative. "To be a girly girl in Pakistan is amazing because you'd go off to the market to get glass bangles and the vendors would sweet-talk you. It's a bit like having your nails painted or having a makeover but I was quite a serious child, so I'd find that all a bit strange."

Zohra and the Englishman she imagined as a child were married in a registry office followed by a traditional Muslim wedding. "It was very short and sweet. Someone read through the ceremony, we said, 'Yes', and that's it," laughed Zohra. Her younger sister had paved the way in marrying a German man. "She did all the hard work, so it was easier for me. My other three siblings have married people from Pakistan. We were all exposed to the same things, we just made different choices."

Whilst working at the V&A Zohra had two children, now teenagers. "It's hysterical because they look exactly like me. If my husband walks out on the street with them, they think a stranger is abducting two Pakistani children." Zohra's children are no longer untypical. People of mixed heritage are one of the fastest growing population groups in Britain. Zohra regrets she has not passed on more of her heritage. "I've always wanted to improve my Urdu so I could teach my kids. I don't write Urdu, although I can speak it. It's a beautiful language. Partly because I was working, I just wasn't around a lot. They were with child minders. Now I'm trying to get them to speak Urdu, and it's ridiculous because they won't. My daughter's quite happy to say, 'I'm half English and we've been brought up here'".

Zohra returned to Pakistan, for the second time, with just her father, when she was twenty-one and at art school. "We travelled together so I could visit museums and see a bit of the country. I remember I went to Murree, a hill station in the Swat Valley, up north. It's the most stunning place – Karachi's quite rough and ready. I remember seeing this clearing, and there was a little homestead, a woman and kids running around, and it looked like the most idyllic place in the world, lush and green with mist coming from the hills. It was just beautiful. I imagine this parallel universe where there's another house where I married a Pakistani guy speaking Urdu, doing Asian cultural things. I have a deep connection with Pakistan, but I'm also Western and have chosen something else for myself. It doesn't negate my Pakistani identity."

Despite the racism and isolation that Zohra experienced in Glasgow, being 'Scottish' was, and to some extent remains, a strong part of her identity. "I wasn't born in Scotland, and I don't have Scottish blood, but I considered myself Scottish for a long time. I would say, 'Scottish and Pakistani'. I loved Scotland because it suited my character – the directness, warmth and friendliness. I'll still go back to Glasgow, start chatting to somebody at the bus stop. You can have a lengthy conversation with a complete stranger and no one would bat an eyelid."

There is no mistaking Zohra's Glasgow roots – her strong accent is one of her many attractive attributes. "Some Scottish accents are very harsh but mine is soft – someone told me it had softened into some Mid-Atlantic drawl – I take that as a compliment. I remember when I came to London, people wouldn't be able to understand me because of the speed at which I spoke. I get back into it when I'm in the company of other Glaswegian people or visit Glasgow."

As we ended the interview, I looked again at Zohra's jewellery, seeing more clearly how she integrates contemporary Western minimalism with her Asian, Muslim heritage. "I like using cultural references, something religious and spiritual, like Islamic art. I remember glimpses and flashes that I try and put into my work but they're just pretty patterns as well. I won't do it for the sake of it. I'm hoping it comes out naturally."[3]

Zohra decided to do a PhD in the representation of South Asian culture and engagement of South Asian audiences in museums, taking the V&A as a case study. At her request I rooted out photos of Sikh warriors slicing melons perched on top of fellow warriors' heads, of V&A visitors learning how to tie a turban, yards of cloth trailing across the gallery floor. She phoned me about her father's sudden death in Glasgow. I wondered if the distance she spoke of, partly but not solely, created by his absence in the first seven years of her life, was ever bridged. But there is no doubt of her admiration for her father who had, as a child, migrated from India to Pakistan during partition, and then as an adult, to London and to Glasgow, who had abandoned his career as a barrister but who had supported his family throughout. Zohra has inherited his resilience and fighting spirit, qualities needed to survive not only on the rough streets of Glasgow but in the corridors and galleries of the V&A, a leading British institution struggling with its colonial past. She challenged, with justification and energy, why her post of South Asian Education Officer was paid at a lower grade than other education officers and why, many years later, the post was one of the first to be made redundant.

CHAPTER 8
OUT OF HER DEPTH
Linh Vu who arrived, aged seven, from Vietnam in 1979

"I'd love to go back to Thorney Island," Linh mused, as we drank jasmine tea in her restaurant, the side exterior wall decorated with multicoloured Chinese lanterns. Thorney Island was the British military base where Linh and her father, Thanh Vu, stayed in a refugee camp when they first arrived in England in 1979. Some months after the interview Linh's husband, Colin, drove Linh, her father, Mitch and I to the south coast. Linh had agreed her story would form the basis of a short film and, as part of this, I had negotiated with the Ministry of Defence, to gain access to Baker Barracks.

Soon after we arrived military officials escorted us to an impressive, red-brick building where most of the Vietnamese had lived when they first arrived in Britain. We walked up the sweeping driveway, into the stately entrance hall and peered into the dining room where the Vietnamese used to eat their meals, now an officers' mess. Linh turned to her father, "Do you remember how Vietnamese families smuggled noodles into their rooms, adding spice to make them palatable?" Thanh laughed, the twinkle in his eye reminding me of the charming man I had met in the mid-1980s when working in Hackney adult education. I had helped Mr Vu, as he was then called, set up English and other classes for newly arrived Vietnamese refugees.

Since we worked together in the 1980s, Thanh had served as a Hackney local councillor and been awarded an MBE for his community work. He had never told me he made the perilous journey across the South China Sea with his seven-year-old daughter, leaving behind the rest of his family in Vietnam. After a delicious lunch in An Viet, the community centre where Thanh set up the first Vietnamese restaurant in Hackney, Thanh not only suggested I interview Linh, but handed me an A4 folder. This was his typed autobiography, recounted through hours of interviews with Tina Puryear. I stayed up all night to read it and contacted Spread the Word, London's writer development agency. Three years later *Catholic with Confucian Tendencies: The true story of the extreme adventures of a Vietnamese boat person*[1] was self-published. It was launched in Linh's Vietnamese restaurant alongside a screening of *Passing Tides,* the film based on Linh's life.[2]

We said goodbye to the Military of Defence staff and drove around permitted routes across the island. "There's the house," shouted Linh, pointing at a red-brick house, guns firing in the background. "It looks quite grand." Linh and her father had not lived in the main building with other refugees but with the staff – Linh's father, an ex-university professor, had acted as an interpreter and advice worker in the camp. "It did seem very different from scenes in the camps in Calais and the rest of Europe," Linh reflected. "I think that welcome makes such a difference as to how a person, never mind a child, perceives their new country."

We piled out of the car to admire the view over the Great Deep that separates Thorney Island from Chichester Harbour. Linh, wrapped in a black coat and stylish green and black scarf, stood with the sea behind her. "To me, water represents fear. Water is not friendly. I tried to swim as a child, but I never felt warmth with water. I fear depth too, from hiding in the reeds up to my neck, waiting for the boat in the dark." Linh looked back across the sea towards the Sussex coast. "When I see those images of migrants in the Mediterranean I go straight to their faces. That could have been us. Lots of Vietnamese drowned and were captured by pirates. It was sheer luck we survived." Between 200,000 and 400,000 Vietnamese died at sea in 1978/79.[3]

Linh was born in Biên Hòa, a small town thirty-five kilometres from Ho Chi Minh City, still known by many southerners in Vietnam as Saigon. She lived with her father and mother, both university lecturers; her younger sister, Tâm; and baby brother, Toan. Maternal grandparents and aunts, who helped care for Linh and her siblings, lived down the street – her father's family lived in North Vietnam, at least those who had survived the famine in 1945 when Thanh's mother and two of his siblings had died. Linh and Tâm, one year younger, attended a school on the edge of a paddy field, singing under the shadow of hibiscus trees in the school forecourt during assembly. They played marbles and hide and seek in the street outside their home, "Just simple games you didn't need toys for." At night Linh listened to the rain dancing on the corrugated roof of their back yard, unable to sleep for fear of ghosts. One of her worst memories was being forced to eat deep fried silkworms, a delicacy in Vietnam.

To supplement their income the family ran a small shop next to a butcher's where you could hear pigs squealing. "Life is much more out in the open in Vietnam. It was hot and humid too." Linh and Tâm helped behind the counter, selling home-made ice cream and lollipops made of squashed banana, dipped in coconut milk and sprinkled with nuts. "Tâm was always the tougher one. I remember one child tried to take a sweet from the shop. I didn't dare tell my parents, but my sister watched out for her and caught her red-handed."

Linh's family, like many in the town, was Catholic. On Sunday mornings the streets would empty – everyone went to mass. At Christmas, households created huge, mechanical figures out of recycled material – Mary cradling Jesus, a shepherd stroking a lamb, three kings bearing gifts. At Easter, people queued up to kiss the feet of a larger-than-life Jesus. "I remember one year he was lying on a bed of popcorn in a makeshift coffin," Linh laughed. "I'm sure I picked one or two." Although predominantly a Christian town, most families followed certain Buddhist traditions. They kept shrines to venerate the ancestors, wafts of incense billowing across the street, and everyone participated in the Mid-Autumn Festival dating from when China's emperors worshipped the moon, praying for a good harvest. Linh loved the night procession of candle-lit paper lanterns that would often get knocked over so the lantern would go up in flames. "My favourite was a cockerel with a long tail and big head."

In April 1975, during the Fall of Saigon, the capital of South Vietnam was seized by communist forces and the government of South Vietnam surrendered. U.S. Marine and Air Force helicopters transported more than 1,000 American civilians and nearly 7,000 South Vietnamese refugees out of Saigon in an eighteen-hour mass evacuation effort. In July 1975 North and South Vietnam were formally unified as the Socialist Republic of Vietnam.[4] The Vietnam War was over.

Many families in the South, including Linh's, became victims of the hard-line communist rule of the Republic. Her uncle, her mother's only brother, was sent to a concentration camp. "The night he died, there was a giant moth and all the family said, 'That's him returning'. We never spoke much about him again." 'The re-education camps were monstrous', wrote Thanh in his autobiography. 'They used pressure on the mind and spirit and would push people to the edge … It was very difficult to know what to say when they [the children] asked about their uncle.'[5]

At first, Linh could not understand why her father, a well-respected, councillor in South Vietnam before the communist takeover, hid his political poster on the toilet ceiling. "Why did he not put it on the wall?" Later she began to understand the danger her father was in. "One day there was a raid at the house. I remember thinking *Please don't let them look up there*. I knew what we were running from." At first the communists targeted high-ranking officials from the South Vietnamese government, police, military and intellectuals who needed to be 're-educated'. Then they targeted people with influence and Thanh was suspect. One night, after three failed attempts to escape on his own and once with the whole family, an ex-student, serving in the police, came to warn Thanh that his arrest was imminent. He fled to Saigon, a bigger city in which to hide and heard, through a cousin, of an offer of escape the following day. Thanh arranged to meet his wife in secrecy in the market in Biên Hòa. He tried to persuade her, once again, to flee as a family but Diệp was too frightened. "'No, not with the baby, I can't do it. Also, we don't have enough money to keep wasting on escape attempts.'" Thanh, desperate, explained to Diệp, "'I cannot face another visit to prison … Your brother died in a re-education camp.'" Diệp's snap decision changed the course of her eldest child's life. "'Take Linh with you. I'll stay in the house with Tâm and the baby.'" Thanh was thankful that neither he nor Linh had much time to say goodbye. 'It was too painful to contemplate that I would never see them again … Deep in my heart I did not think I would succeed.'[6]

Thanh had agreed with his wife's decision. 'Linh was big and strong enough to handle the journey … and, if we were successful, I would have one of my children with me.'[7] Linh's understanding was different. "I think he chose me because I wasn't as streetwise as my sister and health wise, I was probably, a little bit weaker and they thought I wouldn't survive in Vietnam. I don't know why they thought I would survive on the boat." Later, when she heard that it had been her mother's suggestion, she laughed, "Perhaps I was sent to keep an eye on him."

Linh and her father travelled 100 kilometres down the coast to Trà Vinh. Linh climbed into a small boat taxi, the size of a canoe, with a woman and her child, whilst Thanh took another boat taxi with a friend, Mr Bao – Linh would be safer that way as the police and officials were much harsher on men trying to escape. After travelling down the river, they kept out of sight waiting for a fisherman's boat to take them to the ship. Linh hid in the reeds in the dark, submerged and struggling for air. Hours later, at midnight, they gathered on the beach and were taken on the fishing boat. But there was no other 'ship'. Thanh had been lied to. The fishing boat, with only two small engines, was hardly suitable for a journey across the South China Sea. "There were about fifty of us crammed together. Even as a seven-year-old, it looked very small, and you could touch the water with your hand. Everyone was lying or sitting side by side – you felt really small in this big ocean, like a dot in the sea. There wasn't much talking or joking – we were told to keep quiet because police were patrolling the waters."

Thanh did everything he could to reassure Linh. "My dad told me 'You're going on an adventure', so some parts of it were really exciting because I saw dolphins and whales that I'd never seen before." The dangers could not be kept from Linh for ever. "When we had only enough water left for a couple more days and Thai pirates were hovering on the horizon – they knew people were leaving with their valuables – then you think maybe it's not going to be all fun."

One night, as a storm was brewing, Thanh woke up his daughter.

"'Look, there's a ship'. It was like an iceberg coming towards us, with multicoloured fairy lights. To be honest I thought I was dreaming. Our boat was rocking back and forth, filling up with water and everyone was shouting to the ship to rescue us." The fishing boat manoeuvred itself under the prow of the British ship to shelter from the gathering storm. "One of the first things they did was hoist down food – cream crackers and green apples – they were the biggest apples I'd ever seen." After two days women and children, with British government approval, were allowed onto the ship but the men, including Linh's father, were forced to stay back. "I didn't really realise why they weren't sending the men up – I thought maybe they were fixing the boat – and then the storm got worse and worse." Finally, Linh and her father were reunited but, during the storm, Thanh lost the only photos he had of Diệp, Tâm and Toan. Two days later another Vietnamese boat approached the ship, hoping to be rescued. The crew instructed the refugees not to look out of the portholes, but Linh ignored them. "I did take a sneak peek and could see pirates on the horizon."

The refugees on board the *Ashford* were well looked after. "Lots of tinned tomato soup. It wasn't the flavours we were used to, but it tasted warm. We were lucky because other boat people were at sea much longer. You hear stories of them drinking urine, even cannibalism, of torture and rape by pirates. I don't think I realised how dangerous it was or that we might never get to where we were planning. Not that we were planning to go anywhere, just to escape and get to another country."

After three weeks Thanh, Linh and other refugees disembarked in Singapore where they lived in a small refugee camp. Unlike camps in Britain, they could leave to explore the neighbourhood. Linh loved peeping through the iron gates at the big houses that reminded her of Walt Disney films she had seen in Vietnam.

After a few months they were flown to Britain where they lived for a few weeks in a military camp in Sopley, near Portsmouth, before moving to a larger camp on Thorney Island where the staff of the British Council of Aid for Refugees welcomed them. Linh was

Figure 9 Linh, aged seven, with her father, Thanh Vu, in first
refugee camp in Sopley, Hampshire, *c.* 1980. Courtesy of Linh Vu.

aware of her privileged position. Not only did she live in better accommodation because
her father was a member of staff, but she had a bicycle. "Being an ex-army camp there
was lots of outside space. I would ride everywhere – along old runways, discovering old
houses overgrown with wildflowers and grass." She was one of three children chosen to
go to a local primary school – others were educated in the camp. "Everyone wanted to be
my friend because I was different and there was such compassion from the headmaster.
That did help me settle. Back then there was a lot of empathy with the Vietnam War."
But once she was driven back to the camp, neither she nor her father was able to leave –
except on organized day trips.

At Christmas, children from the camp were invited to a party in the local area.
"Everyone had a present for us and all the children were fighting to hold our hand."
There were festive celebrations in the camp too. "We would stage our own shows and
we'd invite the English staff to play different parts. They were friendly and tried to get
us to celebrate key events as we would in Vietnam." It was the Vietnamese New Year

celebrations that reminded the refugees of what they had been through. "There was genuine excitement but there was sadness too. It was just trying to put our best foot forward, keeping the tradition alive and reminding everyone who we were."

As the refugees were dispersed to different places across the country, the number of people in the camp diminished. Linh and her father, who helped with the resettlement, were some of the last to leave. Many Vietnamese felt lonely and isolated and, over time, made their way back to London. In Hackney, one of the poorest boroughs at the time, housing was cheap, and the local borough was keen to welcome refugees. Many Vietnamese, including Thanh and Linh, converged on the borough.[8]

The move to Hackney was not easy. "In Vietnam you had the status in the community; again, my dad had status in the camp but when you resettled you had to fend for yourself. You were a nobody amongst the masses and you had to fight for survival." School was particularly challenging. "It was nitty gritty urban, and the headmaster didn't take care of you. You were just one of a number of immigrants and not all children wanted to be your friend." After an unsuccessful meeting with the headmaster, Thanh moved his daughter to a Catholic school in Seven Sisters where she was happier. "You could chat to the headmistress and even as a child you felt she understood. The children were much nicer and well behaved." Linh flourished. "I was good at art. I could sit drawing for hours and ended up doing all the posters and programmes for the school play. I was the first Vietnamese in the school, so I got VIP treatment and felt I could show the others around if they needed help."

During the day Thanh studied for a degree at the School of Oriental and African Studies but took on jobs to keep them afloat. "I went with him to clean offices above Waitrose in Holloway. I didn't mind it too much, but I remember my friends saying, 'Did you see that film?' There's a big chunk of kids' culture that I missed out on." After a couple of years, Thanh set up An Viet, to support other newly arrived Vietnamese, negotiating with Hackney Council to use disused public baths in Englefield Road. He organized English classes, training in clothing skills – local manufacturers needed workers – and lunches for pensioners followed by *Mahjong* and table tennis. Vietnamese New Year in Hackney Town Hall became an annual event attended not only by the Vietnamese community but local politicians. Linh always helped. "I was often the narrator with speeches Dad translated – as a child you don't like the attention. But I liked congregating with other Vietnamese."

The only communication with Linh's family in Vietnam was through a monthly air mail correspondence between her parents. "Every time he [Thanh] got a letter he would sit on the sofa. He had one or two CDs from America of famous musicians who would sing about their experience of leaving Vietnam that would be playing in the background. He wasn't sobbing, just silently tearful. It was very moving – something I just accepted." Linh had no direct communication with her mother. "There is a strong hierarchy in the Vietnamese family. My dad didn't encourage that either."

Although, in 1979, Thanh gained permission from the British authorities to bring over his wife and remaining children, it took five years for them to arrive. The obstacle seemed to be in Vietnam, with Diệp having to bribe officials to progress the paperwork. In 1983, when Thanh was admitted to hospital with appendicitis, he asked a friend to write, on his behalf, to the Prime Minister, the Queen and others. He believed royalty stepped in. 'I got a letter from the Queen's secretary saying, "Sorry to hear your story". Two weeks later my wife had a visa … I was so nervous I don't remember the journey to the airport at all. We were all crying when we walked into the concourse. It was overwhelming. So many tears and smiles.' For Linh, too, it was a momentous occasion. "I remember the build-up and collecting them at the airport. My brother saved me a little orange juice carton that he had on the plane. When they started my school, everyone had presents for them."

The transition was not as smooth as Linh had hoped. "I was very happy to see them but my dad had to spread his love – I'd got used to being the centre of attention and the freedom I had with him was gone." Neither did her mother's presence compensate for this loss. "My mum was so busy adjusting to life in Britain she didn't have much time for me either. Suddenly there were loads of culturally strict rules – rules never make sense anyway – saying prayers before meals, going to church every Sunday and every time someone came to our house you had to bow. It was so extreme. In Vietnam they think you are a good mother if all the children are well behaved, bow, and observe their Ps and Qs, and she tried to hang onto these ideas."

Relationships with her siblings were not straightforward either. "My brother was eight years younger, so he was cute but with my sister it was much harder because she was popular at school. I was used to being the star of the show." Thanh recognized Linh's difficulties. 'Tâm and Toan settled into life in London but Linh struggled. She had to adjust to having siblings again. My wife was very homesick, she had a hard time adjusting and her sadness caused Linh distress. We were happy to be together, but it took a couple of years before we were truly whole again.'

Linh and I stood outside Woodberry Down estate, built after the Second World War, where Linh first lived with her father and then with the rest of the family when they arrived. "Even as a child I knew the stigma of what it was like living in a council flat. The interior was fine because you decorate it how you want, and it was quite homely. But the exterior was typical red, brown brick. I ended up not having any birthday parties in the flat or inviting my friends or boyfriends back. They had private houses or one or two of them lived in flats, but they were much brighter, painted white. In Vietnam my parents did well, and we lived in a nice house."

The family would escape the "nitty gritty urban" by going for days out to Hastings or Margate. Linh was always impatient to leave. "It used to take us ages to get ready because, in our culture, you don't have fish and chips or pack a sandwich. When we got there it was fine. We had grilled chicken, sticky rice and coconut rice on the beach." Linh also went on day trips organized through An Viet as part of holiday play schemes. "One of the trips that dad organised was a cultural convention in Brussels where there were Vietnamese from other countries. That was fun."

In the early days the Vu family found it difficult to source Vietnamese ingredients – unlike today when every other food outlet along Mare Street in Hackney sells fresh ho fun noodles or pho herbs. Ridley Road Market in Dalston, which has served immigrant communities since the 1880s, was the only place they could find kohlrabi or coriander.

The family had to go further afield to buy shrimp paste, to capture a real taste of Vietnam. "Every nine months we would go to Paris for the day – that was our nearest corner shop. Once I came back with forty Vietnamese baguettes." Vietnamese food has a long history in Paris. The first waves of Vietnamese immigration to France started when the French colonized the country in the nineteenth century, but with the largest influx arriving after the Fall of Saigon.[9]

As a young child Linh loved Enid Blyton – the only Vietnamese literature available was a monthly newspaper suitable for adults. "Now you can get satellite TV from Vietnam." As a teenager she was an avid fan of Stereotypical, U2 and went through a Madonna phase, wearing fingerless lace gloves and Madonna inspired hats. She dipped in and out of Vietnamese culture, attending concerts across London when superstars, who had left Vietnam, and emerging artists based in Paris or America, came over on tour.

Being a teenager brought additional pressures. "We had the usual conflicts, but the biggest difference was that my parents still wanted us girls to marry a Vietnamese. Even when I had English boyfriends my dad would whisper under his breath, 'Vietnamese, Vietnamese!' It was hilarious, thinking he'll convert me." But helping out on a busy night in the restaurant in An Viet changed her father's attitude. "One Friday or Saturday night, the busiest night of the week, they were short of a washing up guy and my dad said, 'Do you think Colin can help?' 'He won't understand the chef's instructions' I replied. 'But he can wash up.' I never heard dad whispering, 'Vietnamese' again. People have a stereotype of English people as being unfaithful, so they think you're not going to be as secure in your marriage," Linh explained. "Now my parents have two English sons-in-law and they're very happy. It doesn't matter at all."

Linh met Colin when they were both studying architecture at university but waited fifteen years before getting married, partly because of the long training to enter the profession. She had her daughter, Mai, when she was thirty-seven. To wait so long would have been unacceptable in Vietnam – pressure from the community, and particularly from the elders, would have been unbearable. Indeed, her mother had warned Linh not to do a degree that took so long. "By the time you finish it's too late to have children."

Linh, like Zohra, feels guilty she has not taught her daughter her mother tongue. "I think more in English now so teaching her Vietnamese is a conscious effort. I'm trying to slot in a few words and sometimes I try whole sentences, but she goes, 'I don't understand.'" Linh was keen to avoid putting too much pressure on Mai, as she felt her parents had on her. "We all knew, when we came over, that the only way to fit in and make something of ourselves was through education. So that's why many immigrants over-push their kids, otherwise you'll be discriminated against. If it was left to me, I would have done more arty, creative courses, whereas architecture was a bit too disciplined and after six years I gave it up. If Mai's happy at something, I'll guide her towards that, but I still like to push her a bit."

Linh remembered with pride the moment the Vu family gained their British citizenship. This allowed them to travel more widely including to Vietnam, something Linh's father had always opposed, a sentiment that affected Linh and her siblings. "We resisted returning for a long time until we realised it's part of us." She first went back with Colin, who had already visited Vietnam as a tourist. "When the aeroplane landed, and my foot stepped onto the tarmac, I felt quite emotional." The fourth time, during the Easter holidays, she and Colin took Mai who delighted in the life-sized Jesus lying in a coffin on a bed of popcorn – Linh had not been dreaming. Seeing family meant there was often not enough time to tour the rest of Vietnam, but she was determined to experience the country of her birth beyond the reasons that drove her family away. "I'd like to rediscover the purity and beauty of Vietnam with my daughter, without the conflict, the politics and all the associated problems."

....

In May 2016, Linh, Mitch and I stood on the quayside, ushering people onto the Floating Cinema on the Regent's Canal in Mile End. It was the launch of *Passing Tides*, the title that Linh chose for the short film based on her migration to Britain as a child. People of all ages and backgrounds sat enthralled, watching video footage of Linh and her father returning to Thorney Island; old photographs of Linh, aged seven, standing next to her father. But most of all they sat spellbound to see Linh, head down, drawing in thick charcoal stokes – images of her head peering out of the reeds that threatened to submerge her; lying side by side with others in a cramped space reminiscent of a slave ship; of the small fishing boat tossed by huge, swirling waves, sheltering under the prow of the British ship decorated with fairy lights. There was silence after the film ended. Then huge applause as Linh came forward to answer questions.

Linh is no longer out of her depth. She feels comfortable living in Hackney with Colin and Mai. "The way people might look at you twice when I'm not in[10] London reminds me *Oh, I am different*. That's one of the best things about London. You can forget your skin and colour." Linh is wary of screening *Passing Tides* within the Vietnamese community. She feels others have suffered far more than she has. There are other reasons. "It's never really talked about, never dealt with, so it's a big black hole, which people try to forget. In the early years, things were whispered from parent to parent, at get-togethers and in community centres, but it was never talked about in the open and not to the children. Mental illness is frowned upon in our culture. I'm surprised there's not more psychological problems."

Passing Tides has been shown in many settings followed by Linh answering people's questions with delicacy and warmth. When tears slip down her cheeks a young girl, tall like her father, but with eyes and jet-black hair inherited from her mother, goes to comfort Linh. Mai no longer laughs at her mother when she refuses to follow her fearless daughter into the waves; is no longer puzzled when her mother stares at footage of migrants, fear in their eyes, crowded onto unseaworthy inflatable dinghies, floundering in the waves. In 2016, the year we visited Thorney Island, at least 3,800 migrants died, or went missing, in the Mediterranean Sea.

Vu Khanh Thanh MBE died in April 2022. Linh cooked his meals twice a day for the last eighteen months that he was in a care home. The strong bond that was formed on the South China Sea, during the five years that they lived together, before the rest of the family arrived, was never broken. "I think it is sheer luck how we survived. It's pure luck. You can't explain it any other way."

CHAPTER 9
A CHILD SOLDIER WHO KNEW TOO MUCH
Henry Bran who arrived, aged seventeen, from El Salvador in 1981

Henry was playing the organ in the Catholic church opposite his house in San Miguel, the third largest city in El Salvador, when one of his older brothers burst in.

"Your father wants to see you."

Henry continued to run his fingers over the keys. *What could be so urgent?* He hated to be disturbed when he was playing.

"Now," insisted his brother.

Henry found his father in the large living room of their colonial house which the four brothers had transformed into a roller-skating rink to entertain themselves during curfew. His father could barely look at him.

"I'm sorry, Henry, but for your own safety, I've decided to enroll you in the army. The guerrillas aren't going to kill you because they're your friends, but the army will."

Henry backed away.

"No way am I going to join the army."

Henry knew what the soldiers, including the infamous death squads, were capable of. They had killed some of his friends.

"That's the only way you can be protected."

There seemed no alternative. If Henry's father did not enroll his youngest son into the army, he would be conscripted. The army liked to recruit young boys when they could be manipulated, corrupted by the promise of power, seduced by the feel, smell and sound of a gun and before they were politicized. Not that Henry had shown any interest in firearms. At least his father had a plan for his artistic, sensitive son. He had talked to the sergeant and organized for Henry to join the army band.

I first met Henry Bran when he was employed during Refugee Week for the initiative, *My V&A tours* where refugees devised tours at the museum based on their life stories told through selected objects.[1] Henry chose Christian crosses and colourful cloths to represent his childhood in El Salvador, performing songs, accompanied by his guitar. It was a surprise to meet him again in a dimly lit bar in Hackney where my Brazilian friend was playing bossa nova. Over the silky strains of a saxophone, we discussed our shared love of Latin American music and talked about my research. Henry, a short man, with dark hair, deep brown eyes, came to my house a few days later – he was living with his elderly parents nearby, caring for his father who was ill. His parents had left El Salvador after the rest of the family had escaped to the United States or to Britain.

Henry staggered up my front steps with a huge bag, his guitar slung over his shoulder. We sat in my front room and drank tea. The large bag lay unpacked as Henry talked about living in San Miguel.

When civil war broke out in 1979, Henry was living with his parents and three older brothers in their huge colonial house with an extensive garden. It had been bought by Henry's grandfather who had gained his wealth from owning cinemas but who had escaped to Honduras as a political refugee. He had opposed President Hernández Martinez, a supporter of Hitler, who, in the 1930s, led *La Matanza* (massacre), murdering thousands of indigenous Salvadorans.[2] From a young age Henry used to sneak through the door of the Catholic church opposite, turn on the organ and teach himself to play. The priest even called upon Henry to ring bells for church funerals. Henry loved San Miguel. "Beautiful, quiet. You can sleep in the street and people will look after you." But when civil war broke out, it became dangerous. To keep his four sons occupied, Henry's father bought a ping pong table. This did not prevent one of Henry's brothers from clambering across the roofs, after the curfew, to meet his friends, one of whom invited his brother to join him in collecting milk at night from a nearby farm. The friend got killed. No one was safe. Aged fifteen Henry was sent to a private school in San Miguel – students in public schools, his friends amongst them, were being slaughtered. One evening, as Henry was celebrating his birthday, he saw the death squads killing a young boy yards away from him. The boy had witnessed a kidnapping. After that Henry was never able to fully celebrate his birthday.

As a child Henry did not understand the politics behind the conflict between the leftist guerrillas of the Farabundo Martí National Liberation Front (FMLN) and the military junta's army, the Fuerza Armada de El Salvador (FAES) that, between 1979 and 1992, left 75,000 dead and thousands missing.[3] This changed when he came to Britain. "I started seeing documentaries, films and photographs, testimonies of people – then my eyes were opened." Henry always admired Oscar Romero for speaking out against the civil war and the rampant injustice that had led to it – the country's wealth was concentrated in the hands of just fourteen families. When Romero, the much-loved priest, was assassinated during mass the Catholic population was outraged. "I remember people saying, 'If they don't respect the man of God, who is going to respect us?'" No one was convicted for the crime but investigations by the UN-created Truth Commission for El Salvador concluded that the extreme right-wing politician and death squad leader, Roberto D'Aubuisson, had given the order.[4] For the Bran family Romero was not just a compassionate man of God, who sought peace and justice, but a close, intimate friend. Henry pulled out crumpled black-and-white photographs from his large, leather bag. They were of his parents and grandparents, married on the same day, posing with Romero who had conducted the ceremony. Romero had insisted that if he was to marry Henry's parents, then his grandparents' union should also be legalized. "He was from my city, married my parents, my grandparents and baptised my sister. That is Oscar Romero for me."

The Bran family became a particular target when Henry's brother-in-law, a university lecturer, took refuge in their house after being kidnapped by government forces but then released by Amnesty International. "Anything that was education was a danger." Henry's brother-in-law insisted on going back to work. 'En route', a university caretaker warned him that death squads were waiting for him. Henry's brother-in-law escaped but the caretaker was killed. The military knew, no doubt, that Romero, a saint in people's eyes, was a close family friend. Henry's older brothers worked as radio journalists which meant they, too, were suspect but Henry, as the youngest, was the most vulnerable. About 80 per cent of the 60,000 military personnel in the Salvadoran army were under eighteen as compared to 20 per cent in the 8,500-strong FMLN guerrilla army. It is more common for child soldiers to be used on the rebel or guerrilla side of any conflict. Henry's father could see no alternative. If his son was not recruited into the army band, he could be abducted by government soldiers.

Henry's induction into the army was frightening. "The soldiers said, 'You're lucky, you're one of us. We can't kill you now.' It was like being in the mafia." But the army band members took to Henry and lent him their instruments. Soon he was teaching himself to play the trumpet, trombone, tuba and the clarinet. This angered the sergeant.

"No one lends Henry their instrument until he learns to read music. If you do, I will put you in jail."

Henry had some protection as his cousins, working as army mechanics, were high-ranking officers. He also learnt to ingratiate himself with fellow soldiers whilst working in the army shop. "I was told not to sell them beer, but I used to hide it behind the counter and fill their flasks." Army friendships also brought dangers. Soldiers would tell Henry, "'If you have a girl you like, tell us and we'll kill their boyfriend.' I knew who was going to be killed and that was scary because, if I warned them, I, too, was going to be killed. I began to like the taste of power, but I didn't want to go to the next level." Henry's parents realized their youngest son was in a compromising situation and determined to get him out of the country. His sister and brother-in-law were now in London, and this seemed the safest option. Most painful for Henry, on leaving El Salvador, was saying goodbye to Napo and Omar, his closest friends. "When they dropped me at the stop to take the bus to the capital, they started crying. We knew then that was it. They're the ones I left back home."

Henry had never travelled out of El Salvador and never in an aeroplane. "When I saw the jumbo jet that was going to bring me to London, I thought, how is that thing going to stay up there? I didn't go to the toilet just in case I fell down the hole." On arrival at Heathrow Henry was hustled into a room where he was questioned by men in uniform.

"I'm coming to study music."

"How much money have you got?" asked an immigration officer. "Music college is expensive."

Henry pulled out crumpled notes from his pocket and laid them on the table.

"Twenty-five dollars?" laughed the officer.

Henry was annoyed. Twenty-five dollars in El Salvador was a year's wages. He was worried, too, that the officer would take all the money away his father had given him.

"That won't even cover your trip from the airport. Even if you walk some of the way. Which music college are you going to? Where did you say you came from?"

Henry kept to his story that he was going to study music but could not name a college. He did not mention the war in El Salvador or that he had been a soldier. He knew not to trust men in uniform. These men, photocopying every paper Henry had in his possession, taking down details and addresses of his friends and relatives, could be anybody.

Henry waited for what seemed hours, even days, in a cold, bare room. After twelve hours, an immigration officer came back into the room.

"Your sister is outside with the Human Rights Campaign. Why didn't you say you were seeking political asylum?"

"Because you might kill me. Now I know you have talked to my sister I can speak openly."

The civil war had taught Henry that a man in a uniform can pull a trigger at a moment's notice. A neighbour, or even someone considered a friend, can report you to the enemy. Only those closest to you can be trusted, and not in every circumstance.

It was Henry's brother-in-law who organized Henry's escape. He feared, with justification, that Henry was being brainwashed in the army. Within days of arriving in London snow started to fall. Henry rushed out of the terraced house in Hackney where he was staying with his sister and brother-in-law, lifted his face to the sky, opened his mouth and let the snowflakes land on his tongue. "I had arrived in Slush Puppy land and wanted to put a flavour on it and lick it all up." Henry was still a child at heart.

Henry was keen to resume his education – he had progressed well in his accountancy studies at his private college in San Miguel but because of his limited English, he was placed in a basic numeracy class in Tower Hamlets College. Henry was outraged. "I ended up teaching all the other students." It was Henry's sister who put him back on his feet. She had heard about a Latin American music festival in south London. "Take your guitar, Henry, just in case."

Henry, his sister, and brother-in-law settled into the front row seats of a draughty hall in south London to listen to Brazilian, Chilean and Peruvian musicians. Then the organizer announced, "Tonight, we have a singer from El Salvador." Henry turned to his sister, "El Salvador?" "Yes," said his sister, "It's you." Handing Henry his guitar, she pushed him onto the stage. Henry stumbled forward, faced the audience, unsure what to sing. Then he remembered a song learnt in his youth, then another. The audience applauded "Encore." Henry's brother-in-law smiled, imagining Henry as a cultural ambassador for El Salvador, introducing his country's music to Britain, to the world. There were few Salvadorans in London, but Henry had other ideas. "I don't feel what other people write so I started composing my own songs."

Henry wrote about war, its effect on children and the plight of refugees, not just from El Salvador but from other troubled areas of the world. He began to get gigs through Latin American, refugee and human rights networks. He laughed as he told the story of being invited to perform for the Labour Party Conference in Blackpool. "When I arrived at the hotel where all the members of parliament were staying, a crowd surrounded the taxi. 'Who the hell is he?' someone asked. Somebody else shouted, 'I don't care, I'll take a picture in case he's famous.' As soon as he clicked the camera, brrrrr … they all started taking photos."

Henry was meant to perform a song on the *BBC* about the devastating effect of landmines on children, planted by the El Salvadoran government, no doubt funded by the US government who backed the right-wing junta. The United States were determined to defeat the guerrillas at any cost so as not to lose the country to communism. But most of the guerrilla army was made up of peasants seeking a better life – only one branch of the FMLN was overtly Marxist. The *BBC* cancelled the programme without telling Henry the reason. It had been replaced by coverage about a lady in London playing with a dog. Henry's fury drove him to compose the song, 'Broken Children.' He reached for his guitar, his voice barely audible as he sang in Spanish, "They care more for dogs and cats than for broken children in my land."

Henry reached into his bag and unwrapped the tissue paper from a wooden cross, thirty centimetres high and fifteen centimetres across. On the left of the horizontal bar he had painted a white peasant house with a red tiled roof, sheltering under the volcano near San Miguel; on the right a row of Hackney terraced houses, Tower Bridge, the London Eye and the Houses of Parliament. On the central spine Jesus held up the world in his hand; above Christ flew the Dove of Peace, wings outstretched, below a blazing sun; at the base stood a young couple in love, a red rose between them. This was Henry and his first wife, a childhood sweetheart, who came from El Salvador to marry

Figure 10 Henry with his many guitars in London, *c.* 1984. Courtesy of Alicia Mc Keown, daughter of Henry Bran.

Henry when he was just nineteen and she was twenty. He had met her at the private college he attended in San Miguel.

Some years after the war Henry returned with his wife to El Salvador, to stay with his in-laws. Early one morning, he decided to visit his former home. As he approached the old colonial house, he felt himself getting smaller and smaller, roller skating in the living room, catapulting his brothers from the fruit trees in the garden, entering the church to play the organ or pull the bells. It was no longer a "wonderful, happy house," the centre of life in San Miguel but "a sad, haunted house," covered in cobwebs, its inhabitants killed in the war, or so the neighbours thought. Henry, wearing white trousers and a white T-shirt, sat on the wall in front of this abandoned house. A bus screeched to a halt. The passengers piled out and stared at this figure clothed in white. The bus driver approached, followed by other passengers, not daring to believe. Then the driver cried, "Henry, you're back. You gave us such a fright because everybody assumed you were dead. And suddenly we see this haunted house, and you sitting outside wearing all white." "He's back," echoed the whole bus. "Oh Henry, you gave us such a fright," repeated the driver, laughing and shaking his head as he ushered his passengers back onto the bus.

Henry brought out a canvas from his bag, eight inches wide and twelve inches high. It was a painting inspired by a photograph in a newspaper of a father in Iran, kissing the hand of his dead child. Henry cradled it in his arms but so that I could see it. "I thought to show what it's like to lose somebody you love so much. It was sad to see parents grieving – they didn't know what to do." He paused, looked up at me. "We didn't know who was next." I motioned for Henry to prop the painting on my windowsill. It could not be put away so easily.

Henry picked up his leaflet of poems with bold illustrations in thick black pen – of Jesus weighed down by the weight of a cross; of a peasant girl carrying a jug of water on her head.

"It's called The Dove of Peace."
Henry read.
"The Dove of Peace came to drink water.
They caught her.
She fluttered.
She could no longer fly.
They put her in a cage and shut her up.
They tortured her, pulling out her feathers one by one.
When she was naked, they raped her, they beat her and then they let her go.
She was just a girl of fourteen years old."
I did not ask who the girl was, if Henry knew her, what he had seen, or even experienced, of rape during war. It seemed too intrusive.

Henry had penned a novel about Jesus living in El Salvador. It centred on two characters, Jesus and a boy orphaned during the civil war who Jesus took care of. "The little boy doesn't know anything but is trying to catch up whereas Jesus knows a lot of different things. I'm a combination of the two." The little boy was Henry who feared the jumbo jet carrying him to London would fall out of the sky but with an adult's knowledge, like Jesus, of the violence and corruption of war. Henry's story ends with Jesus, killed because of his belief, being resurrected, not in person but in the faith of El Salvadorans. It was a story of hope, sustained by faith, that Henry held onto throughout his life. "Christianity has been an escape from pain. Something I can turn to, forget, and give everything to."

Henry loved El Salvador but had no wish to live there. "Hackney has given me all the culture, colours, cosmopolitan of everything. El Salvador is just a dream that I left behind. I can always go back and dream again, but Hackney is my home." He often went out at two or three in the morning – meeting shift workers and night-time revelers – as a break from looking after his father. He tried to reassure his mother about his nocturnal wanderings. "Everybody says 'Hi, Henry.' I know everybody and they look after me." There were other reasons for these night-time ramblings. "Sometimes I have nightmares. My dad asked, 'Why don't you sleep?' and I said, 'I just can't. All these memories come back'. You live in fear, you're scared of everything. You've seen things …" Henry trailed off. He was typical of child soldiers who continue to have nightmares throughout their lives. They, even more than children who are victims of violence, may suffer trauma because of their war times experiences. I wondered if Henry's father ever regretted recruiting his son into the army although Henry claimed, "It was the right decision to protect me."

A few weeks later Henry rang from Homerton Hospital asking me to visit.

"I have liver disease," he said as I stood by his bedside.

He had other sad news.

"My father died yesterday. I am so worried about my mother. She is alone now."

Henry's mother, an artist and designer, had held the family together, through the civil war and the migration of her family across the world. Henry was keen to get back on his feet again, to look after her.

Henry talked of children, his two daughters from his first wife. He talked, too, of a more recent partner whom he had met after his divorce, with whom he had a son but from whom he was now separated. Both mother and son were living in Ireland. I was relieved his ex-wife, who still lived in Hackney, and his two daughters were visiting him, that Henry had not been abandoned. A priest, who was chair of a local organization that works with refugees, arrived. I left them.

Some months later Mitch and I started to produce our first film *Child Migrant Stories: Voices Past and Present*. To open the film, we chose Henry's story about fearing the jumbo jet to London would fall from the skies. To end the film, we chose Henry's love of Hackney and about El Salvador as a place he can return to in his dreams. We began to source a music track for the film.

"What about Henry's music?" I suggested.

Mitch searched the internet until he found,

"There isn't any place safe to live
There isn't any place for the refugees.
Where their children can play their games
And not a real war
And not a real war
And not a real war."

I rang Henry's mobile, but the line was dead.

"Look at the attribution," said Mitch. "RIP."

I felt shock, guilt, regret that I had not followed up on my hospital visit. The RIP gave no indication of when Henry had died, and I had no way of finding out. I sought out the bag he had left with his objects inside – the painting of the grieving father inspired by Henry's empathy with grieving parents in El Salvador; the large, decorated wooden cross – he had given a smaller version to Bishop Sentamu, Archbishop of York to wear round his neck. I reread the poem about the rape, felt tearful but grateful, too, that Henry had shared the stories of his life, both tragic and funny, before his death.

It took some weeks to track down his daughters through the priest I had met at Henry's bedside. They were thrilled to receive the objects Henry had left with me – they had contacted the V&A Museum of Childhood to no avail. And they were delighted to give permission for the use of Henry's music as soundtrack to the film. The youngest, Gabriela, who has inherited Henry's artistic flair and who was studying for a degree in animation, helped us organize the first screening *Child Migrant Stories: Voices Past and Present* on the Floating Cinema. She assisted with a stall in Stepney Green, illustrating people's responses about welcoming child migrants. I asked her if she would help produce a film about Henry's return to the site of his beloved, colonial house in San Miguel.

The House That Is Not There[5] opened with a painting of the countryside in El Salvador by Henry's mother followed by animated scenes of Henry looking to the guerillas, to his left, and government soldiers, to his right. Then the scene shifted to Henry approaching the old colonial house as he grew smaller and smaller, sitting on the wall, in front of the abandoned house, dressed in white; of people piling out of the bus to gaze at what they thought was a ghost but was their old friend, Henry. The voice over and music were Henry's – talented members of three generations of the Bran family contributed to this short, animated film by Gabriela. It was first screened at the Geffrye Museum, now the Museum of the Home, during a conference about home and child migrants. Several members of Henry's family came – his mother, Henry's first wife and his two daughters. There was a mini-Henry too. Henry's second partner had brought over her seven-year-old son from Ireland. Henry's personal life, particularly in later years, was often fraught but here was a demonstration of love and solidarity, despite the challenges Henry faced in his life.

When I think about Henry's story I think, too, of those 300,000 young people in the world today, often teenage boys, who are recruited as child soldiers; to fight on one side or the other, of wars they do not understand; who, like Henry, have to choose a side; to join the Taliban in Afghanistan or be killed; to leave Syria before they are commandeered to kill their own. No wonder their families, if they themselves have not been murdered, send their boys away hoping they will find safety. Do we think of this when we see teenagers, often male, crossing the Mediterranean in leaking dinghies; caught up in fires in refugee camps in Greece, camped in appalling conditions in Calais or Dunkirk, trying to find safety? Henry did find safety. His music allowed him to express children's experiences of war. He contributed to Britain's rich diversity, raised early awareness of the presence of Latin Americans in London and, in later years, became well-loved in El Salvador. He bore three children who have inherited many of his talents as well as an interest in social justice – Gabriela worked on an animation in Rome related to Little Amal, the giant puppet of a ten-year-old Syrian girl who walked across Europe, mirroring the journeys many child refugees endure.

When I reflect on Henry's story I wonder if he had not experienced the civil war and life inside the army, whether he would have been so troubled with nightmares, and whether he would have died so soon, in his fifties, just days after his father who had so wanted to protect his talented son.

CHAPTER 10
"CAUGHT IN A FLOW OF WATER"
Eylem Binboga who arrived, aged twelve, from Turkey in 1987

Brew for Two suggests a chintzy tearoom and, indeed, there were 'English' touches – a row of vintage plates perched on a picture rail, shelves of floral tea pots and gold-rimmed china cups and saucers. But an Ottoman-style Turkish coffee pot stood on the sideboard and seats of various wooden chairs, painted in blue, had been upholstered in African wax prints. Trailing plants in hand-painted pots enticed customers to an outdoor courtyard – tradescantia purple passion and green peppers or *biber* as they are known in Turkish. The sage green walls were covered with framed photographs of doors of every style and colour – some unmistakably London but others? Doors upon doors upon doors.

Eylem, the café owner, switched on the crystal chandelier that seemed more suited to an Italian villa. She made Turkish coffee that we drank at a small table. Her clothing was as stylish and eclectic as her taste in interiors. "I dressed up for you," she said, smiling. She wore a sleeveless, three-quarter length black dress with a black net skirt over a fuller beige net skirt. Such feminine flourishes were tempered by black tights, trainers and a red and black neckerchief. Her sleek black hair, red lipstick and black eye liner, framing her amber eyes, enhanced her handsome face. But behind this stylish and creative exterior lay a more vulnerable woman. Eylem, aged twelve, had been wrenched from her place of birth, with no warning or say in the matter, to join her parents who had migrated to Britain two years earlier. She felt she had been "caught in a flow of water and was just being dragged."

'Participation' is one of the four principles laid out in the UN Conventions on the Rights of the Child. 'Protection' from discrimination, neglect and exploitation, 'provision' for children's basic needs and 'prevention' from harm are the other three 'P's. But at what age, how and in what context children can participate in such life changing decisions as migrating to another country is difficult to judge. Is it even possible to consider individual children's rights without looking at the interests and quality of family life as a whole? Would Eylem have fared better if she had stayed in Turkey?

Eylem Binboga was born in 1976 in Kayseri, Turkey, an industrial city in central Anatolia. She lived with her parents, older sister and younger brother in an Armenian house close to Kayseri centre. When Eylem's grandmother died the family moved to her grandfather's farm outside the village of Kumarli Köyü so her mother could take care of her father. Eylem loved the farm. "It was hilly, a bit barren but there was space after space, field after field. I was out as the sun rose and came home when it was dark." Her uncle, on his way to work one morning, was astonished to find his seven-year-old niece in a rubbish bin at sunrise.

Figure 11 Eylem in her café Brew for Two, May 2014. Courtesy of
Eylem Binboga, Copyright © Eithne Nightingale.

"What are you doing there, eating half a watermelon, with the other half on
your head?"

"I must have stunk," laughed Eylem. "I was covered in soot and dirt."

Eylem's siblings and cousins, who lived nearby, often joined in the mischief. "My
granddad had just cows and sheep, so we ended up exploring other people's farms. One,
belonging to a person who had settled in Germany, had cherry trees around his pool.
We made a pouch out of our shirts, climbed the tree and picked as many cherries as
possible. Cherries stain your teeth, clothes and hands so they knew we'd been stealing.

I loved sunflower seeds. Sunflowers grow quite tall so to find the seeds, we had to break the stalk and check if they were ripe. Once, when the owner appeared, I managed to run, undiscovered, through the stems as far as my granddad's farm. I didn't have the strength to run further so I undressed this scarecrow where my mum was growing Turkish peppers. I put on his black hat full of straw so nobody could see my face, my grandad's *salwar* trousers and an enormous raincoat. Then I stood perfectly still ... I could see my cousins and friends running up the hill to hide in the caves left by the Armenians. I could see my grandfather boiling with fury just ten or fifteen metres away. 'She has the devil in her, *şeytan, şeytan*' he called but he didn't spot me."

Between playing and getting into trouble Eylem helped on the farm. "We worked hard, milking and feeding the cows, carrying hay and watering the plants. Sometimes we were out in the fields for hours, under the sunlight, waiting for someone to bring us food. Once, when I was playing, six of the turkeys wandered onto the rail tracks and got butchered by a passing train. Turkeys are such stupid animals. I knew I was going to get in trouble, so I decided to run away to my granddad's. I remember putting potatoes, tomatoes and spring onions in my apron and just leaving. I walked for an hour, maybe more." By this time Eylem's family had left her grandfather's farm to live near an uncle in Kaybasi.

"You turn around and go home," said Eylem's grandad, giving her a good spanking.

Eylem's father, who hated to get his hands dirty, had fallen out with his father-in-law. "My father was not your typical farmer, but he was a good tailor – he left, for a year, to earn money in Paris but nothing came back. My mum said he gave money to his brothers or his dad. He had a habit of going to Turkish men's cafes and would say, 'I'm only going for an hour,' but would forget the time. My mum had to look after three children, the house, the land. On top of that she would crochet or make rugs, finding other ways of earning." Eylem's mother felt the only solution was for her and her husband to migrate, earn money and return, leaving the children in the care of an aunt and uncle.

"I remember there was something exciting happening, mixed with a little bit of worry. It was summertime, there was watermelon every night and a lot of money being counted. I think they explained what was happening to my sister, but nobody told me." Thirty years after the event Eylem still remembered feeling resentful and confused about not being forewarned or consulted about her parents' departure. "I don't remember them leaving us with my uncle. Maybe it was too painful, my memory blocked it out, or maybe I was so overjoyed that I was going to my uncle's house. He had four children, so we were getting together. And I don't remember saying goodbye to my mum and dad although my sister probably does." Did her parents think that Eylem's sister, just two years older, was more able to understand the reason for their departure?

Eylem thought her parents' decision to migrate was both economic and political. "We were Kurdish Alevis. One of my uncles still can't go to Turkey because of his political involvement in the 1970s, another uncle had about six months in jail." Alevis, who hold beliefs distinct from the Sunni majority, have endured centuries of persecution in Turkey, even branded heretics by the Ottomans. In the political upheaval and repression of the 1970s, resulting in the military takeover of 1980, dozens of Alevis, who have traditionally voted for the left, were murdered. Kurdish Alevis experience persecution and discrimination for their religious identity, political leanings and ethnicity.

"As a child, were you aware of this discrimination?"

"My parents and grandparents spoke Kurdish. I didn't because they wouldn't speak it in front of us in case we spoke Kurdish in school, which would get them into trouble. They were very hush hush about it."

The European Commission Against Racism and Intolerance, even as late as 2010, reported, 'The public use by officials of the Kurdish language lays them open to prosecution.'[1]

Eylem knew her parents' religion differed from most people in the area but not why or how. "We knew we weren't Sunni. We were Alevi, but what Alevi meant I didn't know." She was aware, too, of secret comings and goings, that neither she nor her siblings were allowed to be part of. "My grandfather was a *dede*, the equivalent of an imam, so the doors would be locked, and we wouldn't be let in. My grandfather used to be a good *saz baglama* player, and there were songs he would play, but in a very secretive way. If we spoke about it at school, they could have been taken to jail, tortured and if the local Sunni Muslims heard about it, they could have burnt the place down." Eylem's family differed from Sunnis in other ways. "My mum didn't cover her hair and my parents didn't encourage us to go to the mosque. During Eid, we butchered animals, but certain neighbours wouldn't take our meat. Now it makes sense but then I didn't understand why."

Only when Eylem came to Hackney and attended the *cemevi* in Dalston, Hackney did she learn that the secret happening in her grandfather's house was a *cem* service. "It's more of a chanting, a celebration with dance and music. We believe God exists in everyone – we don't pray in a certain direction or to a certain object but in a square. I only found out who I am in this country." Men and women pray together and although Alevis observe a fast they do so during the month of Muharram, the first month of the Islamic calendar, rather than during Ramadan. They allow the consumption of pork and alcohol and whilst some, but not all, believe Alevi to be a branch of Islam, others, like Eylem, question this. "They have pre-Islamic beliefs, but I think Islam was such a powerful religion that they adopted Islam to survive, so it somehow merged. Some Alevis might say, 'We are Muslim,' just to be safe."[2]

Eylem's love of the farm and surrounding landscape helped her survive her parents' absence. "I was out at sunrise and came back when the sun was going down so my parents' departure didn't feel such a big loss. But when they phoned or a letter came, or when we remembered, it was very emotional. We had maybe four or five letters, two or three telephone calls during that time – it had to be in a post office in a village. My uncle and my aunt were good to us, especially my aunt but there wasn't that physical closeness – I missed my mum's smell and her cuddles. Mind you, my aunt wasn't physical towards her own children either. She didn't have time for cuddles, bless her, she worked too hard. But it's something different not having your mum or dad around."

It was over two years before Eylem would be wrapped up again in her mother's cuddles. Not that she was prepared for it. The first sign she would, once again, be overpowered by events was when, in August 1988, her uncle took her and her siblings to get new shoes and clothes. "It was like *What's going on?*" Eylem started to beat her chest. "I remember my auntie, with her scarf falling across her shoulder, squatting and beating like this, almost wailing." Again, amnesia seemed to have affected Eylem's memory of leaving her aunt, with whom she had developed a close attachment. "I don't remember saying a proper goodbye. The next thing we knew we're in a big coach to Istanbul where we stayed maybe seven days. It was surreal. I'd never been to a big city before and never been on a plane." Leaving her uncle, who had taken them to Istanbul, was painful too. "He was very emotional – there were tears in his eyes." The excitement of flying softened the loss, for a time. "I remember looking at the airhostess thinking *They're so glamorous, like movie stars. I want to grow up and look beautiful like them.* Mind you, at that time I had a flat chest and looked like a boy." The glamour soon dimmed on arrival at London's Heathrow airport. The Home Office required forms to be completed and a barrier prevented Eylem from embracing her mother. "This lovely black lady from Cyprus got to cuddle us first, because my mum had to be kept to one side. She looked old. She looked modern."

Finally, in the back of the van that Derya Abla, the "lovely Black lady," drove back to Hackney, Eylem got to cuddle her mother. "But it was different. Or I was different. It was dark inside the van but outside London was sparkling with lights." They drew up outside İşçi Birliği, the Workers Union Party, in Dalston where the children were welcomed by a sea of faces, amongst them their father. "I remember the warmth and the smell of Turkish tea. I remember my dad's smell, his hug, his tears and prickly moustache. It was so surreal. I think my brain has blocked out quite a lot of it, but it was a joy to be with my mum and dad."

At first the family lived in one room of a three-bedroom terraced house in Hackney Wick. It was August, so schools were on holiday. "My mum managed to stay with us for a week, but she had to go back to work as a machinist, and they just locked the door and left us. You're in a box, with no way of leaving. Doors were always open in Turkey. We never even locked the door when we went to bed. I've taken down all the doors in our flat in Bethnal Green – even in the bathroom. I take a lot of pictures of doors now."

Within weeks the family was moved to more suitable temporary accommodation in Walthamstow. "It was even bigger than the house we had in Turkey, but it was still claustrophobic because there were lots of streets, houses and doors." Eylem missed the chance to be out from sunrise to sunset but she liked how, in her new uniform for Walthamstow School for Girls, she merged into the landscape. "In our green uniforms, we had to go through the churchyard full of trees. After the rain, when the sun came out, everything would sparkle. It was lush green, and we were green too, almost camouflaged. I loved it. I kept saying in my head *How well the cows would have grazed in this country.*"

Eylem's initial challenge, entering the first year of secondary school, was the English language. "I'm a talkative person – my grandfather used to say I yelp like a puppy but I didn't speak a word of English." The one person she was able to speak to was Pinar, a Turkish Cypriot. That is before she finished eight months at a language school. After two years the language barrier evaporated, prompting Eylem's English teacher to say, "I regret the day you learnt English because you never stop talking." Eylem loved English because she loved her teacher and she loved art, because it didn't need much language.

She liked sports too. "I'm not academic, more of a practical person. In Turkey, I hated education – we were sixty or seventy in the same class, and it was neither interesting nor exciting. British education seemed so liberal, and you got attention from your teacher." Her best friends were Zoe, a British born Jamaican; Sadia, a British-born Pakistani; Pu Ling, a British-born Chinese; and Joanna who was British. "There were people from different ethnicities, different countries. I didn't feel the only foreigner, I felt part of this world now."

Eylem took up as many after school activities as possible – drama, long distance running on Walthamstow track, sailing on Chingford Reservoir. In the second year she went on a camping holiday. "If I used the word 'school' my parents supported me, but I didn't get up to anything bad. I just found school comforting." Home was not so comforting. "My parents had a troublesome marriage. As machinists, making ladies' coats and jackets, they would get up at six. They came home with work to do, like turning out pockets or collars or belts so didn't have time to take us to the cinema or swimming. They didn't know anywhere, and they couldn't speak English."

"Were you involved with the Alevi community in Hackney?"

"When I was fourteen, fifteen, we went to İşçi Birliği where there were lots of Alevis, socialist people. Once we went on a big march against the British National Party. It was great fun, but they gave you chores to do – interpreting, translating and form filling. New Year and wedding parties were among the Turkish Alevi community, but religion was not a subject in our house and, although I call myself an Alevi, I'm more of an atheist."

Eylem went onto Epping Forest College and then to the University of Brighton where she studied three-dimensional design and craft, specializing in plastics and ceramics. "I managed to get away from home using the word 'education'. I loved it. A brilliant course, brilliant people, beside the sea, away from family but I knew I had to come back." Eylem sold a couple of ceramic pieces and was invited to exhibit in a couple of galleries. She found a studio space with Kate Malone in Balls Pond Road and another space in Dalston to do plastic work, but she needed financial help. Her father agreed to support her – at least initially. "I was so excited about it but when my dad didn't help, as he had promised, my mum secretly gave me money. Then he accused her of stealing and me of coming between him and his wife saying, 'She came back and messed everything up'. I was like, *What?* There was a bowl of fruit, I just picked up the knife and stabbed myself. It was like *This is how much it hurts.* Having had four years in Brighton, where I was my own person, I felt dragged into this chaos again. After I self-harmed twice, the doctors realised there was something stressful going on. I had therapy and they said, 'You cannot live in that house'. Put the financial thing aside, there was no support at all. They didn't understand what I was doing, and I felt lonely. My sister was an angel even though she herself was having problems."

Graham, now her partner, had gone to South America for a backpacking trek. "What was I going to use as an excuse? I couldn't say *I'm going with my boyfriend.* After Graham came back, we managed to find a place. I moved out at one o'clock in the afternoon. My dad was still in bed, pretending he was asleep, but my mum was helping me pack, in tears. To have her daughter go away without marriage, to live with another man, was hard. She kept saying, 'I wish it wasn't done this way, I wish you wouldn't go', but I told her it was going to harm me to stay. My mum liked Graham and believed in him, so helped me move. Later Dad told his brothers and sisters he didn't know I was leaving, that I ran away. I wasn't that young, twenty-two, twenty-three. People around my age were all doing the same, but for my community it's a major thing. They encouraged education but they wanted me to then marry. I wanted to exhibit my work, to make beautiful things, to have the freedom to do what I wanted."

Eylem's siblings reacted differently to their parent's troublesome marriage; their expectations and that of the community. "My sister could not cope with the idea that her parents were going to split up. As the eldest she felt she had to take care of us and her mum. She had this nine-year relationship with a Nigerian guy, that she knew wasn't going to be accepted by the community. My parents didn't want her to go with a Black guy nor me with an English guy. They were hoping we would marry someone within the village or a cousin. Academically, my sister was good but because of the language she struggled. She stuck with the community, went to Hackney College and never got to university. My brother, he's like a Cockney guy and very much a lad. Everybody loves him because he's a blabber. He runs his own kebab house, owns this building and married a Kurdish Alevi girl from Turkey. Because he's the boy, he has the support of my uncle and dad." As the middle child Eylem avoided the feeling of responsibility that plagued her older sister but, as a girl, she was denied the financial help her younger brother received. Perhaps supporting a kebab shop seemed more familiar territory than establishing an artist studio.

"It wasn't just immigrating to a country, it was also living with parents, who didn't love each other. People left Turkey thirty, forty, fifty years ago, but they hold onto something that has evolved, become better in Turkey. My mum has many cousins [in Turkey] who have left their husbands or wives. My parents finally divorced. Now I think we've grown to understand it's not that bad a thing. If two people have nothing in common, it's better they are not under the same roof. I don't want my child to go through what I went through. I don't want her to be in a house where there is no love, no warmth, no respect. She was sensing it, 'Why doesn't granddad eat the food nana cooks?' They see it."

As I listened to Eylem's story it was hard to imagine her without a voice when she first arrived. The independence and initiative she had shown as a child, roaming the fields and Armenian caves on her own, had laid the grounds for forging her own path, as an adult – defying restraints set by her parents and the wider community. The conversation turned back to Turkey and the manner of her parents' and her own departure. "I didn't get a chance to say goodbye. I constantly dreamt about not being able to reach my grandfather's farm, just a field away, but it was full of lurking, muddy creatures. Weird dreams. When I went back for the first time, in 1995, the village had become a town; the Armenian houses had disappeared; the caves were closed up. Land was being sold off to property developers, so there were concrete buildings everywhere. That nostalgic, romantic childhood had gone and so the dreams stopped. It felt like closure."

I asked Eylem how she imagined her life would have been if she had stayed in Turkey. Her answer surprised me. "I was interested in sports but there was no way of doing that. I was interested in drawing, but nobody encouraged me. I would have been frustrated and rebelled. Maybe I would have fallen in love too soon, run away with someone or wed early, probably with a cousin. I don't think I would have got as far as university." I wondered if Eylem would have felt less resentment if, like her older sister, she had been forewarned and prepared for her parents' and her own migration. Then, perhaps, she would have felt as if she was swimming with the tide rather than against it. This despite the currents that threatened to endanger her in London, but which she had overcome with such flair and *esneklik* (resilience).

I stayed with Eylem as she waited for Graham to collect her – it was ten o'clock at night. We talked about the décor – where Eylem had sourced the African material to upholster the chairs, her green fingers and her wish, one day, to live on a farm – not in Turkey but in Spain where women can live more freely. I admired, once again, the photographs of doors of every size and colour covering the café walls. As I walked the 400 yards to my home I reflected on the significance of doors in Eylem's life – the open doors of her grandfather's farm but the closed doors when her grandfather, a *dede,* performed a *cem* in secret; the locked door when her parents had to go out to work, a week after her arrival, but the unlocked door to her Alevi Kurdish identity; the barriers to her early artistic career but how she had broken free from expectations of her family and community to forge the relationship she wanted. As I put the key into my own front door, I smiled at the thought of Eylem and Graham returning to their open plan flat with all internal doors removed, decorated no doubt in as much style as the café I loved.

. . . .

Eylem did not move to Spain but has moved with her family to Essex outside London where she is building an art studio in her garden. Her teenage daughter has followed in her parents' creative footsteps. Her film script, about a mixed marriage between an Alevi Kurdish woman and an Icelander, has been selected to be filmed in Iceland and Los Angeles, under her direction.

CHAPTER 11
LOVE OF THE MOTHERLAND

Ahmed Ali, originally from Somaliland, who arrived, aged eleven, via Djibouti in 2004; Said who arrived, aged sixteen, from Somalia in 2012

Ex-seamen, with wizened faces weathered by the high seas, sat round tables playing *shax*, a traditional Somali board game. Jama, the community worker who runs the luncheon club in Granby Hall off Bethnal Green Road, stepped forward to welcome me.

"Stay and eat with us."

Over *maraq*, a delicious stew, I learnt that the ex-seamen had joined the British Merchant Navy or the Royal Navy before, or during, the Second World War. Although many now lived in social or private housing, some still lived in the Queen Victoria Seaman's Rest on East India Dock Road where Somali sailors have lodged since the end of the nineteenth century.[1] Most were originally from Somaliland, previously British Somaliland. In the early 1960s, after a brief period of independence, Somaliland, in the north, united with the Trust Territory of Somaliland (former Italian Somaliland), in the south, to form the Somali Republic. The union was short lived because of the assassination of President Sharmarke and the subsequent military coup by Siad Barre in 1969. Tensions rose between the north and south, eventually leading to a civil war in 1991, leading to the start of one of the largest refugee crises in the history of the region and with Somaliland declaring itself autonomous, a status still unrecognized on the international stage.[2]

Many attending the luncheon club were unsure of the exact age they had become seamen, or when they had arrived in the UK – the date of their birth may not have been registered. Jama offered to find younger people many of whom had arrived in Britain due to the conflict before and after 1991. He arrived at my house with Ahmed, a tall, confident 24-year-old, with a disarming smile and infectious laugh. Ahmed and I sat together whilst Jama sat to the side, dealing with his emails.

Ahmed was born the youngest of seven in Burao, the second largest city in Somaliland. His father worked for the water company; his mother ran a fruit and vegetable market stall. Aged six Ahmed and his family left Burao for their ancestral village seventy-five miles away. As a child Ahmed was unaware of the unrest in his country. "I only found out there was a war when I came here." Ahmed loved the village. "It was beautiful and natural – nothing was man-made." The family lived in an *aqal*, a traditional Somali hut constructed from poles covered in fibre mats, hides and colourful cloth. Ahmed enjoyed the intimacy of his new home. "I remember waking up in the middle of the night, next to my mum and dad, and they'd still be up, having a conversation." During the day life was spent in the open unless the heat forced the family to retreat into the cool of the hut. Ahmed played football with his siblings and, even though it was forbidden, swam in the pond used for drinking water. There were animals too – foxes, wild dogs and the occasional lion. "I was not constantly checked up on, like in Burao where I wasn't allowed to go anywhere. I never asked myself *Why am I not going to school?* I never questioned anything." The war drove many members of his clan to the village. "Everyone there was somehow related to me."[3] Away from the violence villagers were able to gather, dance, recite poetry, share stories and proverbs passed down from generation to generation. Men and women performed courtship rituals through song and call-and-response. "Women are always involved when there's moments of joy," mused Ahmed.

When Ahmed, as the youngest, was teased he would run to his mother. "They [older siblings] didn't like that, so they would beat me up, but it wasn't a proper beating. I was very much a mummy's boy." Ahmed would help his mother with chores – tidying the house or fetching things from the local shop. He helped her, too, with the domestic animals – cows, sheep and goats, fencing them inside the paddock at night. Sometimes his father would hoik Ahmed onto his shoulders and walk off with their one-humped camels for miles across the savannah in search of food and water. "It was really good fun." In the village Ahmed was cushioned from the conflict and poverty affecting his country.

Determined to find a better life for her and her children, Ahmed's mother took one of her daughters across the border into Djibouti to study. "She knew that, to improve their situation, one of us needed access to education. It's interesting she chose the girl. She was the right choice because she did well." Once her daughter was settled Ahmed's mother arranged to take the rest of the family to Djibouti – except for Ahmed's father who refused to leave. In Arta, a town twenty-five miles to the west of Djibouti city, Ahmed's mother rented a two-bedroom house next to the railway tracks. Ahmed attended the madrassa attached to the mosque behind their house. He liked his teacher, a Pakistani, but he had to be taught one-to-one rather than in a class, "I was just messing about." Once Ahmed settled, he enjoyed his studies – he learnt about Islam, the *Hadith* – the sayings and teachings of Prophet Mohammed – and some Arabic but to this day he cannot read or write in his mother tongue.[4]

After studying English at university in Djibouti, his sister came to London. "My mum sent her so she could get the rest of her family here.[5] At the time Britain was accepting people from war-torn areas." Ahmed's father was reluctant to leave. "I think he was fearful of the unknown. Maybe it's a gender thing. He could handle what was happening in Somalia with the war, but mum, as a woman, didn't think she or her children could. My dad's brother was also offered to go somewhere else, but said no. Maybe it's wanting to stay on their land." Ahmed was ambivalent about coming to England. "I can remember other people being really excited about going to Europe but, as a child, I didn't know what the fuss was about. I just thought, *The family's moving like they've always moved.* I had no image of what it was going to be like." On a cold snowy morning in 2001 a family member picked up Ahmed, aged eleven, his mother and older brother, from Heathrow airport, and drove them to where Ahmed's sister was living in Fulham, west London. Ahmed's first taste of school was not encouraging. "I didn't enjoy it at all as I didn't speak English. There were no Somalis – just a lot of different ethnicities I'd never come across. It seemed nobody cared about me at school or at home, except for my mum."[6]

Within six months tragedy struck. Ahmed's mother, the backbone of the family and driving force behind the family's migration, was rushed to Chelsea Hospital suffering from liver disease. "They tried treating her, but she passed away in hospital." Jama, who had been scrolling through his emails, sat up. He did not know this part of Ahmed's story. "The operation damaged her to the point she couldn't get out of bed. That's what broke her. They weren't held to account and got away with it. Obviously, it's a question as to whether they thought it would make her better or whether they did it on purpose." Ahmed's grief no doubt fuelled such beliefs, but he is not alone among Somalis in distrusting the health system.[7] Ahmed was unable to turn to his father. "I wasn't close to him and communication wasn't there."

Ahmed's sister could never fill the vacuum left by his mother. She left early for work, came back home late and there was no Somali community in west London to step in. Aged sixteen, Ahmed, his sister and brother moved to the Ocean Estate in Tower Hamlets. This was an opportunity for a new start, but Ahmed made few friends at St Paul's in Stepney Green where most pupils were of Bengali origin. Long-running tensions between Bengali and Somali youth, the latter in a minority both at the school and in the area, often erupted.[8] When Ahmed got caught up in the conflicts, Tower Hamlets Social Services got involved and he was placed into foster care. "They weren't problems that couldn't have been fixed. It was more to do with school … That put a distance between me and my sister – I didn't see her at all. I saw my brother but that didn't have an impact on what was going on."

When Ahmed's foster placement with a Pakistani family didn't work out, Ahmed's uncle in Sheffield offered to care for him. He stayed there for two years and took his GCSEs but on his return to London, he became homeless. As he had previously been in care, social services accommodated him in a shared house with other young people but with no staff in residence. "It was horrific. You're exposed to people who are violent and use drugs. The walls vibrated with people making music so I couldn't even get a good night's sleep. If you complain they say, 'That's the harsh reality. Get on with it.' Maybe I was partially to blame but there was no one from my background to help."

Ahmed's experience of independent accommodation was not unique. Citing a report in 2019, Enver Solomon, then chief executive of Just for Kids Law, said he believed the state was not fulfilling its role as a corporate parent by dumping thousands of teenage children in unregulated homes, abandoned to organized crime gangs.[9] Ahmed was well able to identify the support he needed. "Although I'd learned the basics in English, I couldn't read up on my rights. Social services should have tried to allocate someone who was Somali to represent me. Then they would have had more understanding of my background, my cultural values." Jama and I nodded in agreement. There were few

Somali people employed by Tower Hamlets at the time. This contrasted with the Bengali community who Tower Hamlets Council had made efforts to employ in public facing services. Had they not seen the need to adopt this strategy with the Somali, albeit smaller community?[10]

On leaving local authority care, Ahmed rented a place in Stepney Green. "I've been there for eight years, on my own. I'm very happy. It's a Victorian house with a garden." He found a job doing night shifts in a warehouse in Barking, but the work was so gruelling that, after six months, he left. Ahmed returned to study at Tower Hamlets College, improving his English and maths and progressing onto an access course leading to university. Key to his progress was his tutor. "I still remember John. He was like a parent, pushing you, constantly advising you. At the time I thought being dyslexic was a bad thing, but you learn Einstein was dyslexic." He was unable to take up his place at the School of Oriental and Asian Studies because of his immigration status. When this was regularized and he received his British passport, he enrolled for a course at London Metropolitan University. This was an impressive achievement, given only 13 per cent of care leavers go onto higher education compared to 43 per cent of all young people by the age of nineteen[11] and given Ahmed's first experience of formal education was within a year of arrival in London aged eleven, whilst still grieving for his mother.

To support his studies Ahmed worked part time in retail for Arsenal Football Club. "I wanted to be a footballer but there were no scouts watching me," he laughed. Ahmed was a keen boxing fan, but his interests were cultural too. He enjoyed Somali comedy, poetry and plays. Ahmed was no longer isolated. "I spend a lot of time socialising at the Somali café opposite the Somali-run Al-Huda mosque – it's like our second home." The café is one of a cluster of Somali businesses that line Mile End Road to the west of Stepney Green tube station. Ahmed values the friendship of the UK Somali community and is keen to repay their support. "If there is something that I can do for a Somali person, I'm up for it." He talked with pride of his charity work in collecting money for a school in his village in Somaliland, something that did not exist when he was a child.

The previous summer, Ahmed had visited his ancestral village, returning to see the fruits of his charity work. "I went with a group of forty people from my clan who live most of the time in Europe, America or elsewhere. We slept under the stars. There's no light, so the heavens are open to you. Just remembering it gets me going. It was during Ramadan so we had our *iftar* in the village and we could hear the *adhan* call to prayer, which was beautiful. The villagers are still the same, in essence, but they've changed in that they want more of a modern life now. Poverty is big so if you could tackle the roots of it, through education, that could make a huge difference." During two decades of conflict, famines and floods, the money – known as 'remittances' – sent by over 1 million Somalis living abroad has been instrumental in keeping Somalia afloat. They not only support more than 40 per cent of Somali families, providing crucial resources for their survival, but help build schools and hospitals.[12]

Ahmed returned too late to see his father – he had died a couple of years before his visit. "I wish I'd gone say when I was fifteen. With my mum passing away I think that would have helped. I would have known there was a foundation."[13] His insecure immigration status had prevented him from returning earlier. Ahmed did not grieve at his father's death as he had at his mother's. "I wasn't close to him, so I didn't experience that intense grief." This lack of attachment did not colour the relationship with the three wives that his father married in Burao after his mother died. "I call them 'mothers' out of respect and because they were my 'mothers' – they were that good. They were hospitable, bringing things to my hotel without me even asking. Anything they wanted for their actual son they wanted for me." Ahmed had found a maternal love from an unexpected quarter that had been missing from his life since he was eleven. This did not stop him questioning his father's actions. "He was sick and didn't have a job, so I don't know how he provided for three ladies. They don't live in the same house. If they did, they might be at each other's throats. If their relationship is not good how are their children, as brothers and sisters with the same father, going to get along?" Ahmed is critical of the way some people interpret the practice of polygamy within Islam. "When a man marries more than one wife it creates barriers. Maybe that's why, in Islam, there are strict rules in place before you marry another woman, but people don't follow them."

Ahmed is serious about his responsibility to his new family in Burao. "There's a duty upon me to send money because they're my siblings. Who else is going to be there for them? They seem poor but they have all the necessities – shelter, health and they go to school, so they have some form of education." He is clear where his future lies. "I will definitely go back. It's where I belong. You won't find everything you find in London but it's peaceful although this is home as well, but it seems like travelling here and getting all these opportunities was an aid in the process." I was curious as to where Ahmed would settle in Somaliland. "I would live in the village because of the nature and the open sky." Would this 24-year-old, who had spent years in London, a keen boxing and football fan, be able to settle in the village? Would he want to herd the camels that belonged to him and his siblings, carrying his child on his shoulders, just as his father had carried him? "What are you going to do with thirty-six camels?" I asked. "Buy more," he laughed. But Ahmed had more ambitious plans. "Because of my mum dying and the negligence she was exposed to, I'm going into homeopathy. I want to use plants that have been used in Somalia over centuries. That is the medicine they practice in hospitals in the countryside." He paused, "But you never know with life." Ahmed had learnt that plans can be overturned and tragedy strike when you least expect it.

His sister, a teacher, married to a Somali man with six children, saw a different future. "She sees her life here and would never go back." The conflict with his sister had been resolved long ago and now he met up regularly with her and his brother with whom he came to London. His other siblings had migrated to Norway. Like Eylem Ahmed did not want to migrate to Britain and felt aggrieved he was not consulted but unlike Eylem, he wanted to return to the country of his birth.

……………..

Ahmed had not answered my emails or phone messages, so, on a Sunday morning in February 2023, I popped down to see him. I wanted to make sure he was happy with what I had written and, if so, to sign the necessary consent form. He greeted me with a warm smile even though he had been on a night shift at a hostel for the homeless and was about to return there. This was in addition to a day job during the week, working as IT support for the NHS. He had not completed his degree realizing academic study was not for him.

As we sat outside a café in Whitechapel, he explained why he had several jobs. He, along with his two siblings, was still supporting his deceased father's three wives and children in Somaliland but he also had new responsibilities. He had married since we last met eight years previously to a woman of Somali origin with whom he had two children, aged three and five. A return visit to Somaliland, with its poverty and lack of infrastructure, had dashed any dreams of returning to live in the land of his birth.

As we said goodbye, he explained why he had not responded to my emails and phone calls. "It's not just you. Since COVID-19 I've had difficulty communicating with people. It's much better to chat, like this, in person."

Said who arrived, aged sixteen, from Somalia in 2012

Jama arrived at the V&A Museum of Childhood in Bethnal Green with Said, both wearing pristine white prayer caps and jalabiyas. They were dressed for Friday evening prayers at Al-Huda mosque. We settled in a back storeroom surrounded by display cases full of dolls house furniture, mechanical cars and puppets – toys that Said, born in 1996 during the civil war in Mogadishu, the capital of Somalia, had never had access to.

"You can choose what you tell me," I said, trying to reassure Said who seemed nervous. Said looked to Jama to interpret.

"You can also choose the name you use."

"Just Said."

Although he understood many of my questions, Said often relied on Jama to interpret his answers. He had been in the country for one year and eight months.

In contrast to Ahmed, whose family was shielded from much of the violence by retreating to their ancestral village, Said had known nothing else. The bombshells and noise of artillery in Mogadishu, a virtual no-go zone for decades, were relentless. "It was frightening, particularly at night." Whole swathes of the city were destroyed, with buildings shattered and riddled with bullet holes. There were moments when he played as any normal child. "If the bombing ceased for a short time, I could play football." If for longer, volunteers set up makeshift classes to teach Somali or the Quran. But there was little permanent infrastructure and no access to schooling or health services. "Everything was chaotic." When the shelling got worse, Said and his family fled to the bush on the outskirts of the city, sleeping in Somali huts until the conflict lessened.

Said was born in 1996, the year that the United Nations' four-year intervention to restore order in Somalia failed. In 2000 the rebels reached a peace agreement, and a transnational national government was formed, but it was weakened by regional instability such as the break-away of Somaliland and the threat from armed groups. In 2006, when Said was ten, Mogadishu was overtaken by the al-Qaeda-backed Islamic Courts Union who took over much of the country, leading to the intervention of the Ethiopian military and forces of the African Union. After three years of conflict a compromise was reached between the government and the Islamists, but civil war continued between the moderate Islamists in power and radical Islamist groups such as Hizb al-Islam and al-Shabab. In 2012, the year that Said arrived in Britain, a new internationally backed government was installed, but Somalia still faced a challenge from Islamist groups.[14]

In some ways, Said's family suffered less than their neighbours. "We were better off than other families because dad was over here to support us. At least, most of the time, there was bread on the table." In other ways, they suffered more. There was no extended family around, and with no husband present, all the responsibility lay on the shoulders of Said's mother. The experience of war created strong bonds within the family and with near neighbours, at least those they could trust. "You cannot go anywhere freely so you have to be close knit." What happened next threatened these bonds.

Said's father, who had lived in the UK for ten years and was a British citizen, applied for visas to bring over his family as refugees under the provision for family reunion. The Home Office refused his application. On appeal he was granted permission to bring over three of his children. His wife had to stay in Somalia and care for the remaining three children. Jama was horrified.

"They split the kids in two!"

"Extraordinary," I replied.

"Yes, extraordinary," Jama echoed.

I could not understand the rationale of dividing the family, all equally in danger in war-torn Mogadishu. After all, Said's father was employed and able to support them. I tried, too, to imagine the seeming impossibility of deciding which of the three children should come to Britain. It was a cruel decision, one that tore apart the emotional bonds developed through the civil war.

The court in Britain sent instructions to the British Embassy in Ethiopia to issue visas to Said, an older brother and older sister. A month later Said got on the plane with his two siblings, leaving behind his mother and three siblings. Said had mixed feelings. "I was excited to join my father I hadn't seen for ten years. But I was worried. I was leaving the other children and my mum – we'd been through everything together." Said looked me in the eye for the first time. "It was very difficult, very emotional."

Said had seen footage on television in Addis Ababa so was prepared for the beautiful sights of London but not the cold. He settled in the flat in Stepney Green with his father and older siblings and enrolled at Hackney Community College to study English, maths and information technology for fifteen hours a week, his first real experience of education.

"Who are your teachers?"

Said's smile grew as he realized I knew some of the people who taught him. I felt relieved knowing the college, where I used to work, was continuing to offer opportunities for people like Said just as Tower Hamlets College had supported Ahmed. Such second chances are essential for refugees whose schooling has been interrupted. Said had an advantage over Ahmed when he first arrived – he had a network of Somali friends and extended family in east London who helped him, including with his homework.

Said developed a love of running when he came to London, inspired, perhaps, by his fellow countryman, Mo Farah, who also came to Britain as a child from Somalia. He enjoyed watching athletics on television and was able to access Somali channels for other programmes. But he missed his mother, siblings and friends he had grown up with in Somalia. And the weather.

"Have you encountered any racism?"

Said shook his head.

"He's a very straight guy," confirmed Jama. "He keeps away from troublemakers and avoids confrontation."

But initially Said had problems communicating with English speakers who he found less tolerant than people in Mogadishu to non-Somali speakers. "Somali is an oral society and if a Somali person meets someone who doesn't speak Somali, they try to help." Said had clear ambitions. "My goal is to get a qualification, start working as an electrical engineer in this country and apply to become a British citizen. If God willing, my mum is still around, I want to apply for her to join me." Settling in this country was not the only future Said saw for himself. "If war stops and reconstruction starts, I will probably go back and rebuild the country."

Towards the end of the interview, I asked Said if it was difficult to talk about what he had experienced during the civil war. Jama interpreted for him.

"Yes, he says it's difficult to remember that time, he doesn't want to."

Had I been too intrusive, even though I had stressed he did not need to answer any questions I posed? Was it too soon for him to talk about the suffering he and his family had experienced? I walked with them to the front of the museum.

"Thank you Said, it's been lovely to interview you. And to you, Jama, thank you. Hopefully you'll be in time for prayers."

I was glad Jama was with Said, that they were going off to Al-Huda mosque together, that they would meet Ahmed, perhaps, and the ex-seamen with their wizened, weather-beaten faces.

. . . .

Said responded well to the chapter that I sent to him. 'It's beautiful how you have written it and I liked it very much.' It was good to hear his news too. 'Currently, my life situation is very good and I am doing a painting and decorating apprenticeship. My mum still lives in Mogadishu and I am always in contact with her. She is very good now.'

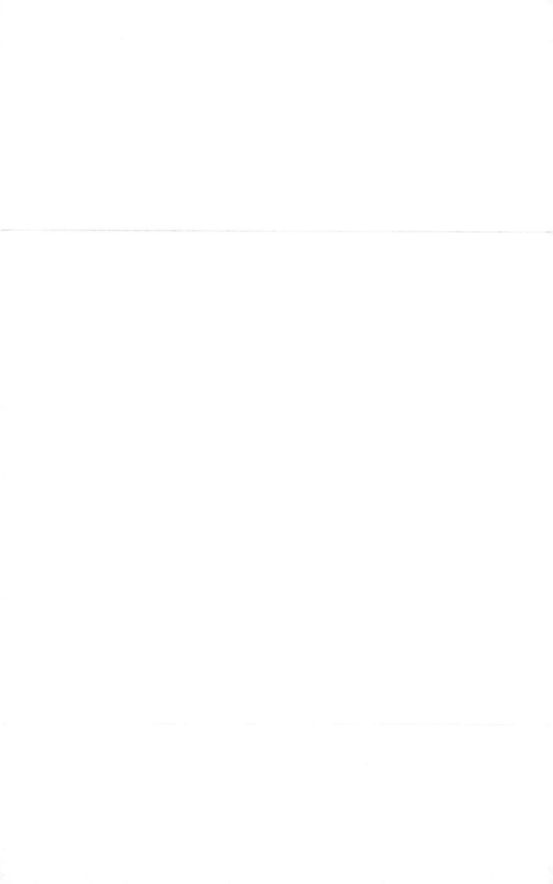

CHAPTER 12
GIRL POWER – FINDING A TALENT AND FOLLOWING A DREAM

Bilqis who arrived from Yemen as a teenager in 2005 and Nimo Jama who arrived, aged fifteen, from Somaliland, in 2009

As I walked through the lobby of the arts block of Queen Mary University of London, I noticed a young woman in an elegant black burqa, setting up an information stall for a summer university.

"Could I place my research leaflets on your stall?"

She read the leaflet closely.

"I came here as a teenager from Yemen. Can I help?"

Two weeks later we met at the V&A Museum of Childhood.

This assured 23-year-old chose 'Bilqis' as her pseudonym. Bilqis was the name of the Queen of Sheba who, according to some historians, ruled Yemen from 950 BC. There are different Muslim, Christian, Ethiopian and Yemeni versions of the Queen of Sheba's life. I had learnt, from the Bible, about her visit to the Israelite King of Solomon to 'test him with hard riddles' and bring offerings of 'spices, a great quantity of gold, and precious stones'.[1] I remembered, too, my mother using it as a taunt, "Who do you think you are? The Queen of Sheba?" Arabic and Islamic folklore paint a more interesting picture of this powerful woman who, through skill and wisdom, united her country following years of conflict between Ethiopian and Yemeni tribes. Today, both Ethiopia and Yemen claim her as their own.[2] As the life story of this young woman unfolded, I realized the appropriateness of her choice of pseudonym.

Bilqis was born in 1990 to Yemeni parents who had crossed the border into Somalia to escape war. Within a year war broke out in Somalia so the family moved back to Hadhramaut on the Gulf of Aden in the southeast of Yemen. Hadhramaut has a dramatic topography. To the south precipitous mountains rise from the coast of the Arabian sea. *Wadis*, dry waterbeds that swell during the rainy season, course through the inland valley. The northern edge of Hadhramaut slopes down to the Empty Quarter, the southern edge of the Arabian desert with its endless, undulating sand dunes.[3] The Republic of Yemen was founded in May 1990, when the Yemen Arab Republic (North Yemen) merged with the People's Democratic Republic of Yemen (South Yemen). North and South Yemen had very different histories. North Yemen became an independent republic in 1918 following the collapse of the Ottoman Empire whereas South Yemen fell under British influence when Britain captured the port of Aden in 1939. It remained part of the British Empire until 1967 when Britain withdrew.[4] For centuries Hadhramis, the people of Hadhramaut, have migrated abroad.[5]

Bilqis was the fifth of eight children. Her father used to be a skilled tailor but, on return to Hadhramaut, set up a small grocery shop. The income from the shop, supplemented by the sale of samosas, spring rolls and falafels, made by Bilqis's mother, just about kept the family afloat. They lived in a one-storey house surrounded by sweeping sand dunes. "After sunset we'd take our mattresses onto the roof, have dinner and then sleep under the stars. It was fun. When the sun rose, we went downstairs – no one can take that heat." Bilqis had other good memories of Yemen. "I remember getting dressed up. Then I'd go out with girls from my town. You had to be home by sunset unless you're with your brother, other family or an older woman. If you go out alone people think *What is she doing?* My auntie chose to live in Ta'izz in the North because she knew she would have more freedom and her children would have a good education and work."[6]

Hadhramaut was so hot that, sometimes, the family would escape to a beach, forty-five minutes away. "We used to rent a car, but it wouldn't fit us all in, so we squashed into the boot. We'd arrive by noon, swim, play in the sand, and throw rocks and stones. They were so beautiful – different textures, colours and sizes – that I used to collect them." Freya Stark, one of the first Western women to visit Hadhramaut, described the rock formations along this coast as, 'Smouldering and dusty, as if the black volcanic points were coated with desert sand and the red sandstones subdued by ashes of volcanoes, like embers of coal dying in a crust of cinders.'[7]

Bilqis took her studies seriously. "I was a good, intelligent kid." But coming from a poor family affected her education. "I love art, but then I hated it because they'd ask you to buy materials and, because we couldn't afford them, I got told off." It was a struggle to survive. "Having eight kids to feed, used to be stressful so, although my dad, who has blood pressure and diabetes, is chilled, sometimes he got angry." The situation worsened when Bilqis's mother got injured in a car crash. "My dad had to look after us so we were kicked out of our house because we couldn't afford the rent. One of my relatives spoke to my dad and said, 'Why don't you go somewhere else?' He wanted us to have the best education ever because he never had the chance. He was taken out of school to support his family." Neither did her mother benefit from much education. "In Somalia the schools were mixed so my mum, whose father was strict, just went to a madrassa where they taught her to read the Quran and write Arabic – that's all she had – and when she hit puberty, she had to leave." Bilqis's father announced his plans when the family were driving back from a relative's. "Dad was like, 'Do you guys want to go to London?' I thought he was joking. So we went to Sana'a, stayed with a cousin and went for interviews twice."

Bilqis, now a teenager, left Yemen with her mother and siblings – her father had left nine months before. "I've never cried so much in my life, driving past the house we were kicked out of, leaving everything behind." Bilqis soon got caught up in the excitement of the journey. "We flew from Sana'a to Qatar and stayed there overnight. The hotel was so lovely that I jumped up and down on the bed. Even the flight was comfy." Next morning the family flew onto London. "I thought I'm watching a movie.

I never thought London would be this diverse, so many people of every colour and nation." Bilqis's father met his family at the airport and took them by taxi to a relative's house where they stayed one night. The housing department, where Bilqis's father had already registered, referred them to London Metropolitan Hostel, a former hospital in Hackney. "We were given two rooms and a kitchen, that everyone used, a toilet and shower. It was weird. I remember crying because it was the first Eid I had spent away. We didn't know where to go, what to do or how to celebrate. We stayed there for about two weeks and then, for one week, they moved us into another hostel in Swiss Cottage."

Bilqis was refused entry to Clapton Girls' School in Hackney as she was told there were no places. Instead, she was accepted onto a nearby college course for English Speakers of Other Languages. "I had a lovely teacher. She realised my sister and I had just arrived and made us feel comfortable. It was different from school in Yemen as we had to mix with boys." In Hadhramaut boys and girls shared school premises, with the boys attending in the morning and the girls in the afternoon. This did not stop them interacting. "The boys left secret letters for the girls. In return, the girls left letters for the boys." In London there was no need for secret messages.

Even though the family moved out of the borough, first to a hostel in Swiss Cottage and then, on a permanent basis, to a house in east London, Bilqis continued her college studies in Hackney. After studying English for two years, she progressed onto a BTEC diploma in media. "I didn't want to do a course that involved a lot of writing." When the government stopped funding the course, she moved to a sixth form where her sister studied science. "I did two years of a media diploma – sound recording, live production, studio setup, vision mixing and animation."

After two years Bilqis got accepted onto one of the most prestigious media courses in the UK. "It was the dream of my life. I loved the atmosphere and the artwork. The first two years was a foundation degree in media production, and then I did an extra year for a BA." Within a decade Bilqis had progressed from being a student in Yemen, ridiculed for not being able to afford art materials, to graduating with a degree in media in Britain. A summer university was another influence in her life. "I took part in their workshops and short courses – collage, digital photography, animation and website design. It was girls only and about the power of women."

Bilqis returned to Yemen eight years after she had left, for her cousin's wedding. "When I first arrived, I felt at home, that safe feeling of being where I belonged. We stayed at my uncle's house with other families. It was fun, but there were lots of kids and sometimes I couldn't take it. I hated the fact we had to stay home all day, as it was so hot, and the electricity cut out every two hours." Bilqis was happy to return to east London. "I felt I'm home again. I still share my bedroom with two sisters, but I have a place where I keep my artwork – my sketchbooks from those summer courses. I have shelves of books that I've read, or I want to read." There was something else Bilqis kept on the shelves – beautiful rocks and stones from the sea shore in Yemen.

I asked Bilqis whether she mixed with other Yemenis at the equivalent of Al-Huda mosque, for example, for the Somali community. "We don't have a mosque close to us with space for women and, to be honest, we only go on Eid days. I think most of the Yemeni community live in Sheffield, not London." Yemenis first arrived in Britain as seamen during the nineteenth century, often through the Port of Aden, with many settling in Cardiff, Swansea, South Shields and Liverpool. Some moved to Sheffield in the 1960s to work in industry. The community in London is smaller but connections with other Yeminis are still important. "My sister met a friend recently and we met her family, then we met another Yemeni family so every month we gather in someone's house and cook together."

It was clear, even though Bilqis was sad to leave Yemen, that she had no wish to return. "If I were still there, I wouldn't have had a future. I wouldn't respect myself so much, had the education I had and the confidence I have now from all the people I've met. I would have been an absolutely, different person, probably married at home with kids running around, going crazy." Bilqis, who cried on leaving her home in Hadhramaut, but Bilqis, too, the powerful African queen who had learnt about female empowerment, forging her own future. Within months of the interview Bilqis was employed by *Al Jazeera* television news channel.

Yemen, one of the Arab world's poorest countries, has been devastated by civil war since Bilqis left in 2005. An Arab Spring uprising in 2011 forced its authoritarian president, Ali Abdullah Saleh, to hand over power to his deputy. But Abdrabbuh Mansour Hadi has struggled to deal with attacks by jihadists, a separatist movement in the south, the continuing loyalty of security personnel to Saleh, as well as corruption, poverty and famine.[8] By migrating to Britain, Bilqis's family had escaped civil war in Yemen, having already crossed between Somalia and Yemen to avoid conflict.

I asked Bilqis, as is my usual practice before saying goodbye, what it was like to be interviewed. Her response surprised me. "I don't think I've shared so much information with anyone before. If I'd known you, I think it would have been much harder. It's better if it's a stranger." I had assumed knowing the person would enhance the interview. Bilqis agreed to a second interview but then I received an email. "I wanted you to know I don't have much to add to the story. Good luck with your research! If I could help in any other way, please let me know." Bilqis was happy for her testimony to be included in the research but not to revisit her own story. Perhaps, its telling had provoked feelings she had not expected.

Nimo who arrived, aged fifteen, from Somaliland, in 2009

"Don't you want tourists in Somalia?"

"No, I hate them."

"Why?"

"They want to attack people, Al-Shabaab, ISIS!"

"Oh, you mean terrorists!"

"Yes, terrorists."

"I'm so sorry. I thought you said tourists."

"Oh my God! No. We like tourists."

Nimo, sitting in my front room in Hackney, was at pains to reassure me that Somaliland, as opposed to Somalia to the south, from where it had separated in 1991, was safe. "You can go out at one 'o clock at night, dressed how you are, without a scarf. No one is going to say, 'You're not Muslim, you're white'. You should go there." Now we had cleared up my mishearing of 'terrorists', it seemed an attractive suggestion. Many Somalis in the UK originate from Somaliland, a British protectorate from 1884 to 1960 when it united with Italian Somaliland to create the United Republic of Somalia, and from which it separated in 1991.[9]

Nimo had arrived full of apologies. She had missed our previous appointment at her flat in Bethnal Green where I had met her mother, a care worker and cook for Somali luncheon clubs. It was also Ramadan, so she had not gone to sleep until 5:00 am and had got up at 7:00 am. She was fasting and, in the evening, attending Al Huda mosque in east London or Finsbury Park mosque in north London.

Nimo, like Ahmed, was born in Burao in Somaliland but unlike Ahmed had stayed in Burao rather than going to the countryside. By the time Nimo was born in 1995, four years after Ahmed, Somaliland had become more peaceful. Although belonging to the same clan as Ahmed's family, Nimo's family was in a better financial position. Her father had spent years in Dubai, attending university and working for the police before returning to Somaliland and setting up his own business. When this closed, he worked for Dahabshiil, Africa's largest money transfer company. As he and Nimo's mother often travelled for business Nimo, her younger brother and sister lived with their aunt, uncle, cousins, nieces and grandmother in a one-storey spacious house with seven bedrooms, two sitting rooms and a large garden. "There were ten people in that house – everyone lived together."

Between three and seven Nimo attended Islamic school twice a day to learn the Quran. She progressed onto primary and then to secondary school where there could be up to eighty in a class and the teachers, understandably, "talked loud and screamed." Children were obliged to take notes from the blackboard and some subjects you had to memorise. "Now I need my laptop and Smartphone – I can't memorise anything." Nimo did well at school, particularly in science and Arabic. "I liked the teachers. Even now when I contact the students, they tell me to come back."

Nimo relished the freedom she had in Burao. "In Somaliland you can go out and play, come back when you're tired, wash, sleep, eat and go to school. It's not like here, where you have the police." Nimo defied gender expectations. "I always liked playing with the boys. I made cars, played football with them, basketball, everything." Nimo's preference for playmates was acceptable when she was five or six but as she approached her teens it became problematic. "People said, 'what's wrong with that girl? Why is she playing with the boys?'"

When Nimo was seven her mother made the decision to leave the country – after her divorce she wanted to go somewhere different. Her five-year-old brother was upset by this development. "Why is he crying?" Nimo asked her father. By contrast Nimo took it in her stride. "It was fine. I didn't feel that lonely. My aunty is very lovely. I love her even more than my grandmother, more than anyone else."

Aged eleven, Nimo, along with one of her girl cousins, went to stay for two years with her father in Hargeisa, the capital of Somaliland. "The school was similar to the school in Burao and I enjoyed living with my dad." But after seven years in Britain Nimo's mother returned to finalize the process of bringing her children to London – her aunt and grandmother had already taken the children to Addis Ababa to progress the application. Nimo, aged fifteen, opposed her mother's plans.

"I want to stay with my friends."

Her mother tried everything to persuade Nimo.

"You're going to have a playground, a park to play in. You'll see a different lifestyle, you're going to finish your education and be a doctor. Everything is easy in the UK." Nimo still resisted.

"Have you watched TV? Have you seen what Europe looks like?"

"No," Nimo replied, still adamant.

Right until the day of departure, Nimo opposed her mother's plans. The idea of parks and playgrounds, an easy life and becoming a doctor did not replace Nimo's fear of losing her teenage friends and the love of her extended family in Burao, especially of her aunt, and of her father in Hargeisa. "I was excited to see my mum but, after seven years' absence, I wasn't used to her and when you're a child all you think about is how you're going to play with your friends." Again, it was Nimo's younger brother who expressed his emotions. "'Daddy, I'm not going to see you for a long time and you haven't even got a passport to visit us … blah, blah, blah.' I just gave dad a hug and said, 'Bye, daddy, call you when I get there.' My sister was three years old when my mother left so it was even harder for her, because she didn't have the same attachment. She talked to her on the phone, but always said, 'I want to see mummy because I don't know what she looks like.'"

The three children, accompanied by their mother, were collected from London's Heathrow by an uncle. They stayed with family members before being moved into temporary accommodation – a house in Poplar, until they were finally given a secure tenancy of a two-bedroom flat in Bethnal Green. "We wanted to stay locally because everyone lives in Tower Hamlets, but my brother has to sleep in the sitting room, and I share with my sister." The promises that Nimo's mother had made to encourage her daughter to leave Somaliland reaped consequences. "I was expecting to see massive, nice houses, but I was like, 'It's even worse than where we live [in Burao]'. I was expecting to have more money, drive at any age, free uni, free stuff, free money, but you need to work hard to reach where you want to be. I had completely different expectations."

Nimo joined year 11 of George Green School in Docklands for a year, went to Tower Hamlets College to study English for Speakers of Other Languages (ESOL), went back to the Sixth Form at George Green to do a BTEC in Business and then to Newham College to do an Access to Higher Education course which she had just completed when I met her. "I got my results yesterday – a distinction and merit." She could now take up her place at university to study business and accounting. Nimo explained why she had moved between schools and colleges. "People asked me, 'Why don't you study in one place?' I told them I don't like to mix just with Somalis and Tower Hamlets College is mainly Bengali. At Newham College there are Black and white, Chinese, Lithuanian, Eastern European, Italian. I prefer the mix." George Green School was where she felt happiest. "I was the student ambassador even though my language was poor. They're always inviting me back to encourage other children." But education was not the easy passport to university that her mother had led her to expect. "English was very hard for me, I was always crying, I had headaches, because the students were abusing me, 'My God, she's year 11, she doesn't speak English'. Bengali girls, boys too, upset me every day. I told them 'Guys, even your mum, your sister when they came to this country, they didn't speak English'. Then I met a boy who went to them and said, 'Are you trying to bully my cousin?' They were scared of Somali people, especially the boys."

Nimo's preference to play with boys, rather than girls, raised eyebrows in east London as it had in Burao. "My school said, 'How did you learn to play football like this?'" At first, because of her lack of English, Nimo did not understand that girls were only allowed to play with boys after school and not during PE. But the boys recognized her talent. "'Come play with us!' they said." Nimo is a keen supporter of women's football and was a supporter of Manchester United but when it came to the African Nations Cup it was Somaliland that she supported, travelling every day to West Ham Memorial Park to support them. "They beat three big countries, Kenya, Rwanda, and Nigeria. It was their first time. I was so wild and proud of them. We got to the quarter final and then we made one mistake and Burundi won."

Nimo flicked up different photos of herself on her mobile phone – in football gear and wearing a white turban, draped in a dress made from the Somali flag. It was taken at an event in Troxy Hall, Tower Hamlets, attended by Mo Farah amongst other Somalis, with performances from well-known Somali singers and comedians. "Eighteenth May is a special day because that's when in 1991 we [Somaliland] made our flag. It's been peaceful since then." Nimo searched her phone of herself dressed in a hijab. "To be honest I prefer to wear a hijab when it's hot because I don't wear anything underneath." Unlike other women in her family, she did not feel obliged to wear the hijab. "I'm different." Perhaps, the situation would change in the future. "It's nice to wear a hijab when you get old. It's part of our religion."

Nimo missed her family in Somaliland but, unlike children who had migrated in previous decades, was in constant contact with them. "I call my grandmother but she's always busy – she's got too many grand-kids – and I call my dad all the time. He and my mum got divorced in 2003 but they're best friends now. They always contact each other, just to find out how we're doing, so I don't feel split between them." It struck me how different was Nimo's experience of staying in contact with those she left behind, to previous generations of child migrants, who waited weeks on the doorstep for a letter to arrive. It struck me, too, how different was her experience of divorced parents to Argun's who suffered not only from his parents' split but from strained relationships with his stepparents.

One of Nimo's uncles encouraged her to get involved in politics – he had stood as a Labour councillor in Tower Hamlets. "I was fifteen when I started campaigning, just handing out leaflets because my English wasn't that fluent. I'd love to be a politician." Because of her family connections, Nimo thought it would be easier to become a politician in Somaliland but did not discount the possibility of pursuing this ambition in Britain. "After university I want to be a local councillor, then mayor, and then, go to the ... House of Lords, what do you call it?"

"House of Commons?"

"I would love that. I don't want to be a prime minister, that would be too much."

She would also like to work for the United Nations with her father. "Helping them with finance and my dad, he can do management." Or she might set up a Morrisons or Asda in Somaliland. I was impressed, if a little overwhelmed, by the extent of Nimo's youthful ambition, wary that her hopes would be dashed along the way. But nothing was going to stop Nimo and certainly not marriage. "My friends who are married, say, 'You're twenty, so you should have two or three kids.' 'No, that's too much!' I reply. I'm too young."

Nimo felt arranged marriages were a thing of the past. Nowadays, Somalis marry people from different backgrounds – Jamaican, Eritrean, Ethiopian, Italian, English, Moroccan, Turkish. She explained that whereas a man can marry a non-Muslim, on the basis he can persuade his wife to convert, if a woman marries a Christian and converts, she cannot revert to being a Muslim. Nimo would not be constrained by this. "If I loved an Englishman, I'd get married to him, or a Jamaican, anyone." She was in no hurry. "I just want to enjoy life!" Having a boyfriend was a complicated, clandestine matter. "If you're going out with him, don't tell your mum, your dad, or your brother. If you feel free to tell your mum that's fine but otherwise keep it separate." She was clear about the need to get to know a potential partner first. "How are you going to love someone you don't know? You need to meet the boy, talk to him on the phone but he cannot touch you. When you are 100 per cent sure you want to get married, he's going to come to your family and ask their permission. Nowadays we do the engagement and marriage on the same day."

Nimo hoped to return to Somaliland for a holiday the following summer – her studying had prevented her from returning earlier. "I think you should come. Somaliland is lovely," she insisted, repeating her assurance I would be able to go out at night, dress how I wanted and with no questions asked as to where I was from, or what my religion was.

"And there will be no terrorists?" I asked, smiling.

"No terrorists," she laughed. "Only tourists."

CHAPTER 13
ON HER OWN
Mariam who arrived, aged sixteen, from Guinea in 2006

"Men are like kings," said Mariam, a touch of irony in her voice. Was this part of the reason why this handsome, young woman from West Africa had found herself, aged sixteen, alone in Hackney, knowing no one and with no word of English?

When hearing about my research Rayah, my neighbour and retired academic with a lifetime involvement in refugee issues, rang Mariam who agreed to be interviewed. Rayah had been a lifeline to Mariam. "Only Madame Rayah helped me. Any problem I just call her." Not that Rayah, an energetic woman of Jewish heritage with an abundance of grey curly hair, knew the full story. She had not wanted to pry into why Mariam had left Guinea.

As a way of starting the interview, I suggested Mariam draw her childhood home. "It was one of the poorest parts of Conakry, but the neighbourhood was friendly because we were all at the same level." She produced an Escher-like drawing of an aerial view of the compound, shared by two families, but with an upright two-dimensional house, drawn in yellow, placed within the perimeter. This was where Mariam's family lived. Bursts of green represented a mango tree outside the open-air kitchen; an African apple tree dominated the central courtyard and a cocoa tree towered above the outside toilet. "Only boys could climb trees," said Mariam. "They believe women should be in the house – cleaning, washing, cooking." Mariam added a fridge, an outside tap and a well from where she collected water from the age of seven. Drinking water, from the communal tap, was chargeable and might only come on, just for an hour, at three in the morning. Someone would shout, Mariam would get up to fill the bottles and place them in the fridge – that is, if the electricity was working.

Mariam drew bowls, too, that caught drips from the leaky roof. There was an open wood fire where Mariam's mother would cook rice with a curry sauce and sometimes fish – meat was for special occasions. The family ate off "a disabled table" – one leg was damaged. When her mother was at work, Mariam often cooked for her younger siblings. Mariam laughed remembering how, after serving a meal, the disabled table collapsed, and the dinner slid onto the muddy floor. The children howled and went hungry that day.

The two families who shared the compound prayed together on the veranda of Mariam's house. "My dad or the family man at the front, the boys on the second row and the girls at the back." Prayers were held five times a day, that is unless their father, a strict Muslim, was out and prayers were abandoned. Mariam's father laid down certain rules. Music was forbidden except during weddings – only cassette readings of the Quranic verses were allowed but as soon as their father left the house the children would put on their favourite music. "Immediately we see him, we turn it off," laughed Mariam. There were two toilets, one inside used by Mariam's parents and one outside for everyone else. Mariam giggled at how she and her siblings would sneak into her parents' toilet when they were out, making sure they left it spotless. The outside toilet, just a hole in the ground, attracted mosquitos that flew into the bedroom that Mariam shared with her sisters. The nets, full of holes, were no deterrent – the children often caught malaria.

Mariam drew a small rectangle in the top left corner of the drawing – this was her father's nearby shop, selling Fanta, cigarettes and sweets. "He does not have good customer service," laughed Mariam. "He's always shouting. He thinks they're family." Mariam was much closer to her mother. "She's a funny, jovial woman. It's my dad that is a terror. If you're not a slave to your man, you're not a woman." The money her mother earned in a pharmacy kept the family afloat. "Just a small shop – it didn't have many medications."

Mariam started to sketch her old bedroom, separate from the main house, that she shared with her two sisters. She drew a mat on the floor on which her younger sister slept, then the bed where she and her older sister snuggled together under the hole-ridden mosquito net. "She was like a twin sister, my best friend. We used to be always together but after her death I became lonely. I used to dream of her so I would take a prayer mat and lay it here and sleep." Mariam pointed to a space near the outside fire, well away from the bedroom which reminded her of the nights she had slept in her sister's arms.

Mariam's sister was eighteen when she died. Mariam was fourteen. "My dad, being a strict man, wanted my sister to get married, but he wanted her to get circumcised first." Mariam's mother, working in a pharmacy, understood the dangers of FGM but exerted little influence over her husband. "In our culture the man has the final say." The practice of female genital mutilation, commonly known as FGM, has been illegal in Guinea since 1965 but there have been few prosecutions. According to a United Nations report in 2016, 97 per cent of females, between the ages of fifteen and forty-nine, across all ethnicities and religious groups, had undergone FGM and/or excision. Many believe this helps girls and women abstain from sexual activity until after marriage and gives them 'an identity, a certain social and adult status, collective recognition and a sense of belonging to a community.'[1] To oppose FGM has consequences. 'Social pressure is such that girls may request excision for fear of being excluded or forced to remain unmarried if they do not suffer the practice.'[2]

Mariam's family was too poor to take Mariam's sister to a registered medical centre. Instead, she was taken to a traditional practitioner, mostly women, who carry out 70 per cent of FGM procedures in Guinea. Only 30 per cent are carried out by health providers.[3] Groups of girls from different families are usually excised together, either at home or in special camps. Girls are given a bath, dressed in towels, blindfolded and placed into height order. The smallest is operated on first, meaning those further down the line hear screams when the girls are cut with knives or razorblades without the use of anaesthetic, sterilization or professional surgical instruments. The wound is treated with traditional mixtures of plants, ash and mud. Such procedures can lead to heavy bleeding, urinary tract infections, cysts, infertility or sepsis. Girls are sometimes made to dance, even when in extreme pain. After leaving the excision camps, they receive gifts of food, clothes and jewellery.[4]

After Mariam's sister returned from the operation, she became feverish and weak. Mariam saw, at close quarters, how her sister suffered. "The area wasn't getting better. Then one night she was really sick." Mariam's mother tried to raise money to take her oldest daughter to a registered hospital. "By the time my mum got the money, it was too late." Mariam went back to school after the summer break – the procedure is often carried out during long holidays to give girls time to recover. She tried to concentrate on her studies – maths was her favourite subject, but sums danced in front of her eyes, mocking her, evading her. At home she would read the Quran before joining her family for prayer on the veranda. She focused on her chores, waking up at three in the morning when the outside tap started to gurgle; filling the fridge with drinking water, hoping the electricity would last until morning. But every chore reminded Mariam of her sister. "On Sunday when she cleaned the house, I'd wash the clothes. And then next week, I'd clean the house and she'd wash the clothes."

Just two years after her sister's death, Mariam's father announced,

"It's all arranged."

One of his friends wanted to marry Mariam but before the ceremony she would have to undergo the cutting.

"How can you do this when we lost the first one?" cried her mother.

"That was God's will," argued her father. "Most people do not die."

"You don't read the newspapers," shouted Mariam's mother. "People die every day from this practice."

Mariam's father dismissed his wife's concerns. She was, after all, in a minority, even amongst women. In 2012, 76 per cent of women in Guinea were in favour of FGM, an increase from 65 per cent in 1999.[5] Mariam realized she would have to take things into her own hands. She threw back her shoulders and looked her father straight in the eye.

"I don't want to get married. This man has wives. I don't want to get circumcised. I'm still young. I want to go to school."

Her father ignored her wishes. Mariam was sixteen, a woman now. His friend was a good bet. The tension in the house increased. Mariam was scared she would die from the cutting, just as her sister had. Mariam's mother did not want to lose another daughter.

One morning, after Mariam's father had gone to work, a man who Mariam's mother had contacted for help drove up in his car to take Mariam and her mother to Sierra Leone. Mariam, clutching a few sparse belongings, did not have time to say goodbye to her younger siblings, playing nearby. After a long, tiring journey they arrived at the airport in Sierra Leone. It was late and dark.

"How can you leave me here?" Mariam cried when her mother told her to embark on a plane with the man who had helped them. "How will I survive?"

"You will be fine, just go," said her mother. "God will be with you."

Mariam's mother left. She did not want to know where her daughter was heading for fear that her husband would bully the information out of her.

There were worrying details in the story. Was this man paid for his services or did he do it voluntarily? How well did Mariam's mother know this man? On the flight, the first she had ever taken, Mariam asked herself the same questions. The stranger made little effort to reassure his charge. He wasn't even talking to her.

As the plane soared over deserts and oceans, barely distinguishable in the dark, Mariam became more and more anxious.

"I want to go back," she said, breaking the silence.

"And have your father kill you?"

Mariam sunk back into her seat. Only when the wheels ground to a halt at Heathrow airport, after a ten-hour flight, did she dare to ask,

"Where are we?"

"London," replied the man.

"London in England?"

"Yes," he replied, with more than a hint of frustration.

As they approached the immigration desk the man whispered,

"If they ask, just say you're my daughter. Otherwise keep quiet."

Mariam did what she was told. "I don't know what happened because he was speaking English, but they just let me pass. I don't know whose passport it was."

Mariam's fate, it seems, was in the hands of a man who had barely spoken to her for over twelve hours. "I was crying inside of me. I didn't know if I would ever see my parents or siblings again."

When they arrived at a terraced house in Hackney, the man pointed to a couch in the front room.

"You can sleep there for a couple of days."

On the third day he said,

"I'm taking you somewhere people can help you."

Mariam was distraught.

"Will I see you again? I don't know anybody here. I can't speak English."

She still didn't know who the man was, or whether she could trust him, but at least he was a connection with her mother.

Mariam was left on the steps of a local children's centre. Inside, with the help of a French interpreter, Mariam explained her situation. She was given a bed for the night in a local hostel and, the following day, a worker took her to the Home Office. The immigration officer did not believe Mariam was only sixteen. This is not uncommon. The Refugee Council revealed that 94 per cent of the 233 migrant children under eighteen that it supported during 2021 had been wrongly assessed as adults and housed with older people. Further evidence suggested it was a widespread problem showing that at least three quarters of 450 young people referred to eighteen local authorities over concerns they might be children were in fact found to be children.[6] This culture of disbelief on the part of the Home Office can seriously affect young people's access to their rights and appropriate services, as well as their mental health.[7]

After the interview Mariam was taken back to Hackney Social Services who accommodated her, on a temporary basis, in a terraced house in Lower Clapton shared with two other girls. It was far from ideal. Her housemates held parties and entertained male visitors late into the night, keeping Mariam awake – there was no qualified person on site.[8] Mariam was desperate to resume her education – one of the reasons she had defied her father. To pass the time she walked to Hackney Marshes, searched local take-aways for cheap fried chicken, ate alone in her room and watched television to learn English. Her social worker said she had no time to accompany her to the local education offices or find her a solicitor.[9]

On a visit to social services to collect her two-weekly allowance, Mariam heard someone speaking French to a Congolese woman. In desperation she approached Rayah. Encouraged by a sympathetic ear, Mariam told her about the confusion over her age, that she did not have a lawyer and that she was not going to school. Rayah rang an activist working with young unaccompanied migrants who suggested a good immigration lawyer. An appointment for Mariam was fixed. Later Rayah accompanied Mariam to the Learning Trust. The officer was helpful, said there were no places in schools, but she would enquire at the local sixth form college and to come back after the Christmas break – it was late December.

Meanwhile the Home Office had rung Hackney Social Services to say that Mariam was not who she said she was. She was a woman of twenty-two, with the same first name but a different surname, from Sierra Leone. The housing provider sent a worker, who generally visited to change a light bulb or get rid of the mice, to tell Mariam to go to Hackney Social Services' office. She was being evicted. Mariam, hysterical and refusing to move, rang Rayah who advised Mariam she needed to go to social services but that she would go with her. Otherwise, Rayah warned, they would call the police. Rayah asked social services staff why they would not challenge the Home Office. They implied it was not in their financial interest.[10] Rayah pleaded to let Mariam stay in the house until the confusion was sorted but without success. The last straw was when Mariam found her belongings in the social services' waiting room stuffed into 'refugee bags'. "It was altogether dreadful," said Rayah.

Rayah went with Mariam in the taxi, arranged by social services, to the Refugee Council in Brixton. Rayah was prepared to let Mariam stay at her home, but this would not have helped. "The lady there told me that, if I want my case to be looked at, I should go to the hostel." Meanwhile the woman at the Learning Trust had found a place in BSIX Sixth Form College in Hackney. Mariam did not let the distance deter her, "Monday to Friday, I wake up at five, even in cold weather. Three buses to go, three buses to come home." At BSIX she studied English, maths, physics, chemistry and biology and soon progressed onto A levels.

Mariam missed her family. She was worried about what had happened to her mother on her return from the airport. There was no way of contacting her as there was no phone in the house in Conakry and, if she wrote, her father might intercept the letter. Six months after she arrived, when looking through an old diary, Mariam stumbled across the scribbled phone number of the neighbour, a friend of her mother's, who shared their compound. "I was so happy like I had won the lottery."

With the last £2.50 in her purse Mariam bought a card to call Guinea. The neighbour picked up the phone.

"Please don't tell anyone. Is my mum there?"

"Your mum is not in Conakry anymore. She divorced your dad, collected the kids without him knowing and left."

"How will I reach her?"

Mariam started to cry.

"I will write to her – she left an address in case you rang. Phone me in two to three weeks."

After receiving the number from her old neighbour, Mariam rang her mother. The news was not good. Although her mother had gone to live near her brothers, she had little money as she had lost her job and was seriously ill. She needed money for treatment. "I couldn't do much because I was only on £35 a week."

At least her mother was able to send Mariam her birth certificate, showing her true age. Under pressure from her lawyer Hackney Social Services agreed to house Mariam again. She moved in with other students but found it hard when they started to apply for university. She had heard nothing to clarify her status, either from Hackney Social Services or the Home Office but, encouraged by her housemates, still applied.

Mariam got accepted onto a nursing course at City University, but the offer was withdrawn when she was unable to produce the necessary papers. "I cried that day, *Oh my God, I'm so tired of this life.*" She was accepted by three further universities to study biomedical science but again was refused entry because of her lack of status. Then she received a letter from the University of Westminster saying she had been accepted as an international student. This meant she was ineligible for student finance and would have to pay overseas student fees. "Where do they want me to get £12,000?" Mariam cried. "I don't have a job or even papers to work."[11] Mariam went to see her solicitor again. She had lost her ID card showing she was an asylum seeker and wondered if a replacement would support her case. The solicitor set up an appointment with the Home Office who told Mariam she didn't need her ID anymore and to contact her solicitor. This could mean one of two things. Either Mariam was on the plane back to Guinea or she had been granted leave to remain.

Every day Mariam rang her solicitor but there was still no news. Undeterred, she attended university, showed her admission letter to gain entry, but was unable to access the computer without a student card – her friends printed off the lecture notes. Neither could she afford to eat in the canteen – the £35 a week barely covered her fares. She would wait until she got home to eat. "I'd be famished."

On the last day, when the £12,000 payment was due, Mariam sat in the library, perhaps for the last time. Her phone rang. It was her solicitor. Students looked up from their books at Mariam screaming down the phone. It took some time for Mariam to notice them. "You don't know what I was going through," she explained to an open-mouthed, curious, even disapproving crowd after she finished the call. "I have indefinite leave to remain. I no longer have to pay £12,000 for my fees," she shouted in excitement. Some students cheered; others looked nonplussed. Mariam went to pick up her papers. She had been waiting four long years. "I was a student now."

Mariam believed the confusion over her identity was unnecessary. The man and woman from Sierra Leone, living in the UK, whom the Home Office believed were Mariam's aunt and uncle, could have been contacted sooner to establish the truth – they were clear she was not their 22-year-old niece. Mariam, now able to work during the holidays to supplement her student loan, got a job serving food at football stadiums. After paying for her rent, travel, food, books and application for her British citizenship, she put money aside to send back to her mother and for a phone card so she could talk to her family. After six years in Britain, Mariam had saved enough money to go back and see them.

"When I met them at the airport, we all cried. I couldn't believe it. All my siblings have grown. They are free now." While in Guinea, Mariam opened a Facebook account for her sister. "Now you can go to the cybercafé to give me news." Mariam did not visit her father. "I was still scared. He was a terror and doesn't give up easily." She tried to build bridges with his family. "They said I'm the cause of my mum and dad being separated, that I'm an evil child."

Mariam was surprised at how much older her mother looked – her illness had made her lose weight but, after Mariam returned to the UK, things improved. "She's doing business now, selling things." Perhaps Mariam's visit had given her a boost.

One day Mariam's mother rang to say she was getting remarried.

"He's a good man, he likes the kids."

"That's your life, I'm not against it," laughed Mariam. "So, don't be against my man. He's from Nigeria."

"Oh, I want a Guinea man," her mother replied.

"As far as he loves me, that's the most important thing."

Mariam had met her boyfriend when she was working at the football stadium. He was also a student but, unlike Mariam, a Christian. It was he who introduced Mariam to the Kingsway International Christian Centre where she met other worshippers from West Africa. "It's easier for me to worship Christianity than to worship Islam. Religion comes from the heart, not like my dad taught us. I was always moody, but, since I've found Christianity, I feel free." Mariam has not forgotten her Muslim heritage. "I still celebrate Eid. I send money to my mum for her to celebrate. That's her and my siblings' belief so I'm not against it and I don't expect them to be against mine."

On the day of her graduation Rayah and I met Mariam in the lobby of the Festival Hall on the South Bank. She looked radiant and elegant, dressed in a black mortar board and black gown over a dress made of dashiki wax print. We cheered when she walked across the stage. She had never given up – not when her age or identity was questioned, not when she was evicted, not when she was denied access to education or classified as an international student. I asked her how she had kept going. "When I close my eyes and see my mum's face, how she used to suffer and how my sister died, I just get courage. I don't have to sit down and cry. I have to be strong and make mum proud of me. I knew she was going to get hell. It wasn't easy. That was my first time living without my family, but I didn't have a choice. If I hadn't left, I'd be somebody's mum by now, someone's wife, or slave. And I didn't want that."

Six years later, in 2020, Rayah and I caught up with Mariam. By then both her mother and father had died. We learnt she was now a British Citizen, was married and living on the South Coast with two young children – her husband, and father of her second child, was living in Guinea but hopes, one day, to be able to join his family in Britain. Mariam has fulfilled her mother's wishes by marrying a Guinea man – the relationship with the Nigerian student, the father of her first child, had not worked out. We arranged to visit her, but the pandemic disrupted our plans. Mariam, as many migrants in Britain, was contributing to saving lives, working as a student nurse on a COVID-19 ward in Eastbourne.

…………….

CHAPTER 14
"HOME IS WHERE THE LOVE IS"
Yosef, originally from Eritrea, who arrived aged sixteen, in 2011

I made my way to the Southbank Centre to see a performance of *Dear Home Office: Still Pending*.[1] The room was packed – over a 100 people to see the recent play by Phosphoros Theatre.[2] As the lights dimmed images were projected onto a back screen including of a performance at the Edinburgh Festival, with English subtitles when the actors – teenage boys or in their early twenties – spoke in Arabic, Pashto, Dari or Somali. Kate Duffy-Syedi, who had set up the drama group with two other theatre artists, was the only woman on stage.

The play opened with young men, many of whom had escaped war, relaxing in a communal space, replicating where some of them lived together in Harrow. Among the group was Yosef, from Eritrea, operating an Xbox – I had interviewed him weeks earlier. Then the scenery shifted to create a housing office, a court room, a bedroom. I recognized the story of a boy searching for housing as he approached the age of eighteen, of being told he had to claim he was homeless, of having to fill in innumerable forms. Yosef had told me about his housing situation, but it was not Yosef playing the role. Other scenes were funnier. Of a tall, open-faced Albanian boy being told that the college course he was keen on was oversubscribed. Instead, he was persuaded to study childcare – there would be plenty of girls on the course. He took the course seriously, making friends with a white English girl who confused Albania with Bulgaria, where a relative had spent a lovely holiday – few people realize that a high percentage of young asylum seekers have been trafficked from Albania.[3] The English girl, projected onto a large screen, helped the Albanian boy with his studies but when the other boys heard a baby's persistent crying they rushed into his bedroom. They were amused, if bemused, to discover the baby was a doll. There was a sadder thread to this story. The friendship between the fair English rose and the strapping Albanian boy was genuine, innocent, but a tutor warned the Albanian boy against friendship with the English rose. She could do better in life – a touch of Shakespearean tragedy behind a smokescreen of comedy.

There was the story, too, of the boy from Somalia whose application to remain in Britain was refused by the Home Office. Kate, key worker in real life to some of the actors and performing the role of key worker in the play, sought assistance from a lawyer. Behind the boy's back so as not to upset him, Kate scoured the internet for images of war in the boy's village in Somalia – more evidence was needed before the boy could get legal aid. The boy rang a Somali organization in London for more information but the second-generation Somali on the other end of the phone had never been to Somalia and knew little about it. Despite this, essential facts were gathered, and legal aid was granted. In court the lawyer instructed the boy to stay quiet, but he would not be silenced – the boy was an actor. Some weeks later he received a letter – his appeal had been successful. The story rang true. Up to 50 per cent of appeals against the Home Office are successful.[4]

The saddest story was of two brothers. At 3:00 am, one night, the older brother was awakened by knocking on his bedroom door. It was his younger brother who had left Afghanistan after him. For a few days the younger brother slept on the floor, disturbing other residents with his nightmares but he was not allowed to stay. Instead, he got caught up in disputes and bureaucracy as to whose responsibility he was. Some days later a policeman pulled the younger brother out of a river, half drowned. He survived but other young people in his situation have not. In 2019 four Eritreans of the same friendship group killed themselves in the space of one year, youths who had made the same journey as Yosef through Sudan, Libya, across Europe, hiding in refrigerated lorries to cross the Channel from France. The solicitor, representing the family of Ahmed Nur who hanged himself in his bedroom, said: "The outcome of this inquest is an indictment of our mental-health services and the ways in which we fail to look after unaccompanied asylum-seeking children and young people."[5]

The young actors performed other quick-fire scenes about queuing for second-hand shoes to replace plastic bags on blistered feet in the 'Jungle' in Calais; of one boy cutting off electricity in the communal house in Harrow by cooking his supper in a kettle; of another unable to go to university as he was classed as an overseas student – a challenge that both Mariam and Ahmed had faced. One boy, who was paid £3.30 an hour for his job in a fried chicken shop, was ridiculed by his friends, "You are better than this." At the end of the week, he counted out his wages into piles of pound notes. "For my mum, for my socks, for my mum, for my shoes, for my mum, for my chicken and chips." How often do we think of the responsibility such young people bear of sending money back to their families back home, living on £35 a week or working well below the minimum wage?

Perhaps most ironic of all was the scene with a TV producer. He was interested in the work of Phosphoros Theatre after their success in Edinburgh and wanted someone to play the part of a refugee in a new production. The boys, dreaming of Hollywood, vied with each other for the part, but their hopes were dashed. The young boys were just not 'refugee enough'. Far too resilient, keen on telling their own stories in their own way, debunking myths about migrants and refugees they read in the headlines daily.

I congratulated Yosef on his performance and walked back along the South Bank, recalling the scenes – the boy practising his childcare skills on a doll, wondering if this was the river that nearly took the younger brother's life, and remembering the interview with Yosef some weeks earlier.

…………..

"She gave us, what do you call it, 'small tree'?"

"Small tree?" I questioned, nonplussed as we sat together in the office of an Afghan refugee charity in Harrow.

"Broccoli," said a confident voice behind me.

"Yes, broccoli," Yosef confirmed, his face lighting up at Mitch, operating the iPhone behind me.

Yosef had agreed to be interviewed for the film *Child Migrants Welcome?*

"Broc … col … li, broc … col … li," he repeated, enjoying the sound of the word on his tongue. "I still don't eat it."

We were all laughing now. 'Small tree' seemed an apt description for a vegetable that, like Yosef, I have never taken to.

Yosef, with a high forehead framed by dark, swept back hair, wearing a crisp white T-shirt, struck a handsome figure. He had arrived, aged sixteen, in the back of a lorry in a Hampshire village with seven others from Calais in 2011. He made friends with the only other minor in the lorry – a boy, like him, from Eritrea. The migrants reported into a police station where they were questioned and, after a night in the cells, the boys were sent to a foster carer – the adults were sent elsewhere. "Her name was Sarah. She was cool and made us feel welcome, but the problem was the food. We didn't speak the language so we couldn't say what we wanted. We watched television with her and her kids, but we understood nothing." After three days social services arranged for Yosef and his friend to stay with an Eritrean family in London. "It did help she was from our country. We were with her a year and a few months. It gave us some stability. Like our mother." Yosef had left his real mother when he was twelve. "She didn't know I was leaving. I just followed strangers." Yosef's mother must have been heartbroken. Her husband, who had served in the army, had been killed in the war with Ethiopia, the whereabouts of one of her other sons were unknown, leaving her, after Yosef's departure, with one remaining son at home.

Thousands of refugees have fled Eritrea, a small country with a population of about 5 million on the Red Sea. The majority have fled to neighbouring Sudan, Djibouti and Ethiopia but tens of thousands have also made their way to Europe. The most obvious reason for the exodus is the country's national service system that requires all citizens to serve in the army for an unlimited amount of time. Through this, the government controls almost every aspect of a civilian's life, both male and female, from the age of sixteen or seventeen. There are instances, too, of younger children being forcibly recruited. Human rights groups have condemned the practice as being akin to slavery. The only real way to avoid conscription is to flee the country. This appalling human rights record, indefinite military conscription, forced labour and use of torture have earned Eritrea the epithet 'Africa's North Korea'.[6]

The area that is present-day Eritrea was colonized by Italy in 1890 and integrated into Italian East Africa as the Eritrea Governorate in 1936. In 1941, following Italy's loss of the region during the Second World War, it came under British military administration where it remained until 1951 when it fell under United Nations supervision. In September 1952 it became an autonomous part of Ethiopia until its independence in 1991. President Isaias Afwerki, who has been in power since 1993, leads a totalitarian government with no elections, no constitution or independent press. He and his government maintain control by forcing citizens to spy on each another – if they refuse, they might be 'disappeared', perhaps the fate of Yosef's brother. The slightest rumour of political activism, or even sympathy with dissenters, is grounds for arrest and indefinite detention.[7]

"Back home we have deep rooted issues," acknowledged Yosef. He had no plan when he followed others into Sudan, braving the official 'shoot to kill' policy at the border.[8] In Sudan, where life was far from easy, he listened to people's advice 'Go here', 'Go there'; he became fascinated with tales of where people were going and what lay ahead. After a year, he piled into a Toyota car with thirty others headed for Libya. They crossed the Sahara, on unprepared desert tracks where breakdowns can leave people stranded under the hot sun. After seven days, he and his fellow passengers emerged from the cramped car, stiff and famished. Young Yosef had no real concept of what was in store.

Every year thousands of Sudanese, along with Ethiopians, Eritreans and Somalis, travel overland to Libya which, for decades, has provided opportunities for seasonal, temporary employment in the agricultural and industrial sectors. But Libya has been in chaos since the Arab Spring movement and the NATO bombing campaign that toppled Gaddafi in 2011, causing the proliferation of extremist armed groups such as ISIS. Detention centres, with inadequate access to food and water, have become infamous for holding migrants and refugees indefinitely. Those detained are subject to human rights violations such as torture, forced labour and unlawful killings at the hands of Libyan authorities, smugglers and armed groups.[9]

Yosef was remarkably sanguine about his imprisonment in Libya. "I learnt many things from the people I was with. I lay with them, laughed with them. I was young and didn't think about what was going to happen tomorrow." It was eight months before Yosef stepped outside the prison walls. "A friend, a big guy, paid money to the police for me and some of the other guys. He took us to some place next to the sea where we stayed for a month maybe. There was no law, no protection. If you pay enough money to the police anybody can get out of prison. We got on a boat and travelled four days to Syracusa in Italy. We arrived at night. People tried to run from the police. Some injured themselves, but I was OK."

Yosef's second imprisonment was short-lived. "There was a boy who brought us meals. I just picked up food and walked back out with him. I was never afraid to try things then. I have lost that now. The journey changed me. I have become more silent, calculated, concerned about consequences. I miss that small, innocent guy." He had survived crossing the border into Sudan from Eritrea, the journey across the Sahara, imprisonment in Libya, the sea crossing across the Mediterranean and imprisonment in Sicily. Who would not be changed by this? His subsequent journey across Europe, dodging the authorities and avoiding imprisonment, ended in Calais.

Since at least the 1990s, migrants have congregated around the French port, waiting for their French asylum claims to be processed or attempting to enter Britain. A refugee centre at Sangatte, administered by the French Red Cross, was opened in 1999 but, under pressure from the UK government, was closed in 2002. Since then, migrants have set up unofficial camps, with no access to proper sanitation or shelter. They have been regularly harassed and evicted by the authorities. Yosef's stay in Calais in 2011 was before the Calais 'Jungle' grew to over 8,000 during the peak of the European migrant crisis in 2015, attracting global media attention when it was disbanded.[10] It must still have been a dire place for young Yosef to stay. When Yosef set out from Eritrea aged twelve, the UK was not his ultimate gaol. "I learnt a little bit in geography, but I didn't know which country was better." He moved from country to country pushed on by maltreatment and taking advice from others. "There are many boys who say, 'this way is better' and I just went."

Once settled with his Eritrean foster carer in Harlesden, west London, Yosef started college. He appreciated the teachers' professionalism and skill, but it was their personal support that he valued most. "You have to be able to engage with them not just as your boss but as your friend." After a year and several months Yosef, with the support of his social worker, moved into housing accommodation for young unaccompanied asylum seekers in Harrow. He was seventeen and, although grateful to his Eritrean foster carer, looked forward to more independence. Kate became his designated key worker. "She plays an important role in our lives and has become our friend too. She gives us advice, goes into college to tell them what is difficult for us. When we apply for anything, she explains who we are."

I had met Kate at a conference where she and the young people from Phosphoros Theatre gave an impressive presentation about their work. It was Yosef who had partly inspired the formation of Phosphoros Theatre. "Me and Kate were talking about hobbies. I told her I loved writing and asked if there was a possibility to share things that were happening in the house. She said, 'My mother is a TV writer and I have a degree in drama.'[11] She spoke with her mother and later she asked 'What do you think about starting up a drama group? I said 'Go ahead. It's going to be awesome.' We started with funny stories of when we went shopping and couldn't speak English or about sexual health workshops – condoms and stuff but about serious things too. I told my story about being in prison as did my friends from Afghanistan."

Yosef was right in thinking the drama group would be awesome. When I met him, the group had already been booked out at Edinburgh Festival with their second full stage production *Dear Home Office: Still Pending*. Yosef explained the aim of the show, "We want to show that people should not be afraid of us, that we are like them but that something has happened in all our lives that creates a difference. We want to make people open their hearts to us, to impress the Home Office because we can't exist here without documents." The drama group was important to the boys on a social level. "We have become closer and started going out together, like English boys." It was significant in other ways. "I don't think the way I did. I don't believe in what I believed which is a sign of change, isn't it?" When Yosef's college teachers visited the show, they were clearly impressed with the progress Yosef had made. "My favourite teacher, from when I first arrived and did not know my ABC, hugged me." At the time of the interview, Yosef was approaching the age of twenty-one so had to leave the housing scheme in Harrow. "We've searched for a house but just can't find one. Social workers have done what they can, but I feel like they are not helping 100 per cent more like 70 per cent maybe because I'm getting older. The transition has become very difficult."

Yosef wanted to be a psychologist. "My interest in psychology is because of the experience I've been through and from books I've read." He paused. "To understand the mind is to understand the world." Yosef had advice to others who arrive in the UK as unaccompanied minors. "Our past can become a burden, like a burial ground. You have to leave space for new things, the new environment, new people, new love. You have to be open and explore yourself, be around people who are supportive and value you." Yosef stopped. "It feels weird to give advice." It wasn't weird. Who better to share his experience than someone who had been through similar experiences?

"Do you think about Eritrea?"

"Of course. I was born there. I have family there. But it's not possible to go back in real life, only in fiction. I would love to see my mum, if possible, in a European country for a month or two."

The plight of those who return to Eritrea was highlighted by a case brought to court by three Eritreans who campaigned against the Home Office's guidance, updated in 2015. The tribunal rejected the argument that they could return safely by signing a letter of apology and paying a 'diaspora tax'. Signing such a letter could expose returnees to potential danger. The Home Office guidance was revised.[12]

"Our problem goes beyond politics. If the door is open, people can learn and change but they have closed the door. To unlock it is difficult. I don't think politics can fix the problems in our country. Only education can bring about change."

"So where is home?"

"Wherever the love is, that is home."

As we said our goodbyes Yosef offered an invitation. "Come to the South Bank and see us perform *Dear Home Office: Still Pending*."

CHAPTER 15
SEEKING SANCTUARY ON A SCOTTISH ISLAND

Syrian children who arrived from Lebanon, aged six to sixteen, on the Isle of Bute, Scotland in 2015

Road from Damascus

Personal Essay by Malek

'We were spending a peaceful night at my aunt and uncle's house in Damascus, after a week of being trapped. The rebels, who had set up their own checkpoint next to an army checkpoint nearby, had let us leave our houses. We felt human, following a week of terror. The phone rang – it was a call to dad from a friend. "Get out of your house immediately." He hung up without adding a single thing – not when or how or what was happening. We started to panic, arguing what we should do. The rebels and army had already taken up their positions. My parents went to our house above my uncle's. My dad told me to follow, but I stayed. What a decision that was!'

'After ten minutes I wanted to go home so I opened my uncle's door, but a sniper started shooting at me from the roof opposite. I managed to get back into my uncle's house where I waited, stressed and scared, for the battle to begin. As soon as it did, we relaxed – there was nothing more we could do. I sat with my cousins, playing cards and telling jokes, whilst the adults prayed, hoping the enemy didn't take us hostage. An hour before the end of a thirteen-hour battle, a helicopter above us started to drop bombs. After that a deathly quiet.'

'We were afraid to go out. What if the rebels had lost? If the army saw us, they would kill us. My dad came down, "We need to leave." All our relatives lived in the street so we could reach one of their houses, without being seen. A tanker had been destroyed and the rebels, who were still there, told us not to move as there was still a sniper around, hidden from view. My dad asked if he could get the car. We waited a long fifteen minutes for a signal to allow dad to leave.'

'We left to stay with other relatives from where we watched our city being bombed day and night. Then we moved to stay with an aunt who lived in the mountains where I started to go to school. The rest of my family moved to a house in the city where I spent every weekend. It was hard. I wasn't used to living away from my family. After the term had finished, we moved to Jordan, especially for my older brother who was eighteen, the age to join the army.'

'My journey has ended here on Bute. I never imagined I would end up on the opposite side of the world. Despite Scotland having a different culture, we were welcomed. The first time I stepped into the house, here on the island, I felt this was now our permanent home. It was a feeling I hadn't had for a long time.'[1]

....

In 2015, a small boy wearing blue, short trousers and a red T-shirt lay on his front, his arms and head to the side. He looked peaceful, cushioned by the sand, waves lapping around his ankles. The boy seemed unaware that he might get washed away by the Aegean Sea. Minutes later a uniformed official picked up the body and carried it, limp and lifeless, across his outstretched arms. David Cameron, Prime Minister, said he felt 'deeply moved' by pictures of three-year-old Alan Shenu (named in media reports by Turkish authorities as Aylan Kurdi) washed up on a Turkish beach. 'Britain is a moral nation, and we will fulfil our moral responsibilities.'[2] In 2015 Cameron greatly expanded the Vulnerable Persons Relocation Scheme already in place to take 20,000 refugees, identified by the UN from camps on the Syrian borders, by 2020.[3] Scotland stepped up and, in December 2015, the first Syrian families arrived on the Isle of Bute.[4] At only thirty-three miles from Glasgow, and a short ferry ride across the Firth of Clyde, Bute is Scotland's most accessible island. Most islanders, and indeed the Syrian refugees, live in or around the town of Rothesay, known for its Art Deco buildings, palm trees and promenade.

In June 2017 Mitch and I leant over the rail on the deck of the ferry as it left Wemyss Bay, the bracing sea air reviving us after the train journey from London. My phone rang. "I don't know if it's going to happen," warned Pat Till, a close friend and teacher on the island. "I've got to visit their families with the interpreter to get their signatures. I'll meet you off the boat in Rothesay." In the hectic life of the school, organizing the interpreter had been complicated. By the time we reached the Isle of Bute, Pat had secured permission from all the Syrian parents and children. We sighed with relief, deposited our luggage at the B&B overlooking the harbour and went on an evening walk to Scalpsie Bay. Mitch experimented with his new Iphone7, placing it underwater to take shots of the seabed, whilst Pat filled me in on her role with the Syrian children. "I teach English as an Additional Language at Rothesay Joint Campus – the primary, infant and secondary schools all rolled into one. The children are a delight to work with. They love being here and I love being here, so the whole thing is a joyful experience." Pat now spends half her time in London and half her time on the island. She had scheduled two whole days of interviews with five of the Syrian children and two of the staff. There was the possibility, too, that Malek, who had already left the school, might be happy to be interviewed.

In the morning Mitch set up his new Iphone7 on a tripod in one of the classrooms. Having been involved, for decades, in policies and practices that support child migrants in London, I was intrigued, if a little wary. How could a rural school on a Scottish island understand, and meet, the needs of children, with a different culture and language, who had experienced civil war, and whose education had been disrupted by spending months or years in neighbouring countries outside Syria? My prejudice, that schools with a history of accommodating migrant children were in a better position to meet such challenges, was about to be challenged.

First to be interviewed was Maureen Shaw, Depute Head Teacher of the primary school, a compassionate, confident woman, with auburn hair curling past her shoulders. She recalled the exact moment she was told about the arrival of Syrian children. "The headteacher called me into her office and said, 'I have some exciting news. There are twenty-one Syrian families coming to Bute'. I just thought *WOW! What can we do to prepare?* We got lists from the Home Office but that could be difficult because the minute you start to read about children and families you start to make a connection. You'd be practicing their names on your tongue and then further down the line you'd find out some families had not been able to come. Maybe they weren't well enough – sometimes they had to pass a medical. You think about their expectations about coming to Britain and suddenly they are not there, and another family has taken their place. That is a sad thought. We did a lot of work with staff, learning Arabic phrases like, 'Hello' and 'My name is'. We worked with children, finding out about Syria, the culture, the food they liked. It was daunting but exciting." I was impressed. Not all teachers I knew in London practised non-'English' sounding names on their tongues. There were plenty of instances, certainly in earlier decades, of 'foreign sounding' names being anglicized. Pola became Paula or Ali became Robert believing that if the child had an English name he or she might integrate better.

It was one thing for the teachers and children to be on side, but what about the parents and wider community? How were people on this island, with a declining population of 6,000, going to respond to the arrival of twenty-one Syrian families, 100 individuals, making Bute one of the largest recipients of Syrian refugees in Britain relative to its population? "Some parents weren't that keen. European children fine but they're just not sure what they were going to get but everybody is an individual. Once you meet people that just disappears." Lorna Morss, a classroom teacher, was more sceptical. "The community was very much divided. There were people for it and people not so for it, which was a sad reflection on Rothesay." According to Argyll and Bute Council the island had been chosen because it had available social housing and was closer, than other islands, to medical support.

The arrival of the families was a newsworthy item far beyond Bute's shores. "We had to think about how to deal with the press," Maureen explained. "As you can imagine Syrian children coming to a rural school in Scotland was a big news item. We had one press conference, were advised by the council to respect our new families and ensure confidentiality. There were newspapers that thought *What would they want to come to Bute for*? I remember one of the quotes, 'It's just somewhere people go to retire.' I think we've proved them wrong. We gave the newspapers what they wanted and most of what they wrote was positive." Most but not all. Headlines in the *Daily Mail* read 'Senseless! Why are Syrian refugees being foisted on a remote Scottish island with high unemployment and poverty – then given perks some locals don't enjoy?' Concerns in the article ranged from Syrian boys cycling the wrong way down a one-way street to suspicion they might be ISIS terrorists.[5]

It was Maureen's story of how the school prepared to greet the Syrian families that floored me. "I went up to Glasgow airport and it was an absolute privilege to meet people who you feel you know because you've seen their photographs. I remember my son had gone to help with the luggage. I looked out the door and thought *My Goodness, he's got a baby in his arms*. A mum had passed her baby to my son who'd never held a baby before. My son turned to me and said, 'Mum. This one's for Orkney.' I just thought what a moment for him – he will never forget that."

Eighteen-year-old Malek, who had returned to the school to talk to us, confirmed Maureen's story. "There was a bus come to collect us. On that bus, there was the head teacher and six pupils from the school. They welcomed us, they helped us with our bags, we felt comfy, we felt welcomed." The speed with which Malek and other children were registered in school, within two weeks of arrival on Bute, contrasted with Malek's experiences of accessing education in the three years since he had left Syria. In Jordan he attended night school for Syrian pupils because day schools were full, in Egypt he received no education and in Lebanon he was confronted with angry gangs at the school gates. "They beat people as if their life depended on it." Instead, he attended an alternative school for Syrian pupils in an abandoned hospital. "No one would receive a certificate showing they had finished the year but at least it was a place to learn." By the time Malek arrived on Bute he was desperate for some stability. "Staying in a house for a long time was a dream: every time I got used to one, we had to leave."

Lorna was all too aware of the disrupted education some of her pupils had received. "One of the biggest challenges was building trust. One child had quite horrendous experiences at school in Syria and Lebanon, so it was making him realise this is a safe place; that it is me every day." There was no denying the warmth and permanence that Lorna evoked but she did not underestimate the challenge. "It's a complete learning … " She took a deep breath. "It's not even a curve," she laughed. "It's a CLIFF." One of the reasons Pat enjoys teaching the Syrian children is, for the most part, because of their willingness to learn. "Syrians are so aware that education is the key to going forward. You can see that in the way they apply themselves to any task they're doing." Additional resources to help children learn included extra staffing, iPads and educational psychology support as and when required. All the Syrian children had a Universal Child's Plan identifying targets and actions needed to help them fulfil their potential.[6]

The children entered the classroom, one by one, except for two sisters who came together. They were bright and eager, practising their responses to questions about the island, the school and their futures with their English teacher, Ms Till, before facing me and the camera. Rabia, aged thirteen, came first, hiding behind her long black hair. Pat had told me she had recently arrived, had little English and was very shy.

"What do you think about the weather?" I asked, hoping the question might serve as an ice breaker.

"It's so cold and always raining," she said with a shiver, making us laugh.

Fedaa, aged eight, with her wavy, brown hair, tied back with a ribbon, liked, "the sun and a little bit rain so she could splash." Her seven-year-old sister, Jana, with darker hair and deep-set eyes, also liked the rain "because the rainbow comes." I imagined the two of them chasing that elusive pot of gold across Scalpsie Bay. "I like two things," said Fedaa, "Scotland and Syria." Jana agreed, "I like Syria and Scotland." In a softer, more melancholic tone Jana added, "Syria is so big, so beautiful, I miss it."

Ali, a robust ten-year-old, with dark curly hair, was enthusiastic about his new home. "Scotland is a good place to live. My mum's friends are all so nice. They sometimes come to my house and teach me and my mum some English." Safa, aged six, with jet-black hair pulled back into a plait sat with her hands under her knees, her legs swinging. Looking to the left, then to the right, as if searching for words, she explained how she had become her parents' tutor. "When I learn a new word, I help them to learn it. I do a sentence for them." Maureen was proud of the progress the children had made. "There are two interpreters on the island, but we don't use them nearly as much because our older children are now English-speaking – they understand the school much better than the interpreters." Fedaa, reciting an amusing tale of a fish and a frog, demonstrated an impressive command of English but that was not the limit of her talents. "I love art. I'm very good at it because one time I drew a girl and all the class said, 'How did you draw that? It's like a real one.'"

Ali shared a long list of his Scottish friends with whom he learnt Scottish dancing. Malek talked of two pupils who had given him a tour of the school on his first day and of another who took him to every class for a month. He had made friends with two Scottish girls whom he saw outside of school but, as Lorna admitted, there were underlying tensions. "When Syrians are on the football pitch, football being football, or the 'F' word as I call it, they end up fighting, but it always comes back to them being 'Syrian'." She saw the challenge from both sides. "Initially a lot of our kids welcomed them. Then they found it hard to be continually trying to get over what they meant. It's also hard for the Syrian children because they are listening to English all day." Lorna had started bringing the Syrian children together at the end of lessons. "It's a relief for them to get together with someone who speaks the same language and understands where they are coming from." I resisted the wish to hug Lorna for her insight. One of my worst teaching experiences, in 1974, in a primary school in north London, was an 'English only' policy, denying newly arrived children the right to communicate in their mother tongue, not just in the classroom but in the playground. Some children withdrew into their shells; some, in frustration, hit out. Research confirms there is both intellectual and emotional value in supporting children's bi- or tri-lingual skills.[7]

Previous knowledge of the English language did not always help the Syrian children. "I was used to movie accents," admitted Malek in his broad Scottish accent. "I'm also from a different culture. I can't just walk in and do the same stuff." The reality was, as Lorna explained, that often children were required to do "the same stuff." "From day one, we were into Burns – what they made of all that I have no idea," laughed Lorna, reflecting on the absurdity of the children being thrown into a fervour of activity around the famous bard. The Syrian children were not the only ones confused. "Learning about Burns was as new to me as it was to the children," explained Pat. "Any Scot would know all the traditions." She flicked up a video of a Syrian girl who had left the island, and who she had taught to recite a Burns poem.

"Oh, my love is like a red, red rose that … newly springs in June.

Oh, my love is like … the melody … "

Pat had done her best to prepare her students for the Burns night supper to which all students on the island were invited. It was held at Mount Stuart, an impressive neo-gothic mansion, owned by the Marquess of Bute. "Haggis was brought in with pipers and Scottish dancers and there were all sorts of traditional things going on that I didn't understand."

I was careful to avoid questions that might trigger disturbing memories – I had checked the questions in advance with the school and Argyll and Bute Council. This did not always prevent children sharing horrors, unprompted, of what they had seen. One child, slicing her arm through the air, spoke of seeing a man beheaded. Jana, too, shared some of the violence she had seen. "We saw two people in the door who were fighting. And I saw a man he had plasters all over his body." Her older sister, Fedaa, was clear where she wanted to live. "I want to stay here because all the homes in Syria are broken and fallen down." Ali had other reasons. "If I stay in Syria there will be some people who will take me away. I want to stay with my Mum." Ali, whose father had died in the conflict, was concerned that, as he grew older, he could be recruited by either side of the civil war but at some stage he wanted to return. "When I'm an aerospace engineer, I will go back to Syria." Malek, too, had a clear ambition. He wanted to go to university to study immunology. "If I finish my education I will stay here, get a job and settle in. I will only go back and visit if it is safe."

When Malek first arrived on the britain, he was depressed. "I could not imagine how to live on an island, but then I saw how beautiful it was. I think it is even safer here than on the mainland. It is a small community and I know a lot of locals as friends." But Bute is not like Damascus where Malek had everything within easy reach. "There is not much to do for young people here, apart from walking around." Malek was the oldest of the Syrian children, had already left school and was waiting to see if he had done well enough in his exams to take up a university place. He welcomed the chance to talk about Syria. "I will never forget it. I spent my childhood there. They were good days, before the war started in March 2011. We held olive branches and white flags for peace, but the army started hitting people with sticks. A few months later, during a large peaceful protest, the army started shooting. We had to bury three victims the next day. The army weren't just killing people – they would go into their houses, harm people and steal stuff. The rebels had no choice but to defend themselves and fight back. Then all sorts of people came into the country to do their own stuff. Our house has not been burnt down but there is nothing in it. We had expensive furniture, amazing decoration, my own room, but everything has been stolen, even the pipes. I left with only a change of clothes. We thought we would be back in a few days."

Concerned I had not, unwittingly, activated painful memories I asked Malek how he felt sharing his experience of the war. "I don't mind talking about it because it is part of me now, but I don't think anyone has asked me before. I don't think they would like to know, or they would not like to make me remember the things I have suffered." In avoiding discussions about the war Malek never knew whether people were being respectful, not wishing to upset him, or were just not interested.

After buying chocolate for the children, Mitch, Pat and I visited Mount Stuart. We entered the Marble Hall where the children had sat at round tables, bemused by haggis being brought into the room on a silver platter to the sound of bagpipes. I found it difficult to imagine what the Syrian children, unfamiliar with Burns or the brooding works of Sir Walter Scott, would have thought of such a building. So different from the mosques in Syria with their curved mihrabs, minaret towers, gold calligraphy and mosaics.

Mitch and I took the early morning ferry back to Wemyss Bay, happy that we had unique footage to contribute to our film *Child Migrants Welcome?* capturing experiences of child migrants across the UK. "This is a special place," I said as we looked back to Rothesay harbour. "Let's do a film just about the Syrian children on the Isle of Bute."

Seeking Sanctuary on a Scottish Island, after being approved by all participants and Argyll and Bute Council, was first screened at the gallery, Transitions, in Glasgow during Refugee Week in June 2018. Maureen Shaw, Depute Head Teacher of the primary school of Rothesay Joint Campus, and Morag Brown, who oversees the refugee resettlement programme for Argyll and Bute, were there for the post-screening discussion. The film opened with underwater images of the seabed at Scalpsie Bay and ended with the sunset over Rothesay harbour, but it was the Syrian children who stole the show. This tender, fifteen-minute film has been shown to students, teachers, health workers, child psychotherapists and many others. Out of respect for the children and their families *Seeking Sanctuary on a Scottish Island* is not available online but can be screened on request.

In June 2019 Sajid Javid, as home secretary under Theresa May, announced the UK Resettlement Scheme to replace the Vulnerable Persons Relocation Scheme post 2020, consolidating three programmes and broadening its geographical focus.[8] Then, in 2020, COVID-19 swept across the world, borders closed and progress on refugee resettlement schemes stalled. In March 2021 Priti Patel, home secretary under Boris Johnson who having replaced Theresa May as prime minister in July 2019 before winning a general election in December 2019 on the basis of getting Brexit done, spoke with pride in Britain having met its target of settling 20,000 of Syrian refugees since 2015. Over six years, 25,000 refugees were accepted by all UK Government-funded resettlement schemes, around half of whom were children. Priti Patel vowed that "Global Britain will continue its proud tradition of providing safe haven to those in need through safe and legal routes."[9]

....

For this chapter to be included I needed to procure consent forms from all those who had participated in the film and from the parents of children still under sixteen. But how was I to make contact with the Syrian families given they had moved to the Scottish mainland? Fortunately, I was still in email contact with Malek, the older boy who put me in contact by email with Rabia and Ali, now over sixteen, and the parents of Fedaa and Jana. But repeated emails yielded no response – people are busy, the form for the publisher was legalistic in tone and difficult, no doubt, for those less confident in English. I had no means of contacting Safa or her parents.

In January 2023, two days before visiting Glasgow for a Celtic music festival, I sent an email offering to meet people in person – this was my last chance to secure the necessary permissions. Rabia rang back and we arranged to meet in the House of Sher, an Asian shopping mall in a bleak part of Glasgow. She drove in from Motherwell with her mother who went to shop in the Asian supermarket whilst she and I caught up in the Syrian Pie restaurant. This former shy, fourteen-year-old, seven years earlier had hated Scottish weather, was now a confident young woman, dressed in a woollen tartan jacket, who had come to appreciate the cold. Rabia had not only passed her driving test, but gained British citizenship, was working as a part-time carer who enjoyed listening to her clients' life stories and was training to be a dental nurse. As she signed the consent form, I shared my despair at ever contacting Safa. She smiled and took a form, "Safa is my neighbour." When I asked about Fedaa and Jana Rabia introduced me to the man who had served us *zaatar* and cheese pie. "He is their relation." Following a phone call we left a form behind the counter for Fedaa and Jana's father to pick up later. When I asked Rabia whether she was in contact with Ali, she looked up his phone number. I met up with Ali after his shift in a Glasgow luxury hotel. Following a five-month break in his education, after leaving Bute, he was now studying for his higher exams and planned to do an apprenticeship in electronic engineering, his ambition to become an aerospace engineer now tempered by reality. He had a wide circle of friends with young people from different backgrounds, still enjoyed rapping in his bedroom and was clearly a support for his mother and two younger siblings.

I was still reeling with gratitude at Rabia's ability to put me in contact with the other Syrian children when I realized a key contributor to the chapter was Malek who, although supportive, had not returned the signed form. I knew his family had set up a Syrian bakery in Glasgow, having already established a similar successful business on the Isle of Bute. After an internet search I took a taxi to Baljaffray shopping centre in Bearsden, a half an hour drive from central Glasgow. "Malek?" I asked as a young man stepped forward to serve me from behind the counter of Helmi's bakery. He gasped, "I don't believe this. I live in Dundee now. I am only here for the day." We laughed with delight at my unbelievable luck. It was good to catch up. Malek had stayed on in Dundee after finishing his degree course and was now applying for a four-year post-graduate medicine qualification to become a doctor. As I tucked into a raspberry and pistachio cake, a Syrian couple entered the bakery. Malek introduced me. "This is Fedaa and Jana's parents. It's the first time they have visited in over a year." Their father had already picked up the form from the Syrian Pie restaurant. My good fortune knew no bounds. I felt some God, some angel, of whatever faith, was looking out for me.

All the children and parents I met after seven years spoke of their gratitude at finding sanctuary on the Isle of Bute despite Rabia admitting that, at first, she felt scared of the place. The children had received a good education, the locals were friendly and they could take their first steps at integration. But, although city life was challenging, there were more opportunities in Glasgow for study and employment. The children and their families could access a broader range of facilities – mosques, halal restaurants, the House of Sher and there were more opportunities to make friends and things to do. None had plans to return to Syria, although there was concern for family members, particularly grandparents back 'home'.

Although sad to see children leave the Isle of Bute Pat, Maureen and Lorna should feel reassured they provided a temporary sanctuary, a sound education and support for the children to make their own way in the world. In the words of Maureen, whose names, "Fedaa," "Jana," "Ali," "Malek," "Rabia," "Safa" she practised on her tongue, "Children work their own magic."

CHAPTER 16
"WE WILL WIN"
Mariia who arrived, aged thirteen, from Ukraine in 2022

Parishioners, prompted by the Sunday morning peel of bells, opened the doors of their half-timbered houses and headed towards St Mary's church. I followed until I reached The Vicarage. It was not the vicar but Shushik who answered the door, dressed in a cotton dress, the bright yellow centres of white daisies on a blue background, reminiscent, by design or chance, of the colours of the Ukrainian flag.

Shushik ushered me into a large back garden with swings, trampolines, footballs and frisbees. Mariia, Shushik's thirteen-year-old daughter, joined us. She was taller than her mother but with the same dark, wavy hair, reaching past her shoulders. She wore a T-shirt, green and white check trousers, trainers and a denim jacket. Anya, our interpreter, arrived to complete the party. We sat round the garden table eating warm *deruny*, Ukrainian potato pancakes, that Shushik had made. I handed her a packet of macaroons in exchange. "Our favourite," said Shushik. I felt grateful to Shushik and Mariia for agreeing to talk just four months since Russia had invaded Ukraine, causing the fastest and largest displacement of people in Europe since the Second World War. By August 2022, 3 million Ukrainian refugees had fled to Europe, Mariia, Shushik and Anya amongst them; 6.6 million had been displaced within Ukraine[1] and two-thirds of Ukrainian children had left their homes.[2]

I was intrigued as to how Shushik and Mariia, through the government-sponsored Homes for Ukraine scheme, had arrived in Horsham, this quintessential English town, forty miles south of London. The scheme invites individuals, charities, community groups and businesses to sponsor Ukrainians to come to Britain, allowing them to stay for free in their home or in a separate property. Children under eighteen can apply as part of a family unit which includes their parent or legal guardian.

Mariia explained that she had been learning English for ten years every Saturday with Ira, a Ukrainian woman who used to live in Kyiv. Four years ago, Ira moved to Horsham to live with her English husband, so lessons transferred online. When the British government opened the Homes for Ukraine Scheme[3] in March 2022 Ira approached Lisa, the vicar of St Mary's. Lisa was working with Ukrainian residents in Horsham to match British hosts with Ukrainians fleeing war, given the lack of a formal process to do this. "We have a little Ukraine here," smiled Shushik, explaining there were now 200 Ukrainians in Horsham, sixty of whom learnt English every Tuesday in the church. Those who didn't attend had already found jobs.

It was later, though email correspondence with Lisa, that I found out more about the matching process that led to Shushik and Mariia living in The Vicarage. 'We decided we had space for a mum and a child and felt it would be better if the child was a different age to our children, so there were less issues with differing parenting styles, bedtime rules etc. When the photo of Shushik & Mariia was emailed to me … I quickly felt they would be a good "match" for our family. We began getting to know them through messenger and video chats and submitted the visas. They have been the most beautiful family to share our home with.'

Before coming to England Shushik and Mariia lived in a flat in Kyiv with Mariia's father, Sergie, and her dog, Cleopatra. At the beginning of the war the area became a target for Russian attack with regular air sirens and frequent shelling of nearby buildings. "You never knew what to expect," Shushik explained. After four days of bombing the family left for Chernivtsi where Sergei's wider family live. They fled under constant bombardment, joining huge traffic jams, unable to move forward, backwards, to the right or left. As they drew into a petrol station, the sound of sirens warned them of an imminent attack, then missiles started flying overhead. Mariia and Shushik sat in the back of the car not knowing if the vehicles that thundered past them belonged to Russia or Ukraine.

Petrified Shushik burst into tears. The side door of a military vehicle opened, and a woman soldier peered out. "'Don't cry, we will win.' I've held onto that belief so hard" sighed Shushik. "It doesn't make any sense why they started this war," cried Anya. "In the twenty-first century, why would you do that?" "We heard warnings, but we didn't expect Russia would attack and invade" Shushik added. "It's crazy. Unbelievable. It was safe in Chernivtsi but then there was a bomb in neigbouring Vinnytsia which killed dozens of people."

When the visas arrived on 15 April 2022, Mariia and her mother celebrated Easter in Ukraine, then caught the bus to Poland. Mariia's last sight of her father was of him running behind the bus, in tears, prolonging the inevitable departure. Most men, aged eighteen to sixty, were banned from leaving Ukraine, in anticipation that the government would need them to fight – 90 per cent of those fleeing Ukraine are women and children.[4] In the case of Mariia's father, a psychotherapist, his role is to support adults traumatized by war. Shushik's and Mariia's journey to Poland took twenty-two hours, much longer than in peaceful times with long queues at the border as officials checked their documents. Shushik and Mariia spent just a few hours in Poland before flying to Gatwick, each carrying a small backpack. "Some had hardly any clothes or were just wearing socks on their feet." They were met at the airport by Lisa's husband.

Shushik was grateful to her hosts. "They greeted us like family and made us feel at home. We have wonderful people around us." Mariia was excited to be in Britain but the realization of what she had left soon caught up with her. "The first night wasn't bad. It was green, it was beautiful. It's like *Wow, I'm in England* but after that you understand you are not in Ukraine anymore." The vicar's young children, girl twins aged nine and a boy aged six, provided a welcome distraction. "During the day we play together, running and jumping on the trampoline so I can forget about the problems in our country. They [the children] are so funny but every evening, it all comes back. I chat with my dad on the phone. He shows me, Cleopatra, my dog, and I start crying – I wanted to bring her to

Figure 12 Marking the first week as an international household, a week after the arrival of Mariia and Shushik in Horsham in 2022. Courtesy of Riasenko and Barnett families.

England, but this was impossible. It would take longer to prepare documents for the dog than for the visas and she would need to stay in quarantine when she arrived." In Europe entry requirements for transporting pets were relaxed.[5]

Mariia's main fear was for her father's safety. He was working at a crisis centre with people who were affected by war and was no longer using his consulting room as people were too afraid to visit him in his flat. Instead, he supported people online, working at home at night with people as far away as the United States but this too was dangerous. "There is no underground facility – just a wall to hide behind to protect him from the shelling." There were other family members still in Ukraine – Shushik's younger sister and husband and her mother who was seriously ill. Shushik was no stranger to war. As a child, in 1994, she and her mother left Armenia because of war with Azerbaijan.

Mariia enjoyed her new school in Horsham. "I love all subjects but maybe my favourite is music, or English as the teacher is very good." There is no dedicated EAL (English as an Additional Language) support, but Mariia has continued her English lessons with Ira. Sometimes the teachers provided Mariia with Ukraine translations and a Ukraine member of staff, resident in Britain for twenty-four years, worked at the school to support children's welfare. Then there was Google Translate. "I am the only one who can use my phone," Mariia admitted with a smile. She had made friends with a group of girls who, when she arrived, showed her around. If they saw her alone and sad, they helped her, "with my mood, to be happy. They ask me things and we talk about everything." The school in Horsham was very different from the dance academy in Kyiv she had attended since the age of eight and where, three hours a day, she trained as a professional dancer. The school closed as soon as Putin's 'special military operation' began and pupils dispersed across the globe. Only her dance teacher remained. At first, Mariia talked online with her fellow dance students. "Now it happens not very often. I miss them."

Mariia talked of her passion for Ukraine traditional folk dances and of her disappointment at missing out on the next year's timetabled lessons of dances from around the world – Polish, Slavic and Spanish. She pulled up videos of the *gopak* I remembered Ukrainians performing in my hometown, Rochdale, near Manchester – the way they had crouched and kicked up their legs without seeming to touch the floor had mesmerized me as a child. Many Ukrainians settled in the north-west of England after the Second World War. Some were recruited to work in Lancashire cotton mills. Mariia brought up more images on her phone of Ukrainian dance costumes, the embroidery typical of different regions. Mother and daughter exchanged looks and Mariia left to collect something to show me.

I asked Anya and Shushik if they kept up with events in Ukraine. "For the first two months I checked the news constantly, like every fifteen minutes. I still check it but once in every two to three hours," Anya replied. Shushik also kept abreast of events. "I check the news every morning before I call my husband and my mother. If they don't pick up for a long time, I start to worry." Shushik was worried, too, how her family seemed to have got used to the war, that they were no longer scared. "When they see a missile flying above their heads they just wonder where it will fall." Anya and Shushik felt especially for those who had started new lives in one part of Ukraine and then had to move again, losing everything twice.

Mariia returned with two beautiful embroidered *vyshyvankas* (shirts) – one hers and one her mother's. Her father, too, had a 100-year-old *vyshyvanka*, embroidered by his grandmother. I imagined Shushik and Mariia throwing out items from their backpacks to make room for their *vyshyvankas*, poignant reminders of a life they were fleeing and to which they hoped to return. Mariia held her *vyshyvanka* against her chest – white cotton with an embroidered front panel, tied at the neck; the same embroidered design, stitched along puffy sleeves, clasped at the cuff. In another setting Mariia would wear her *vyshyvanka* over a circular skirt, a garland of flowers on her head. The music would start, she would twirl and tap, link arms with her friends and bow to applause. Mariia had started to learn Irish tap at a dance school in Horsham but it reminded her too much of what she had lost. "When we danced [in Kyiv] it was like one team. It was a real childhood. I was happy to be a dancer but not any more. It's hard to be cheerful when your country is in danger." Her mother agreed, "She has turned into an adult faster because of these events." Not only her childhood but Mariia's ambition to be a profesional dancer was a casualty of Putin's war. "If the situation doesn't improve then, probably, dancing won't help me succeed in life."

As a practising child psychologist, Shushik could see the impact of war both on children who had stayed and those who had left Ukraine. "I feel sorry for both. For kids here, maybe it's a bit better because they don't hear sirens every night; they can sleep but they miss their motherland. They worry about their fathers in Ukraine; and about their future. They cannot trust anybody; they have lost hope." I asked Shushik if age affected children differently. "It's probably easier for younger children. They can forget their problems and just play with other children. It's much more difficult for teenagers who are better at analysing the situation. They miss family members and dream about going back."

Galyna, a Britain resident from Ukraine, who has been helping newly arrived Ukrainian families on a voluntary basis, made a similar point – I had interviewed her days earlier in east London. "From what I hear and see from my friends who have teenagers, some children are really struggling. I think because they have deeper connection with friends. My friend's son, he's fifteen and he's refused to leave his room since they came. He doesn't want to go to school. He doesn't talk to people. So, for teenagers, the trauma is being disconnected from life, because they had more of their own life [in Ukraine]. Younger children seem to get on better." Galyna quoted an example of a local primary school displaying welcome signs and how the Ukrainian children had appreciated being stretched academically. One child even enjoyed school lunch. "They have pizza and burgers, I love it. I don't want to go back." But children differed. "A lot of it is how resilient the child is, what they experience … My friend and son, they lived in a basement for three weeks because Kyiv was shelled. Another friend said the child screams at night because they'd been hiding in a basement. Another, their home was destroyed. Children have lost family, fathers have been killed, pets have been killed. For these children, there's no specialist help. What makes it more difficult is they live with strangers. You don't have privacy … to grieve or cry." Shushik, too, found significant variation in how children responded. "Some are good at adapting and some are not. Their mentality, their language, their culture, are different."

Mariia and Shushik were unclear about their future. "We are grateful for all this support and from British people but we understand it is temporary and even though we have this visa for three years, it's hard to plan. We want to be more independent and work; to stay at least until the end of the year and then return, but it's complicated." Shushik had found work in the kitchen of a children's nursery but was hoping to improve her English enough to return to her profession as a child psychologist. I remembered Galyna's words, "For these children, there's no specialist help at all." Education departments in Ireland, Poland and Britain have committed to providing mental health support, but it was unclear whether any services would be available in Ukrainian.[6] I wondered how long it would be before the benefits of employing professionals like Shushik who could speak the children's language and understand their culture were utilized.

I asked Shushik and Anya about the two different schemes – the Ukraine Family Scheme for Ukrainians[7] who have an immediate or extended family member who are British citizens or have permanent status in the UK, as in the case of Galyna, who was hosting her niece, and the Homes for Ukraine Scheme through which Mariia and her mother had come to Britain.

"Glitches? Is that the right word? asked Anya.

"Yes, a very good word."

"It is based on emotion," Shushik explained.

It seemed a polite way of saying, what many professionals, charities and others had expressed, that details of both schemes had not been thought through. Major 'glitches' of the Ukraine Family Scheme centred around accommodation and financial support. "Even close relatives cannot live together in one house for a long time especially when they accept a lot of people and their house is not big enough. At least in Homes for Ukraine the sponsors get some financial support." Those hosting family members are not entitled to any reimbursement whereas hosts under the sponsorship scheme are entitled to a monthly £350 tax free payment. Kate Smart of the organization, Settled, found that the pressure to take in as many relatives as possible led to people agreeing to more than they could cope with so 'people are ending up at the doors of local authorities needing homeless accommodation.'[8] Galyna, who had taken in her niece, did not expect reimbursement. "It's my family, I don't expect to get paid." But she recognized that her niece, as a skilled hairdresser and single without children, would find work and accommodation more easily than women with young children who could not afford the cost of childcare and housing or find employment.

One of the main issues, according to Shushik, with the Homes for Ukraine Scheme was that there was no safety net if the relationship broke down. "It's not that Ukrainians or British are bad. It's just that people didn't expect they would have to live together for such a long time. Now the families can host Ukrainians for one year but, for the majority, it's still unclear what to do next." Galyna had shared examples of where such relationships had failed, the most tragic being of a woman who, on hearing her husband was missing in action, probably killed, started to scream. The British hosts asked her to leave. "I understand they were not cruel because somebody's grief is very depressing, but, if this person's done nothing wrong, why do they have to leave in the worst moment of their life?" Just two months into both schemes, 480 families and 180 single people had been made homeless.[9] Research by the Work Rights Centre, after six months, established that one in ten Ukrainians had been threatened with eviction at some point of their stay in the UK, with risks particularly high for those on the Family Scheme.[10] Galyna believed this was a structural failure – in England at least. "Somebody should be responsible, a trained person or a local authority. It shouldn't be an individual." The Scottish and Welsh governments had, at least, acted as sponsors, until they had to suspend the scheme due to demand. Galyna also knew of generous hosts – one paid for a tutor for a Ukrainian child and arranged for friends in Europe to look after a family pet. "They've gone way beyond what was expected."

The Ukraine Family Scheme was brought in by the British government on 4 March 2022. The Homes for Ukraine Scheme opened two weeks later. Britain's initial response to the crisis in Ukraine was pitiful in comparison to that of the European Union. Whilst Home Office staff handed out KitKat chocolate bars and crisps to Ukrainian refugees from a pop up stall in Calais,[11] the EU acted decisively in activating the Temporary Protection Directive (TPD).[12] Without the need for the examination of individual applications, those fleeing Ukraine were able to access harmonized rights across the EU for three years – including residence, housing, medical assistance, and access to the labour market and education, giving Ukrainians the right to live and work in any of the twenty-seven EU states, as well as Switzerland, Norway, Liechtenstein and Iceland. There was no need for visas, security checks or passports, with airlines instructed to accept birth certificates and identity cards if those fleeing Ukraine had no travel documents. The numbers speak for themselves, with neighbouring countries, many of whom share their fear of Russian aggression, receiving the majority of those who have fled Ukraine. By August 2022 Poland had given protection to 1,274,130 Ukrainians. The number of Ukrainian refugees in Germany was 971,100 and in the Czech Republic 412,959.[13] Yet this solidarity exposed double standards in the EU's deeply politicized – and often discriminatory – nature of providing refugee protection. A Syrian refugee, in a camp in Germany, wrote 'I feel the pain and suffering of Ukrainian refugees more than most. But when … I saw how enthusiastically Polish society welcomed them, it hurt so much. How is it possible that on one border you beat people, and yet on the other you give them soup and cookies? Isn't this racist? … Why are bombs falling on Ukraine more important than bombs falling on Syria?'[14] I had heard similar viewpoints from asylum seekers in Britain, and those who work with them.

The UK's approach to the Ukraine refugee crisis is more restrictive than the EU's as not all Ukrainians are eligible – they need a UK family connection or sponsorship arrangement and they must apply for a visa in advance. Hosts and Ukrainians have struggled to overcome bureaucratic loopholes, visas were issued to some family members and not others, younger siblings were separated from older siblings. Unaccompanied children, even with a sponsor and the parents' permission, were refused initially, although this was later overturned.[15] Those with material and other resources, good networks, proficiency in English language and use of the internet were most likely to get through, particularly at the beginning of the scheme. Anastasia Salnikova, who volunteers helping refugees, commented that the first wave of people who came to Britain were generally those who escaped early and had a bit of money, but those who are only recently free from places like Bucha and Mariupol are 'in a disadvantaged situation.'[16] Certainly, it is unlikely that children from the besieged city of Mariupol whose parents had inserted name tags in their children's backpacks and who handed them over to strangers for safety have arrived in the UK.[17] Nor a woman who Galyna and others are raising funds for, who is sleeping on a mattress in a basement with her child with cerebral palsy. "They're from Kherson and they are now somewhere in Central Ukraine. There's absolutely nothing left of their lives … she wouldn't be able to get anywhere in Europe." Despite these criticisms, 'glitches' and relative limits of the UK's response, as of 30 May 2023 there were 230,800 visas issued to Ukrainians by the UK government.[18] It is too soon to see the long-term impact of the schemes.

Britain's approach to refugees from Ukraine, as with the EU, is more liberal than to other asylum seekers who are not generally permitted to work and can only claim benefits if their asylum application is successful. It is perhaps wishful thinking to hope the schemes for Ukrainians could be an important precedent for treating refugees from elsewhere with more humanity. There are already signs that they might be given as a reason, because of resource implications, not to host refugees from elsewhere. The UK approach to the Ukrainian crisis reflects a broader trend in selecting and differentiating between refugees from different conflicts or parts of the world.[19]

Mariia told me she would be fourteen in a few days. Since her arrival she had held onto the hope that her father would join them for the celebration, a hope that was fading fast. She was doing her best for him to be there in spirit. She planned, on the day, to visit the Sherlock Holmes Museum on Baker Street in London – she and her father shared a love of detective stories. "He dreams and I dream about them, and we read them together as a family." She also hoped one day to visit the Freud Museum in Hampstead based in the house where Sigmund Freud, the psychoanalyst, lived when he fled Vienna before the Second World War. It was her father's suggestion. "You should go. Maybe you will become a psychotherapist too."

"Would you like to be a psychotherapist?" I asked.

"Yes, but I love to dance as well."

I was glad of the long drive home to reflect on the conversations with Mariia, Shushik, Anya and Galyna, merging and competing for space in my head as I ate the left over *deruny* – images of Mariia dancing, trampolining, crying over her dog, missing her father. Just outside London the traffic piled up. I was unable to move forward, backwards, left or right. Then a petrol tanker drove beside me. It was then I remembered the woman soldier who opened the tank door to reassure Shushik that "We will win." It is the image that has surfaced above all else.

To James and Ira Strong, Stephen and Lisa Barnett, we will be forever grateful.

Mariia and Shushik

CONCLUSION
"If I had a magic wand": Final thoughts and insights

A boy, in white shorts, steps off from the Libyan coast onto a line of boats that serve as stepping-stones to Europe. Another boy, with a naked torso, using a huge dice as his life buoy, battles with the waves. A girl, carrying a city of skyscrapers in her backpack, strides over a stretch of water to firmer ground. Another girl in a pink dress, with a boat of passengers tucked under each arm, wades into the shallows off the Moroccan coast. Snakes slithering into treacherous waters and ladders propped against mountains warn and tempt the youth in equal measure.

I stand mesmerized by the fantastical paintings of the Belgian-born, Mexico-based artist, Francis Alÿs. The introductory panel of *Don't Cross the Bridge before You Get to the River*[1] explains that the exhibition is 'a meditation on the political and social barriers that keep the excluded people from the South from enjoying a better future'. In his watery, fluid paintings of blue seas, ochre sands, brown land masses and lithe, young bodies, Alÿs seems to communicate so much about child migrants' lives – their resourcefulness and resolve; the weight of responsibility they carry on their shoulders; their independence, yet solidarity with other children; the element of chance as to where the dice falls.

Yet, as I stand in the Museo de Arte Contemporáneo de Buenos Aires (MACBA), I feel a sense of frustration. We do not know why these young people have left their homes, whether they arrive safely on distant shores. They are, as it were, suspended in motion, on the cusp of life. Then my frustration gives way to gratitude. Those who have shared with me their experiences of migration have shed light on the possible back and future stories of these wanderers and of others too. Children who have migrated in earlier decades with families or without, on fishing boats, cruise ships and aeroplanes; who have found love, had children and grandchildren; who have slipped on snake-filled paths but have scaled ladders, too, not just through the occasional throw of the dice but through their own resilience. But there are other stories that are more difficult to imagine, that none of us may ever know, of children and young people who have drowned or disappeared.

Concluding thoughts on key themes

Departures

Alÿs states that the children, depicted in his paintings, are migrating to enjoy a better future, aspirations the Global North will do everything to block. Such rationale emphasizes the economic 'pull' rather than 'push' factors of war, discrimination, natural disaster or climate change and masks the historical and political ties between the Global North and Global South. The parents of several child migrants featured in this book, particularly in earlier decades, came from countries that were part of the British Empire, some as children of British citizens, and where Britain has participated in global conflicts.

Many children in this study came to Britain with, or to join, adult family members. Where the adults migrated first, factors such as the outbreak of war, a change in family circumstances or the introduction of stricter immigration rules could lead to children migrating sooner or later than the adults intended, if indeed that was the plan. A research project that also included adults could tease out further information about how far they took account of young people's needs or wishes in such life changing decisions. But applying Western-originated views, as enshrined in the UN Convention on the Rights of the Child,[2] to children's participation in decisions around migration is not straightforward. Argun and Eylem were opposed to leaving their country of origin at the time but later acknowledged the wisdom of their elders. On occasion a parent's needs were a major consideration – Linh, for example, was chosen to keep her father company on his escape from Vietnam. Where teenage boys were expected to contribute to the household income, the family's interests, indeed survival, perhaps overrode that of the children's interests or wishes. Parents who, in desperation, sent their children on the *Kindertransport* were clearly thinking of the children's rather than their own interests. But often migration seemed to be of benefit to the family as a whole and sometimes for a mix of reasons – to escape war, discrimination or poverty and to access work or education opportunities – children's interests were 'part of' rather than 'subsumed within' the family's 'broad commonality of interest'.[3] When children came as part of a government resettlement scheme, as refugees from war in Syria or Ukraine, the reasons for migration were more clear cut, as with children who came on their own. Mariam left to escape FGM and forced marriage; Yosef avoided prolonged military conscription under a dictatorship although how far his reasons, at such a young age, were thought through seems in doubt – he followed the crowd.

Journeys

For children, such as Eylem or Bilqis, leaving a physical home or a landscape[4] was significant but, overwhelmingly, for others it was being left by, or leaving, loved ones that was the most traumatic. Saying goodbye was so painful that Pola blocked out certain memories of the final departure; for older children, such as Henry, saying goodbye to friends could be as, or more, important than leaving extended family.[5] Yet even children who were reluctant to leave could get caught up in the excitement of travelling. Long journeys by sea, such as by Linh and Argun, were particularly memorable as was Yosef's journey across the Sahara and then Europe – dodging traffickers, border controls and prison officers. Some children, particularly from Syria, spent years 'to-ing' and 'fro-ing' across borders[6] – moving to the countryside to escape war or spending time in refugee camps. Children, like Ahmed, had little idea of where they were heading whilst others such as Nimo had clear expectations of what Britain might offer, expectations that could lead, on arrival, to disillusion – at the graffiti and grime of dilapidated estates, cramped living conditions and the piercing cold.[7] Yet there were the bright lights of the city to compensate, or the beauty of a Scottish island. It was often the taste and smell of strange foods; the sound of traffic and unfamiliar languages; the sight of different people, clothing and religions, that lingered in people's memories.[8]

Arrival

Children and young people were not only 'to-ing' and 'fro-ing' across, and within, borders but, on arrival, between different households and living arrangements in the UK. Richard went to live with his grandparents when his mother migrated to Australia, Maurice became homeless when the relationship with his parents broke down and Ahmed moved between different care arrangements after his mother's death. Ruhul, refusing to return to Sylhet with his parents, moved in with another Bengali family and then with friends. Pola left her mother and siblings to get married. Again, it was relationships that were most important. Except for children who came with both parents, and left no extended family behind, children's ability to settle was dependent on how well they were able to re-establish relationships with family who they no longer recognized or to whom they harboured feelings of resentment at having been abandoned.[9] Or children had to adapt, as in Argun's case, to new family members – stepparents, new siblings or extended family they had never met.[10] Children invariably missed those they had left behind. Such transitions could be challenging and it seems clear that even young children, such as Richard, would have benefitted, circumstances allowing, if the reasons for migration had been explained and the children more fully prepared.[11] Forced separation by states between child and adult carer during migration, as on the Mexican US border,[12] is, of course, a different matter, but even the *Kindertransport*, where the motivation was to save children but where some never saw their parents again, raises uncomfortable questions.[13]

There is no doubt that feelings of loss, experienced through serial migration, could be important at crucial stages of a child's development and could last a lifetime.[14] During their troubled teenage years Maurice and Ahmed missed fathers, grandfathers or uncles who had remained in their country of origin. Roberta, Pola and others did not return in time to see people who had cared for them in their parents' absence, a regret that could last for years. But children can be resilient and the role of the extended family in migration is impressive, particularly if they are able to sustain a sense of familyhood across borders.[15] New technology has made this easier,[16] although it can never replace the touch of a loved one,[17] as the Home Office, in separating families, sometimes claims.[18] And whilst some relationships were weakened through migration, others were strengthened. Young people formed strong friendships with peers, got involved in collective struggle, found partners, some marrying early. The experience of early loss made Pola and Argun determined, as adults, to hold onto, re-establish and sustain strong family bonds across borders.

Education

Today children in London are unlikely, as did Roberta in the 1960s, to find they are the only Black child in the class. No longer would it be acceptable, at least overtly, for staff to have such stereotypical views as experienced by Pola, of what course of study or work is appropriate along race or gender lines. Indeed, school achievement of girls of Bangladeshi heritage in east London has increased dramatically since the 1970s.[19] For children who arrive in their mid-to-late teens, there are now more educational routes to qualifications than in earlier decades, but new arrivals can still, as did Ruhul, experience long delays in securing an appropriate place in school or college.[20]

It is clear from these testimonies that teachers can have a huge influence on child migrants' experience of education, either believing in them or not seeing their potential.[21] English language provision is patchy, varies in quality, rarely takes account of the time it takes to gain qualifications[22] and has experienced cutbacks in recent years. Few schools build on, and recognize, the multilingual skills that children bring.[23] New arrivals may be made to feel unwelcome by other students, including those whose parents or grandparents were once migrants themselves, as was Nimo's experience.[24] Not all schools, despite today's equality legislation and anti-racist policies, take such matters seriously enough. Neither do most integrate migration studies, including the legacy of empire, into the curriculum.[25] But it is to the credit of good schools, committed teachers but, above all, to children themselves that some have done remarkably well.

Adult or second chance pathways to education and employment opportunities, as well as financial support that avoids young migrants being classified as overseas students, are essential for those whose education is disrupted. Society benefits from the investment in, and skills of such children. Mariam, who arrived aged sixteen, qualified as a nurse and cared for us during the COVID-19 pandemic. Malek, also sixteen when he arrived, having gained a degree in medical sciences at the University of Dundee, is now applying to train as a doctor. But our responsibility should not depend on how talented young people are or how they conform to an idealized view of the 'good' immigrant child. National legislation such as the Children Act in England[26] and the UN Convention on the Rights of the Child[27] requires the government to take account of the 'best interests' and safeguarding of all children, including a right to education.

Stepping out

Particularly in east London there have been spaces for young people to learn, play, pray and work with others who have migrated from the same village, city or country. Places where they do not face racism or other forms of discrimination;[28] where they can explore their identity and pursue cultural,[29] linguistic, religious[30] or political interests. But there are still instances where child migrants may feel isolated if there is no one from their place of origin in their neighbourhood, who speaks the same language or shares their beliefs – Zohra in Glasgow mixed with few other children of Muslim Pakistani background and even in 'super-diverse' east London it took time for Mariam to meet someone who spoke her mother tongue. Nimo and Eylem sought friendships regardless of ethnicity, belief or country of origin, choosing particular colleges and universities to achieve this. Such cross-ethnic friendships can broaden opportunities and allow girls to withstand pressures within the family or specific community.[31] But young people's preparedness to mix with others of a different background, whether in school or in a political party, at a youth club or place of worship, depends on whether they feel welcomed or, conversely, whether they face individual or institutional racism or other forms of discrimination.[32]

Ethnicity, gender and class

Children's gender, ethnicity or socio-economic background all brought challenges.[33] Girls fled from, or had to negotiate, their family's and community's expectations around marriage, particularly if, like Linh, Eylem or Zohra, they chose an English partner. Teenage boys were often expected to support the family income back in the country of origin or in Britain. Gender and race intersected with young Black males, such as Richard, being stopped by police more frequently than their white peers.[34] Whilst migration can be a leveler, some young people from middle-class backgrounds seemed more confident to pursue their ambitions. Ruhul followed his dream to be a filmmaker and Pola rose to the House of Lords. Both grew up in families with considerable social and cultural capital in their country of origin,[35] although they too had to overcome barriers. But other Bangladeshi youth, such as Ayub and Jalal, also found routes out of low-paid, insecure work due to their talent, persistence, activism and second chance educational opportunities – gaining degrees, finding employment in the public sector as well as pursuing political careers.

Impact on adult life

i) Returns Few people visited their country of origin before the age of eighteen. Many did not return for years, sometimes with reluctance, and often with marital partners and their own children. Those not able to return included more recent migrants from Syria and Eritrea where it is still dangerous to do so.[36] People's first return to visit family who had cared for them as children – grandparents, mothers, fathers, aunts and uncles – could be particularly emotional.[37] Some, like Roberta, returned too late, a regret she harbours to this day. A few returned to get married or, later, to pursue charitable, business or unfulfilled political ambitions, as has Ayub, although children and grandchildren, living in Britain, mean people will never sever links entirely. Some, like Linh, returned to fill gaps in their memories or, like Eylem, to explore aspects of identity they had lost or rejected, only to realize, having spent years away, that places and people had changed.[38]

ii) Feelings of home Some people considered 'home' as either England or Somaliland; Great Britain or India – although young children on the Isle of Bute had no such divided loyalties. Straddling continents with ease, they stated that "Home is Syria and Scotland." Such clarity may not last – Malek, the eldest Syrian, was weary of moving. "I have started here so I won't go back and start again." Feelings of belonging shifted over time, back to people's roots or to where they had settled. Conflict with authorities meant people might never feel part of a nation, irrespective of their citizenship status or where they lived. Richard identified as Jamaican rather than British, Maurice as Igbo, rather than British or Nigerian. For many 'home' was a city, region, village or neighbourhood within a country – Biafra or the Isle of Bute, Maulvi Bazaar or Spitalfields but after decades in Britain, some still felt in limbo.[39] Duncan felt, neither at home in the UK nor in India, tossed out by the city he knew as Calcutta, now Kolkata, the city of his birth.

iii) Trauma and the role of creativity Previous research indicates that those children who stay with their parents or adult carers during war suffer less than those who, for safety reasons, leave them – it is being separated from loved ones that can traumatize the child even more than experiencing war.[40] Blanca came back from Shefford, to where she was evacuated, to join her parents despite the Blitz. Even during the conflict in Cyprus in 1964 Argun wanted to stay with his grandparents. Maurice experienced both war and separation, first from his parents and then from his grandmothers, one who died of hunger in front of him and the other who experienced a breakdown due to constant shelling. Yet the presence of caring adults during war may not fully protect a child. Duncan, who lived with both his parents during post-partition riots in India, was only able to unlock and process a suppressed memory of viewing traumatic events from his balcony in Calcutta, forty years later.[41] There are other factors such as perilous journeys and the challenges of settlement in a hostile environment, in addition to war and disruption in relationships, that affect children's mental health and can impact on later life.[42] It is not just the level or nature of trauma that the child experiences but the ability to express and integrate it that can support a child's ability to heal.

It was through music, art and writing, as adults, that Maurice and Henry were able to retrieve and rework traumatic events,[43] often through performance, memorializing those lost[44] and highlighting injustice. The films, *Child Migrant Stories*, were produced with the aim of increasing understanding of, and empathy with, experiences of child migration, and different evaluations have provided some evidence of this.[45] But what has been particularly surprising, and rewarding, has been the impact of the films and post-screening discussions on those with direct experience of the specific conflict represented as well as on their children and grandchildren, whether that is civil war in Nigeria, Cyprus or El Salvador. Descendants of those who got caught up in such conflicts felt that painful experiences had been withheld from them. They, too, considered themselves victims.[46]

Sharing childhood memories including of traumatic events

Many of those interviewed, who had had few opportunities, both as children and subsequently, to talk about their early experiences of migration welcomed the opportunity to talk. Duncan wrote, "I cannot tell how hugely important … was your gentle excavation of experiences and memories which otherwise would have lain fallow. The need to make some, or any, sense of all these years past, from Calcutta to Mile End, has grown and the memories you evoked may otherwise have been lost like some crucial missing pieces of a puzzle." It is, of course, impossible to claim that all research participants viewed the interview so positively. Rather I fear that, for some, the interview brought back painful memories that took time to process. Timing could be important. Eylem, approaching her forties, said she could not have shared her story of immigration earlier.

How those who have experienced traumatic events as children, should share these with others, in what environment and at what age, are complex questions. Studies by PTSD UK have shown that more than 40 per cent of refugees, and as many as 90 per cent of refugee children, suffer from PTSD.[47] Some who work with asylum-seekers warn against encouraging people to talk of past traumatic events and stress the importance of looking to the future. But is the solution really to shut down such conversations, especially when people talk about them spontaneously? Several initiatives in schools and elsewhere encouraged young people, affected by the Grenfell fire tragedy, to share their experiences through discussion and creativity.[48] Should the Syrian or Afghan conflicts, more geographically and culturally distant from us, be treated differently?

Sarah Temple-Smith, who works therapeutically with unaccompanied asylum-seeking children for the Refugee Council, spoke of the reluctance of one child to share her experience: "In response to a client who said, 'I don't want to think about all these bad memories' I asked, 'How is that working out?' 'Not very well' she laughed." Sarah stressed the need for young people, to have the choice of when, and how they open up, allowing them to reconnect with their former lives before they were a refugee. "We know people are resilient because they are here – the dreadful fact is that the vast majority have not made it – and we try to find ways to reconnect them with that; with what they remember, 'What everybody sees is that you are a refugee or asylum seeker, and that is a very important thing right now, but that is only one aspect of who you are … all the memories, way back when you were a kid in your country, if you were lucky enough to go to school, have lovely times with your families or friends.'"[49] On speaking to Sarah, I wondered if life would have been different if some of those I interviewed had been able to rework traumatic events when younger; to talk to someone who had truly listened; to express themselves creatively; to join a group where they could feel solidarity with others.

Sarah, as a psychological therapist, believes others have a role in supporting children who have experienced trauma. Education settings, in particular language learning classes, are seen as potential spaces in which to deliver psychosocial support, without trespassing on the therapist's domain. Teaching strategies, that support students who have experienced trauma, recommended by UNHCR,[50] include recognizing and mitigating symptoms, providing ground rules and routine, allowing choice and developing useful activities such as the language needed for a Home Office interview. Aleks Palanac explains, 'Some would advocate avoiding these topics [traumatic events] altogether; however, this is doing our learners a disservice, as they are likely to require the language necessary to talk about these topics in a variety of situations in their daily lives.'[51] Appropriate training, along with guidance on when to refer to others and the exercise of self-care, would give teachers and others more confidence in the use of such strategies.

"If I had a magic wand"

For the film *Child Migrants Welcome?*[52] I asked individuals across the UK who had migrated to Britain as children and those who know or work with them, "If you had a magic wand what would be your one wish to improve the lives of unaccompanied child migrants?" Sarah chose two. "My first magic wand would be to make therapy accessible for all separated refugee children. For my second I would wish the process of seeking asylum was less complex and difficult to go through." Shekiba Habib who, as a responsible adult, had accompanied young people from camps in Calais to the Home Office stated, "The most unwelcoming thing the moment you step into a new country, has to be referred to as a number." The children were keen to tell their story but were cut off – the interviews were limited to half an hour at most. Zainab Ali El Faki, another volunteer, provided further insight. "As soon as they were taken into the interview room some immigration officers would ask them about their age and say, 'We don't believe you're telling the truth'. All that happiness in a matter of minutes just went down. I think they were too young to digest it." As Kenan Malik writes, 'What has developed … is a bunker mentality in the Home Office in which the starting point is to view asylum seekers – and migrants more broadly – with suspicion and seek ways of rejecting them.'[53]

UNICEF, lawyers and NGOs concerned with child migrants, not just in Britain but internationally, recognize the urgent need for more child-sensitive arrival procedures and speedier mechanisms for assessing child migrants' asylum claims.[54] The number of children waiting longer than a year for an initial decision increased from 563 children in 2010 to 6,887 in 2020. At the end of December 2020, 55 children had been waiting more than five years but[55] by November 2022 this figure had increased to 155, reflecting the huge increase in the backlog for all asylum seekers, with serious concerns about the safeguarding arrangements for children placed in hotels.[56] Such delays and disbelief on the part of the Home Office damage mental and physical health and can lead to self-harm, even suicide.

In response to the question, "If you had a magic wand?" Hackney's Assistant Director of Children and Young People's Services spoke of the need for foster carers "that match some of their [child migrants'] characteristics even if we weren't able to match all of them." I nodded in agreement, remembering the success of Yosef's placement with an Eritrean foster carer but how Ahmed's care arrangements had not worked out so well. Lisa Matthews, from Right to Remain, spoke of the effective guardianship programme in Scotland for unaccompanied minors. "The idea that you have somebody who is on your side to help you, in a consistent linked-up way, has been shown to be really valuable." I thought of how Ahmed, after his mother died, or Mariam, alone in London, would have benefitted from such a guardian – to help access housing, education, legal support over difficulties with the Home Office and being classed as overseas students. Scotland, according to Lisa Matthews, is impressive in other ways. "There is a political and public narrative of hospitality clearly in opposition to what might be happening in Westminster. That does not mean there is no racism in Scotland … but to me the way forward is having these conversations at a community or neighbourhood level. Conversations that solely take place above that … can be problematic." I remembered the warm welcome of the Syrian children by teachers on the Isle of Bute, how it had been important to work with the local community to get residents on side, about how this narrative of welcome is reflected in the term 'New Scots'.[57]

Gulwali Passarlay, author of *The Lightless Sky – An Afghan Refugee Boy's Journey to Escape to a New Life in Britain*,[58] stated it is the press and the government that lack compassion. "Let's challenge the negativity attached by the right-wing media and politicians towards the refugee crisis. People across Britain are sympathetic but it is the government who lacks compassion." Gulwali almost gave up when, after months travelling to get to Britain, the Home Office disbelieved his age – it was teachers and foster carers, among others, who believed in, and supported, him.

British people's sympathy was evident when the Windrush scandal broke; in the collection of money, food and clothing for Afghan refugees in August 2021 and when over 110,000 people offered to accommodate Ukrainians in the Homes for Ukraine scheme in 2022. But that does not replace a sustained approach, a humane immigration policy; that does not discriminate in relation to race, faith or nationality; a Home Office that is 'fit for purpose';[59] that treats people with fairness and respect and works with others across Europe and the world to address the scale of the challenge including climate change …. as many as 1.2 billion people could be displaced due to climate change by 2050.[60] Empathy, that can respond to a child's body washed up on a Turkish beach or sights of young people being tear gassed in camps in Calais, too often evaporates by fears whipped up by governments and tabloid headlines. Our society needs, and benefits from, migration.

My wish – repeal of recent UK legislation on immigration 2022 and 2023

If I had a metaphorical magic wand, my wish would be to repeal the Nationality and Borders Act that came into force in June 2022 despite opposition from the UNHCR,[61] human rights groups, refugee, migrant and religious organizations, politicians and others. This cruel and ill-thought out legislation undermines the universal human right to claim asylum and violates UK's commitment under the UN 1951 Refugee Convention that Britain helped draft after the Second World War.

A key thrust of the act is to differentiate between those who come through 'irregular' means – by a lorry or small boat, for example (Group 2 refugee status) and those who arrive by 'regular' routes – primarily through a government approved resettlement programme (Group 1 refugee status). Those who arrive by 'irregular means', as did Yosef, Gulwali or Mariam, may be removed because of their 'earlier presence in, or connection to, a safe third country' or 'to any safe third country that will take them'.[62] Yet there is no requirement, either in the Refugee Convention or in international law, for people to claim asylum in the first safe country they arrive in.[63] Such a requirement would undermine any global cooperation, putting disproportionate responsibility on neighbouring countries that already accommodate almost two-thirds of refugees and asylum-seekers worldwide.[64] Although Suella Braverman, the Home Secretary, in October 2022, described, small boat crossings in the English Channel as an 'invasion'[65] other countries in Europe take in far more asylum seekers than the UK, notably Germany, France and Spain.[66] People seek refuge in Britain because they have family or community connections here, their country of origin may have historic links with Britain or they speak English.

A further misconception is that people who come by 'irregular' means are not genuine asylum seekers, yet the data shows otherwise. Seventy-five per cent of initial decisions made in 2022 in the UK of those who came by irregular means were awarded refugee status or humanitarian protection and a further 44 per cent, of those refused, on appeal.[67] The percentage is higher for unaccompanied children. The reality is that there are few safe and legal routes. Although, in March 2019, Priti Patel, then Home Secretary, vowed to continue Global Britain's 'proud tradition of providing safe haven to those in need through safe and legal routes'[68] there are no targets for resettlement set out in the Nationality and Borders Act, with only 1,885 refugees, being resettled via the UK Resettlement scheme in 2022[69] – resettlement schemes internationally only reach 1 per cent of the refugee population. The crisis in Afghanistan has revealed serious flaws in UK's ability to manage timely, safe and legal routes leaving thousands of vulnerable Afghans at risk.[70]

The argument for this division into 'admissable' and 'inadmissable' refugees that is, in UNHCR's view, fundamentally at odds 'with the country's long-standing role as a global champion for the refugee cause'[71] is to break the smugglers' business model. But contrary to the UK government's assertion that deterrence measures in the Nationality and Borders Act will achieve this Médecins Sans Frontières argue that they will 'further push people into the hands of smugglers, precisely because there are insufficient safe and legal routes to the UK'. 'We've not seen a single Ukrainian getting in a small boat,' stated Care4Calais founder Clare Moseley. 'If we gave visas to other refugees in the same way we've done with Ukrainians, that would stop people crossing the Channel in small boats. That would put people smugglers out of business.'[72] Many of the unaccompanied children, stranded in Europe, without the Dublin 111 provision previously available under the EU, are now attempting to reunite with family in the UK through irregular means. In 2018, just twenty-five young people under eighteen were recorded as crossing to the UK via the Channel but from January to June 2022 alone this figure rose to 1,866. Such children, according to Beth Gardiner-Smith, CEO of Safe Passage, are forced, 'To either remain in shelters alone, or risk their lives on dangerous journeys to reunite'.

A report on children adrift across Europe states, 'Instead of being seen as yet another migratory flow to be curbed, it is time to see them for who they are: children at risk.'[73] Yet the Act does nothing to address this. In fact, the reverse. A new 'one-stop' appeals process pressurizes children to produce all evidence at the start of the asylum process, yet they may never have had certain documents, or have lost them 'en route'. They may be traumatized, need therapeutic support, legal advice or support in their own language. Neither do the proposals for a more centralized age assessment system, to establish a child's age, bode well[74] as confirmed by the recent Refugee Council report. More children risk being wrongly treated as over eighteen, more will be assessed unnecessarily, and some forced to go through scientific procedures that are not reliable.[75] Although the Act states that children are not liable for removal to a safe country, data shows that in January to March 2022, 150 asylum seekers, placed in adult accommodation or detention and subsequently found to be children, would have been at risk of removal to Rwanda.[76] Young people in detention or threatened with deportation are vulnerable to self-harm and suicidal thoughts. Hundreds are going missing from hotels,[77] increasing the risk of trafficking and exploitation. There were to be no blanket exceptions to children being awarded 'Group 2' refugee status if they came by 'irregular' means although there was 'flexibility' – what this meant in practice was unclear as what happened when the child reached eighteen.[78]

The legislation does not solely impact on unaccompanied children. Thousands of children in asylum-seeking families already experience deep poverty,[79] a situation deemed unlawful by the High Court. This will be made worse if carers, granted temporary protection status as 'Group 2', have no right to work, no recourse to public funds and no possibility of settlement for at least ten years, as opposed to the previous five years.[80] The two-tier system risks preventing 'Group 2' asylum seekers from bringing over dependents, being given leave to remain, gaining citizenship for themselves or their UK-born children or ever re-entering the UK. Children in families are not immune to the insecurity this causes. Nine-year-old Akar refused to attend school for fear his parents, originally from Iran, would be deported to Rwanda in his absence.[81]

Accommodation for asylum seekers is already in crisis with dependence on sub-standard hotels, where families may live in one room with poor food, and on private housing providers who are making huge profits.[82] 'Group 2' refugees may be placed in accommodation centres described by the All-Party Parliamentary Group on Immigration Detention as 'isolated quasi-detention centres', arguing instead for, decent, safe accommodation in the community.[83] Instead the government is exploring the use of former prisons and military bases as well as redundant ferries, barges and cruise ships.[84] There are, at present, no plans to place those with children in proposed 'accommodation' centres[85] but, this is no guarantee. Despite a government promise to end the practice, 317 children entered immigration detention in the year ending June 2022[86] – Britain is the only state in Europe with no limit on the amount of the time spent in detention.

In their report, *Safe Routes from the Perspective of Young Refugees*, 2021, Young Leaders of Safe Passage urged the government to provide safe routes to Britain, including for unaccompanied children across Europe; offer the same protection fleeing war and persecution and right to family reunion to people regardless of how they travelled to Britain; agree a deal with the EU to strengthen family reunion; expand the proposed resettlement scheme to other countries beyond the Middle East and, importantly, 'Listen to those directly affected before taking decisions that have an impact on so many lives'. Home secretary, Suella Braverman, and indeed this government show little inclination to listen.[87]

Instead, the Illegal Migration Act, that came into law in July 2023, goes even further than the Nationality and Borders Act 2022 and specifically in relation to children. According to writers in *The Lancet*, the Illegal Migration Act will, "Violate the rights of children seeking asylum, undermine the Children Act, create safeguarding risks, and exacerbate the toxic stress experienced by children seeking asylum who arrive in the UK by irregular routes".[88] Children who have not arrived through the very limited safe routes will be blocked from protection as refugees or as victims of trafficking, will have no right to claim asylum and potentially be subject to detention and removal. Even Priti Patel, previous Home Secretary, has reservations. 'The word in Westminster is that she is very uncomfortable with imposing a ban on unaccompanied children, which speaks volumes about the extremity of the government's approach.'[89]

The Children's Commissioner for England, Dame Rachel de Souza, who is 'deeply concerned' about the impact of the act stated, 'There needs to be many more safe and legal routes for children and their families who are fleeing war.'[90] She argued all children, whether unaccompanied or with families, should be excluded from rules that would permit their detention, a practice ended by the David Cameron-led government in 2014 in response to overwhelming medical evidence of harm to children[91] – Barnardo's and the Refugee Council urged the government to keep to the strict time limit of twenty-four hours.[92] Dame Rachel de Souza also asserted that unaccompanied children should be excluded from the proposed duty to remove them beyond their eighteenth birthday and, under limited circumstances, beforehand. 'Having the threat of removal hanging over children's heads as they reach adulthood will risk many of them going missing in an attempt to avoid this, leaving them open to exploitation and abuse.'[93] As the Association of Directors of Social Services stated, 'When a child first comes into care our primary focus is to find them a permanent stable home as set out in statute. We cannot carry out this essential work if they are to be removed as soon as they turn 18 years old and despite having care leaving rights and entitlements up to 25 years.'[94] The Local Government Association pointed out that removal at the age of eighteen is incompatible with other legislation, in particular the Children Act 1989. 'This incompatibility would place councils in the position of trying to comply with two sets of legislation as they attempt to fulfil their duties towards children.'[95] In the first three years of this bill becoming law, according to Barnardo's and the Refugee Council, nearly 15,000 unaccompanied children from countries such as Afghanistan and Sudan will be locked up and banned from remaining in the UK when they turn eighteen.[96]

The Children's Commissioner also argued against formalizing the Home Office's role as a potential accommodation provider for unaccompanied minors. 'I do not believe it [Home Office] has been able to adequately care for children in the hotels it has been providing since 2021, and creating this new power would likely exacerbate the issue.'[97] As the Refugee and Migrant Children's Consortium wrote, 'The Home Office has neither the authority, expertise nor mechanisms to care for children.'[98] Besides going missing from hotels, they are often scared by adult strangers with whom they are living, have to cook for themselves and are denied their basic rights such as access to education or English classes.[99] As Dame Rachel de Souza stated, 'Anyone interacting with them [unaccompanied children] … can see they are extremely vulnerable – yet they are left to fend for themselves in ways we would never tolerate for our own children. They should be given looked-after status from the moment they arrive, cared for by the local authority which has a duty to protect them under the Children Act 1989.'[100] A family court in June 2023 ruled that the Home Office has no power to house children who should be looked after by local authorities as the Children Act 1989 requires.[101]

Provisions in the act that disqualify victims of modern slavery and human trafficking from support and protection, as well as the threat of detention and removal, are shocking for all victims but particularly for children. As Theresa May told the Commons during the third reading of the bill, 'Far from making the bill provisions better for the victims of modern slavery, it makes it worse … The government will be ensuring that more people will stay enslaved … because it will give the slavedrivers, it will give the traffickers, another weapon to hold people in that slavery.'[102]

The Home Office's entrenchment of its unreliable policy of border officials deciding age based on 'physical appearance and demeanour'[103] is a further worrying aspect as are plans to introduce X-ray checks to verify the age of migrants without the involvement of child protection experts – the government's own scientific advisory committee, in January 2023, stated it was not possible to scientifically confirm a person's age 'with precision', warning the use of X-rays could cause distress and put children at risk of harm from radiation. But the government proposes that any age-disputed person who refuses to undergo a scientific age assessment test will automatically be treated as an adult with reduced opportunities to a right of appeal and limited access to judicial review.[104] Mariam's and Gulwali's harrowing stories of wrongful age assessment are not isolated cases. Research by the Helen Bamber Foundation and Humans for Rights Network shows that, in 2022, over 850 children were wrongly 'assessed' to be adults by border officials and sent to adult accommodation/detention (some for many months) before being referred to local authorities whose social workers found them to be children. This figure is likely to be an underestimate.[105] Despite the evidence politicians continue to claim that a high proportion of asylum seekers who are adults attempt to cheat the system by saying they are children. "At times, up to 20% of the adult males who arrive at Western Jet Foil claim to be under 18, when clearly the number is substantially less than that," pronounced Jenrick, the Minister of State for Immigration in parliament. In fact, a freedom of information request to the Home Office revealed that between 1 January and 7 November 2022 only about 1% of all males arriving on small boats at Western Jet Foil who claimed to be under 18 were later found to be over 18.[106] 'Even based on the data the Home Office *does* publish, the claim is still false – last year [2022] nearly two thirds of ALL age dispute cases were found to be children.'[107] The impact of a wrongful age assessment cannot be overestimated. The Home Office is facing serious questions after Amir Safi, an Afghan asylum seeker who claimed to be 16, was said to have taken his own life in May 2023 after being placed in a hotel alone on the basis that he was considered an adult and being denied refugee status.[108]

This act will affect a huge number of children. Over the last decade, they have accounted for around a fifth of those applying for asylum. In 2022, there were 15,670 children who sought asylum, of which 10,487 were children with families and 5,183 were unaccompanied children.[109] Many are in limbo because of the huge asylum backlog in March 2023 of 170,000[110] in comparison to a backlog of 14,882 in December 2010.[111] Only 13 per cent of initial decisions have been made on all asylum claims from small boats since 2018.[112]

The situation is exacerbated by 46 per cent of asylum decision makers resigning from the Home Office in 2022. An official, who spoke on condition of anonymity, predicted a 'big exodus if this bill gets passed … Most civil servants accept the fact the work may be unpalatable, but they'll do it as long as it's lawful. If that changes, there are large numbers saying they don't want to do it.'[113] Recruitment efforts for staff from ethnic minorities are also being hampered by 'reputational damage from the Rwanda deal and wider asylum narrative'.[114] Former Home Office permanent secretary Sir Philip Rutnam has also questioned why the UK uses executive officers [second-lowest civil service grade] as asylum decision-makers. 'It's a relatively junior position to be making life-changing decisions.'[115]

The expressed purpose of the Illegal Migration Act is deterrence and yet there is no evidence that 'tough' policies impact on the number of refugee arrivals. 'The Illegal Migration Bill is unlikely to "stop the boats." Worse, it may instead push refugees into deeper and more dangerous forms of illegality, not only 'en route' to the UK but also within it.' [116] Instead of presenting themselves to the authorities for protection asylum seekers will disappear into the shadows, fearful of being detained or deported and posing real dangers in relation to security, health, poverty and exploitation by criminal gangs.

According to Lord Dubs, 'History will judge this shabby government and its weaponization of refugee lives.'[117] He believes, 'It is only public opinion which in the end will influence our Government.'[118] For the first time in 2022, since polls began in 2015, the number of people who supported maintaining, or increasing, migration levels outnumbered those who wanted a reduction in migration – half were positive about both the economic *and* cultural impacts of migration with the pandemic, in particular, laying bare their contribution to the workforce. This attitude change is happening twice as fast with younger voters, graduates and those from ethnic minority backgrounds. Meanwhile Suella Braverman stated that people who come to the UK across the Channel in small boats 'possess values which are at odds with our country' and have 'heightened levels of criminality'.[119] The Conservative peer Sayeeda Warsi believes the government needs a home secretary who would re-establish 'evidence-based policies'[120] and indeed the Oxford Migration Observatory knows of no recent academic research or official statistics examining criminality among recent refugees.[121] Previous research has shown there is no correlation between immigrants and crime,[122] with some data showing that there is less criminality among asylum seekers and refugees than the rest of the population.[123] Young people are not immune to such divisive language and misrepresentation of facts that

'Exposes children seeking asylum to the health harms associated with discrimination, xenophobia, and racism.'[124]

The Illegal Migration Act states that all asylum seekers arriving via irregular means could be forcibly removed to Rwanda to have their claims processed. This may include children with families and unaccompanied minors, if wrongly classified as adults, or when they reach eighteen. In December 2022 the High Court ruled that the UK-Rwanda scheme was lawful but in a case brought by UNHCR, charities and a group of asylum seekers, claiming that Rwanda has a record of human rights abuses against refugees,[125] the Court of Appeal ruled, in June 2023, that Rwanda is not a safe country for asylum-seekers to have their claims processed, although the overall policy was not deemed unlawful.[126] Even if the government appeals successfully to the Supreme Court the scheme is unlikely to be operational for some time. Besides, how many refugees could this small, highly populated country accommodate? Surely not the 24,000 asylum seekers who have been warned they are being considered for forcible removal,[127] at a cost, according to the Home Office's own data, of £169,000 per person.[128] The UK currently has no similar arrangements in place with other 'safe' countries nor bilateral agreements enabling the return of asylum seekers who have passed through EU countries on the way to the UK.[129] Other concerns include the UK's reluctance to condemn Rwanda's involvement in war crimes through support of armed groups in the Democratic Republic of Congo.[130] And what are UK's reciprocal obligations in accepting some of Rwanda's more vulnerable refugees, a clause that has received little scrutiny?[131]

Will Suella Braverman's dream of sending asylum seekers to Rwanda ever be realized given opposition by devolved governments, refugee and human rights organizations, other NGOS, religious bodies and others? In June 2023 the Lords passed amendments that the bill be consistent with international law and that asylum claims of unaccompanied children, exempt from the duty to remove, be admissible.[132] The government rejected such amendments and, anticipating challenges in the courts, introduced measures that allowed them to ignore its decisions, for example to delay or prevent removal of a person from the UK. It did not want a repeat of the interim ruling from the European Court of Human Rights (ECHR), which grounded the government's first attempted deportation flight to Rwanda.[133] Such disregard of human rights risks reputational damage on the international stage, aligning us with Belarus and Russia. It brings us into conflict with the European Union potentially affecting trade, security and the Good Friday agreement, threatening peace in Northern Ireland.

Is this legislation, pushed through at break-neck speed without public consultation, scrutiny including of the interests, needs and rights of children, a political ruse to influence the next election? The confusion, unworkability and ineffectiveness of the government's approach to stopping the boats that, in the year ending June 2022, represented a tiny proportion of overall migration figures[134] was highlighted by a written Illegal Migration Update in June 2023. Communicated discretely without the usual fanfare of performative cruelty this stated that, from July 2023, it was pausing the two-tier system giving some hope to 55,000 people who had arrived by irregular routes since the Nationality and Borders Act came into force just a year previously.[135] Ostensibly this was to help clear some of the backlog in asylum applications. Refugee organisations welcomed this change, senior conservatives considered it a de facto amnesty. But at the same time, the government continued to push forward with plans to ban all new arrivals from claiming asylum "The Bill [Illegal Migration Bill] goes further than ever before in seeking to deter illegal entry to the UK... This approach represents a considerably stronger means of tackling the same issue that the differentiation policy sought to address."[136] Will the Illegal Migration Act and the Rwanda policy be as inoperational as the Nationality and Borders Act? Stephen Kinnock, Shadow Minister for Immigration, has publicly expressed at least on one occasion that a future Labour government would reverse the act.[137] But, if successful, what would Labour put in its place? For children under eighteen will there be safe and legal asylum routes; speedy and inclusive family reunification procedures; protection and support for those who have been trafficked; a child-appropriate asylum system that prioritizes the best interests of the child and safe community-based accommodation with access to education, health, and social support? Will there be opportunities for children to make their lives here, to flourish and contribute? Enver Solomon of the Refugee Council suggests we do not have to trap people in an unworkable, costly system with no apparent exit. 'As the government ramps up its rhetoric against people seeking asylum, we must not forget there are other ways to navigate what is undoubtedly a global challenge.'[138]

A further wish

In addition to repealing the recent UK legislation on immigration of both 2022 and 2023, like Sarah Temple-Smith, I would like to claim a second wish – that the government consider, as recommended in the Windrush Lessons Learned report, 'ending all deportation of FNOs [foreign national offenders] where they arrived in the UK as children'.[139] It does not look promising. A progress report on implementation of recommendations from the Windrush Lessons Learnt report makes no reference to children[140] and rows back on "crucial" measures such as independent scrutiny and reconciliation events with Windrush families.[141]

What next? Ideas for future research

In the introduction I suggested that historical studies of child migration had barely got out of the cradle. It seems incumbent on me, therefore, to at least suggest some future areas of research, not only for historians but for others. One key area, given the above, is how far and in what ways immigration law, and related policy and practice, takes account of legislation regarding the rights of, and responsibilities towards, children. The role of young people in political activism against racism and anti-immigration policies and practice, including of the police, is another area – what are the links, if any, between the Battle of Cable Street in 1936, the fight against the 'sus' law 1970–81, Rock Against Racism in 1976, the Battle of Brick Lane in 1978 and the more recent Black Lives Matter movement; how effective have they been in implementing change and in garnering solidarity from across society? How true is it that the butt of racist abuse is now on those newly arrived rather than on children of a particular ethnic or religious background? Rhetoric and demonstrations against asylum seekers in hotels or those arriving in small boats would seem to suggest this.

According to Elaine Arnold, Director of the Separation and Reunion Forum UK, adults brought over 6,500 children from the Caribbean between 1955 and 1960 and left 900,000 behind.[142] Yet it is children not only from the Caribbean but from across the world and in different decades who shared with me their experiences of being left by, leaving or reuniting with, loved ones, contributing to loss and pain that lasted decades. More research into the short- and long-term effects of such disruptions as well as into those factors that can support children through such transitions, including by the extended family, is an under researched area. Most people identified key adults who made a difference in their lives – within the extended family; neighbours in hostile neighbourhoods; teachers, foster carers, community workers or religious leaders who believed in, or opened doors for child migrants, reminding us that small or large acts of kindness can matter. And is it true that urban rather than small town or rural areas are less hostile, more welcoming to refugees and migrants and to children in particular? The example of Rothesay Campus on the Isle of Bute would seem to undermine such a view.

There is no doubt these testimonies, as evidenced by the *Child Migrant Stories* films, have the power to evoke empathy, highlight agency and humanize lives. But how can their potential to empower, heal, produce counter narratives and contribute to meaningful change be realized? More investment and research into the impact of film, theatre, learning programmes led by, or co-produced with, migrants and refugees, in museums or elsewhere and with different audiences, would help address this.

East London transformed

I have seen many changes over the fifty years I have lived or worked in east London. Blooms, the famous Jewish deli in Whitechapel, has gone but taxi drivers still queue for salt beef bagels at the top of Brick Lane. Vintage shops are replacing curry restaurants and the Truman Brewery development is still a threat, as with gentrification elsewhere in east London, but Brick Lane is still known as Banglatown. There are no longer zones in Tower Hamlets, as in the 1970s and 1980s, that are out of bounds to the Bangladeshi community. This is not to deny the existence of present-day racism by individuals or institutions, nor the growth of the far right.

Vietnamese families no longer visit Paris to buy shrimp paste but congregate at the southern end of Kingsland Road in Hackney, now known as Pho Mile because of its many Vietnamese restaurants. As you travel north, through Dalston and towards Stoke

Newington, the menu changes. Turkish men take long, sharp knives to spinning chunks of lamb and head-scarved women roll out balls of dough on a gozleme grill, folding and filling them with spinach and white cheese. Further north in Stamford Hill Grodzinski's has become the largest kosher bakery in Europe. Migrant communities have transformed the eating habits of east Londoners.

But it is Ridley Road Market in Dalston that holds up one of the best mirrors to east London's history of migration. In the 1940s and 1950s, stall holders were predominantly Jewish. In the 1960s and 1970s, it attracted Caribbean immigrants and, later, Turks and Greeks. Today sequinned sari materials are on display alongside bold African wax prints; stall holders sell handmade Afghan carpets; women shape afro hair into cornrow braids and Cockney costermongers sell cassava and yams alongside carrots and potatoes. Yet in 1947 and 1948 Ridley Road was the site of clashes between Oswald Mosley and Jewish ex-servicemen[143] who broke up fascist meetings whenever and however they could.

My research has deepened my connection to east London. I have discovered Green Street Market in Newham with stalls selling everything from moth beans to papaya, and shop windows shimmering with Indian bridal jewellery. As I walk down Whitechapel Road, I peer into the café, opposite Al-Huda mosque, to see if Ahmed is discussing Somali poetry. I can no longer pass Blanca's house, on the 106 in Stamford Hill, without hearing the laughter but also the cries of forty *Kindertransport* children as they lay on camp beds in Rabbi Schonfeld's house. Or walk across Hackney Downs without remembering how Duncan learnt to chant "som, soi, som, sami" as he marched behind his Russian teacher, plonking a musical instrument. When I drive down Rectory Road, I can't help smiling at Maurice and his brother, scratching out the eyes of Sooty and Sweep in their newly decorated bedroom, thinking they were demons; when I follow the canal towpath where we first screened *Passing Tides* on the Floating Cinema, I remember the moment Linh's daughter first understood her mother's fear of water.

Visits to Brew for Two and Argun Stationers, just yards from my home, used to take longer as I chatted with Eylem, Argun and Hurmus, upsetting other customers as they waited to be served. But now Argun and Hurmus have retired and Brew for Two has closed – Eylem has other exciting plans. But the research has also broadened my understanding of the lives of child migrants beyond east London – in Glasgow and on the Isle of Bute in Scotland, in Horsham, Sussex, in Sidmouth, Devon and in Norwich, Norfolk, challenging views that it is area of historic migration such as east London where child migrants are best welcomed and more able to prosper.

As I walk past Sutton House, a Tudor manor house at the top of my Victorian-terraced street, I remember when we screened *Child Migrants Welcome*? in support of safe routes for unaccompanied child migrants on the eightieth anniversary of the *Kindertransport* in 2018. Five years later the Dubs scheme has been abandoned; routes for children with family in the UK previously possible under the EU regulation have been closed; the Nationality and Borders Act 2022 and the Illegal Migration Act 2023 are in place with no clear plans for additional safe and legal routes. Britain has withdrawn from Afghanistan along with a coalition of international forces led by the United States, Russia has attacked and invaded Ukraine and civil war has broken out in Sudan. In response to Suella Braverman's statement that those fleeing Sudan would not be allowed to apply for asylum in the UK, people rang into the radio to ask why refugees from Ukraine are welcomed and not from Sudan, a country with historic ties to Britain.[144] And in the week that the Illegal Migration Bill suffered twenty defeats in the House of Lords raising hopes for the protection of traffickers and unaccompanied children but that led to minimal concessions by the House of Commons,[145] news leaked of Robert Jenrick, Immigration Minister, having ordered the removal of cartoon characters on the walls of an asylum centre for children in Kent. Mickey Mouse and Baloo from the Jungle Book were considered too 'welcoming'?[146]

My hope, that Gulwali Passarlay's belief in the British people is justified, that it can win out against the hate against immigrants engendered by elements in government and the British press, starts to wane. Then I see a tweet from Marie, who loaned the cloth to the V&A Museum of Childhood in which, in 1996, aged twelve, she carried her baby brother for six months from Rwanda to safety – a story with which I opened this book. She has been awarded an MBE for services to human rights and her local community. The realization that Marie, under the new immigration legislation, may not have been allowed entry to the UK, or granted British citizenship, stirs me to action. God forbid she would have been sent back to Rwanda to where she cannot return. As I join yet one more demonstration in support of a more compassionate immigration system, under the watchful eye of Nelson Mandela in Parliament Square, I remember a favourite saying of the famous anti-apartheid revolutionary, 'There can be no keener revelation of a society's soul than the way in which it treats its children.'[147]

NOTES

Introduction

1. Nightingale, E. (2014), 'World in the East End at the V&A Museum of Childhood', in L. Gourievidis (ed.), *Museums and Migration: History, Memory and Politics* (*Museum Meanings*), 103–22, Abingdon, UK and New York, US: Routledge.

2. UNHCR (2022), *More than 100 million people are forcibly displaced*, viewed 3 March 2023, https://www.unhcr.org/refugee-statistics/insights/explainers/100-million-forcibly-displaced.html.

3. UNHCR UK (2022), *Figures at a glance*, viewed 3 March 2023, https://www.unhcr.org/uk/figures-at-a-glance.html.

4. Grant, H. and Fallon, K. (2021), 'UK accused of stranding vulnerable refugees after Brexit', *The Guardian*, 27 April 2021, viewed 3 March 2023, https://www.theguardian.com/global-development/2021/apr/27/exclusive-uk-accused-of-stranding-vulnerable-refugees-after-brexit.

5. Townsend, M. (2022), 'UK accused of attempting to deport children to Rwanda', *The Observer*, 5 June 2022, viewed 3 March 2023, https://www.theguardian.com/world/2022/jun/05/uk-accused-of-attempting-to-deport-children-to-rwanda?utm_term=Autofeed&CMP=twt_gu&utm_medium&utm_source=Twitter.

6. Townsend, M. (2023), ' "They just vanish": Whistleblowers met by wall of complacency over missing migrant children', *The Observer*, 21 January 2023, viewed 3 March 2023, https://www.theguardian.com/uk-news/2023/jan/21/they-just-vanish-whistleblowers-met-by-wall-of-complacency-over-missing-migrant-children.

7. Nagesh, A. (2022), 'Sir Mo Farah revels he was trafficked to the UK as a child', *BBC News*, 16 July 2022, viewed 3 March 2023, https://www.bbc.co.uk/news/uk–62123886.

8. UNICEF (2022), *War in Ukraine: Support for children and families*, viewed 3 March 2023, https://www.unicef.org/emergencies/war-ukraine-pose-immediate-threat-children.

9. Younge, G. (2018), 'Ambalavaner Sivanandan Obituary', *The Guardian*, 7 February 2018, viewed 3 March 2023, https://www.theguardian.com/world/2018/feb/07/ambalavaner-sivanandan.

10. Kehily, M.J. (2009), *An Introduction to Childhood Studies*, Berkshire, England: Open University Press.

11. Bhabha, J., Kanics, C., and Senovilla Hernandez, D. (2018), *Research Handbook on Child Migration*, Cheltenham, UK: Edward Elgar Publishing.

12. Baldassar, L. and Merla, L. (eds) (2014), *Transnational Families Migration and the Circulation of Care: Understanding Mobility and Absence in Family Life*, New York and London: Routledge.

13. Veale, A. and Dona, G. (eds) (2014), *Child and Youth Migration: Mobility-in-Migration in an Era of Globalization*, London: Palgrave MacMillan.

14. Veale, A. and Andres, C. (2014), ''I wish, I wish…': Reflections on mobility, immobility and the global "imaginings" of Nigerian transnational children', in A. Veale and G. Dona (eds), *Child and Youth Migration: Mobility-in-Migration in an Era of Globalization*, 140–61, London: Palgrave MacMillan.

15. Suárez-Orozco, C., Todorova, I. and Louie, J. (2002), ''"Making up for lost time": The experience of separation and reunification among immigrant families', *Family Process*, 41: 625–43.

16. Veale and Dona (eds), *Child and Youth Migration: Mobility-in-Migration in an Era of Globalization*.

17. Olwig, K.F. (2014), 'Migration and care – intimately related aspects of Caribbean family and kinship', in L. Baldassar and L. Merla (eds), *Transnational Families Migration and the Circulation of Care: Understanding Mobility and Absence in Family Life*, 133–48, New York and London: Routledge.

18. Ni Laoire, C., Carpena-Mendez, F., Tyrell, N., and White, A. (2011), *Childhood and Migration in Europe. Portraits of Mobility, Identity and Belonging in Contemporary Ireland*, Surrey, England: Ashgate.

19. De Block, L. and Buckingham, D. (2007), *Global Children, Global Media. Migration, Media and Childhood*, Basingstoke: Palgrave Macmillan.

20. Ni Laoire, C., Carpena-Mendez, F., Tyrell, N., and White, A., *Childhood and Migration in Europe, Portraits of Mobility, Identity and Belonging in Contemporary Ireland*.

21. Crawley, H. (2011), ''"Asexual, apolitical beings": The interpretation of children's identities and experiences in the UK asylum system', *Journal of Ethnic and Migration Studies*, 37 (8): 1171–84.

22. Lynch, G. (2015), *Remembering Child Migration: Faith, Nation-Building and the Wounds of Charity*, London: Bloomsbury.

23. Kushner, T. (2012), 'Constructing (another) ideal refugee journey: The *Kinder*', in *The Battle of Britishness: Migrant Journeys 1685 to the Present*, 77–98, Manchester: Manchester University Press.

24. Kushner, T. (2018), 'Colin Holmes and the development of migrant and anti-migrant historiography', in J. Craig- Norton, C. Hoffman and T. Kushner (eds), *Migrant Britain*, 22–32, Abingdon, Oxfordshire and New York: Routledge.

25. Gatrell, P. (2013), *The Making of the Modern Refugee*, Oxford: Oxford University Press.

26. Holmes, C. (1988), *John Bull's Island: Immigration and British Society, 1871–1971*, Basingstoke: Macmillan.

27. Ibid.

28. Panayi, P. (2020), *Migrant City: A New History of London*, New Haven and London: Yale University Press.

29. Vertovec, S. (2006), *The Emergence of Super-Diversity in Britain*, University of Oxford: COMPAS: 06–25.

30. Herbert, J. (2008), *Negotiating Boundaries in the City: Migration: Gender and Britain in Britain*, Ashingdon, Oxfordshire and New York: Ashgate.

31. Kushner, T. (2018), 'Places and spaces', in J. Craig- Norton, C. Hoffman and T. Kushner (eds), *Migrant Britain*, 56, Abingdon, Oxfordshire and New York: Routledge.

32. Kushner, 'Colin Holmes and the development of migrant and anti-migrant historiography', 22–32.

Notes

33. Fryer, P. (1984), *Staying Power: History of Black People in Britain*, London: Pluto Press.

34. Olusoga, D. (2016), *Black and British: A Forgotten History*, London: Macmillan.

35. Burrell, K. (2018), 'Framing Polish migration to the UK, from the Second World War to EU expansion', in J. Craig- Norton, C. Hoffman and T. Kushner (eds), *Migrant Britain*, 272–81, Abingdon, Oxfordshire and New York: Routledge.

36. Wilkins, A. (2019), *Migration, Work and Home-Making in the City: Dwelling and Belonging among Vietnamese Communities in London*, Abingdon, Oxfordshire and New York: Routledge.

37. Hoffman, C. (2018), 'Community history', in J. Craig- Norton, C. Hoffman and T. Kushner (eds), *Migrant Britain*, 103–105. Abingdon, Oxfordshire and New York: Routledge.

38. Waters, R. (2018), *Thinking Black, 1964–1985*, Berkeley: University of California Press.

39. Kershen, A.J. (2018), 'From the profitable strangers to the residents of Banglatown: An exploration of the historiography of immigration in London's East End', in J. Craig- Norton, C. Hoffman and T. Kushner (eds), *Migrant Britain*, 59–69, Abingdon, Oxfordshire and New York: Routledge.

40. Kershen, A. (2005), *Strangers, Aliens and Asians: Huguenots, Jews and Bangladeshis in Spitalfields 1666–2000*, Abingdon, Oxfordshire and New York: Routledge.

41. Banton, M. (1955), *The Coloured Quarter: Negro Immigrants in an English City*, London: Jonathan Cape.

42. Fishman, W. (1974), *Jewish Radicals: From Czarist stetl to London ghetto*, New York: Pantheon Books.

43. Ullah, A.A. and Eversley, J. (2010), *Bengalis in London's East End*, London: Swadhinata Trust.

44. Eade, J. (1989), *The Politics of Community: The Bangladeshi Community in East London*, University of Michigan: Avebury.

45. Dench, G., Gavron, K., and Young, M. (2006), *The New East End: Kinship, Race and Conflict*, London: Young Foundation.

46. Ahmed, N., Phillipson, C., and Latimer, J. (2003), *Women in Transition: A Study of the Experiences of Bangladeshi Women Living in Tower Hamlets*, Bristol: Policy Press.

47. Begum, S. (2023), *From Sylhet to Spitalfields: Bengali Squatters in 1970s East London*, London: Lawrence and Wishart.

48. Glynn, S. (2014), *Class, Ethnicity and Religion in the Bengali East End: A Political History*, Manchester: Manchester University Press.

49. Hoque, A. (2015), *British-Islamic Identity: Third Generation Bangladeshis in East London*, London, Stoke on Trent: Trentham Books.

50. Zeitlyn, B. (2012), 'Maintaining transnational social fields, the role of visits to Bangladesh for British Bangladeshi children', *Journal of Ethnic and Migration Studies*, 38 (6): 953–68.

51. Kushner, T. (2018), 'Afterword', in J. Craig- Norton, C. Hoffman and T. Kushner (eds), *Migrant Britain*, 282, Abingdon, Oxfordshire and New York: Routledge.

52. Richie, D. (2010), 'Introduction: The Evolution of Oral History', *The Oxford Handbook of Oral History*, viewed 26 February 2023, https://warwick.ac.uk/fac/arts/history/students/pgr/course-lectures-seminars/the_evolution_of_oral_history.pdf.

53. Oral History Society (including Oral History Journal), viewed 26 February 2023, https://www.ohs.org.uk.

54. Thompson, P. (1978), *The Voice of the Past*, New York: Oxford University Press.

55. Richie, 'Introduction: The Evolution of Oral History'.

56. Thomson, A. (1999), 'Moving stories: Oral history and migration studies', *Oral History Journal*, 27 (1): 24–37.

57. Price, P.L. (2010), 'Cultural geography and the stories we tell ourselves', *Cultural Geographies* 17 (2): 203–10.

58. Adams, C. (1987), *Across Seven Seas and Thirteen Rivers: Life Stories of Pioneer Sylheti Settlers in Britain*, London: THAP books.

59. Adams, C. (1991), 'Across seven seas and thirteen rivers', *Oral History Journal*, 19 (1): 30.

60. Hoffman, M. (2020), *Practicing Oral History among Refugees and Host Communities*, Abingdon, Oxfordshire and New York: Routledge.

61. Gittins, D. (2009), 'The historical construction of childhood', in *An Introduction to Childhood Studies*, 36. Berkshire, England: Open University Press.

62. Hirsch, M. and Spitzer, L. (2011), *Ghosts of Home: The Afterlife of Czernowitz in Jewish Memory*, 156. Berkeley, CA: University of California Press.

63. Brah, A. (1996), *Cartographies of Diaspora: Contesting Identities*, London: Routledge.

64. Dahinden, J. and Efionayi-Mäder, D. (2009), 'Challenges and Strategies in Empirical Fieldwork with Asylum Seekers and Migrant Sex Workers', in I. Van Liempt and V. Bigler (eds), *The Ethics of Migration Research Methodology, Dealing with Vulnerable Migrants*, 98–117, Brighton: Sussex Academic Press.

65. Hashem, R. and Dudman, P.V. (2016), 'Paradoxical narratives of transcultural encounters of the "other": Civic engagement with refugees and migrants in London', *Transnational Social Review*, 6 (1–2): 192–9.

66. Breckner, R. (1998), 'The biographical-interpretative method: Principles and procedures', *Sostris Working Paper* 2: 99–104.

67. Felman, S. and Laub, D. (1992), *Testimony: Crises of Witnessing in Literature, Psychoanalysis and History*, 67, New York, US and Abingdon, UK: Routledge.

68. Hirsch and Spitzer, *Ghosts of Home: The Afterlife of Czernowitz in Jewish Memory*, 163.

69. Alderson, P. and Morrow, V. (2011), (2nd edition) *The Ethics of Research with Children and Young People: A Practical Handbook*, London: SAGE.

70. Temple, B. and Moran, R. (2011), *Doing Research with Refugees: Issues and Guidelines*, Bristol: The Policy Press.

71. Miller, W.R. (2004), 'Motivational interviewing in service to health promotion', *American Journal of Health Promotion*, 18 (3): A1–A10.

72. Clark, T. (2008), '"We're over-researched here!": Exploring accounts of research fatigue within qualitative research engagements', *Sociology*, 42 (S): 953–70, viewed 3 March 2023, https://journals.sagepub.com/doi/abs/10.1177/0038038508094573.

73. The Gentle Author (2019), 'Surma centre portraits', *Spitalfields Life*, viewed 3 March 2023, https://spitalfieldslife.com/2019/10/11/surma-centre-portraits-x/.

74. Swadhinata Trust (2022), *Welcome to Swadhinata Trust*, viewed 3 March 2023, https://www.swadhinata.org.uk.

75. Heywood, F. (2010), 'The V&A through the eyes of refugees', *The Guardian*, 9 June 2010, viewed 3 March 2023, https://www.theguardian.com/society/2010/jun/09/victoria-and-albert-museum-refugee-tours.

76. *Child Migrants Welcome?* [Film] Dir: Eithne Nightingale and Mitchell Harris, UK: Child Migrant Stories, viewed 3 March 2023, https://childmigrantstories.com/films/child-migrants-welcome/.

Notes

77. Dawes, A., Tredoux, C., and Feinstein, A. (1989), 'Political violence in South Africa: Some effects on children of the violent destruction of their community', *International Journal of Psychology*, 25: 13–31.

78. Miller, 'Motivational interviewing in service to health promotion', A1–A10.

79. Merriam, S., Ntseane, G., Lee, M., Kee, Y., Johnson-Bailey, J., and Muhamad, M. (2000), 'Power and positionality: Negotiating insider/outsider status in multicultural and cross-cultural research', *Adult Education Research Conference*, viewed 3 March 2023, https://newprairiepress.org/cgi/viewcontent.cgi?article=2241&context=aerc.

80. Kissoon, P. (2011), 'Homelessness as an Indicator of Integration: Interviewing refugees about the meaning of home and accommodation', in B. Temple and R. Moran (eds), *Doing Research with Refugees: Issues and Guidelines*, 75–96, Bristol: Policy Press.

81. Oakley, A. (1981), 'Interviewing women: A contradiction in terms', in H. Roberts (ed.), *Doing Feminist Research*, 30–61, London: Routledge & Kegan Paul.

82. Denzin, N.K. (1989), *Interpretive Biography: Qualitative Research Methods*, 17, London, UK and New Delhi, India: Sage Publications.

83. Hurworth, R. (2003), 'Photo-Interviewing for research', *Social Research Update*, 40.

84. White, A. and Bushin, N. (2011), 'More than methods: Learning from research with children seeking asylum in Ireland', *Population, Space and Place*, 17 (4): 326–37.

85. Kinney, P. (2017), 'Walking interviews', *Social Research Update*, 67.

86. *Child Migrant Stories* [Film] Dir: Eithne Nightingale and Mitchell Harris, UK: Child Migrant Stories, viewed 3 March 2023, https://childmigrantstories.com.

87. Holmes, S.M. and Castaneda, H. (2016), 'Representing the "European refugee crisis" in Germany and beyond: Deservingness and difference, life and death', *American Ethnologist* 43 (1): 12–24.

88. Lenette, C. and Miskovic, N. (2018), 'Some viewers may find the following images disturbing': Visual representations of refugee deaths at border crossings', *Crime, Media, Culture*, 14 (1): 111–20.

89. Eastmond, M. (2007), 'Stories as lived experience: Narratives in forced migration research', *Journal of Refugee Studies*, 20 (2): 248–64.

90. Khiabany, G. (2016), 'Refugee crisis, imperialism and pitiless wars on the poor', *Media, Culture & Society*, 38 (5): 755–62.

91. Burrell, K. and Hörschelmann, K. (2019), 'Perilous journeys: Visualising the racialised "refugee crisis"', *Antipode*, 51 (1): 45–65.

92. Lynch, B. (2014), *Whose Cake Is It Anyway?*, London: Paul Hamlyn Foundation.

93. Oral history handout from The Writing Center, University of North Carolina at Chapel Hill, viewed 3 March 2023, https://writingcenter.unc.edu/tips-and-tools/oral-history/.

94. Alderson and Morrow, *The Ethics of Research with Children and Young People*.

95. Bhabha, J. (2014), *Child Migration & Human Rights in a Global Age*, Princeton, New Jersey: Princeton University Press.

96. Suárez-Orozco, Todorova, and Louie, '"Making up for lost time": The experience of separation and reunification among immigrant families', 625–43.

97. Ainsworth, M.D.S. (1989), 'Attachment beyond infancy', *American Psychologist*, 44: 709–16.

98. Arnold, E. (2012), *Working with Families of African Caribbean Origin: Understanding Issues around Immigration and Attachment*, London and Philadelphia: Jessica Kingsley Publishers.

99. Kofman, E. (2004), 'Family-related migration: A critical review of European studies', *Journal of Ethnic and Migration Studies*, 30: 243–62.

100. Baldassar and Merla, *Transnational Families Migration and the Circulation of Care: Understanding Mobility and Absence in Family Life*.

101. Bryceson, D. and Vuorela, U. (2002), 'The transnational families in the twenty-first century', in D. Bryceson and U. Vuorela (eds), *The Transnational Family: New European Frontiers and Global Networks*, 3–30, Oxford, UK: Berg.

102. Davies, H. (2012), 'Affinities, seeing and feeling like family: Exploring why children value face-to-face contact', *Childhood*, 19 (1): 8–23.

103. Ackers, L. and Stalford, H. (2004), *A Community for Children? Children, Citizenship and Internal Migration in the EU*, Aldershot: Ashgate.

104. Orellana, M.F., Thorne, B., Chee, A., and Lam, W.S. (2001), 'Transnational childhoods: The participation of children in processes of migration', *Social Problems*, 48 (4): 572–91.

105. Veale and Andres, '"I wish, I wish…": Reflections on mobility, immobility and the global "imaginings" of Nigerian transnational children', 140–61.

106. UNCRC (1989), *United Nations Convention of The Rights of the Child*, viewed 3 March 2023, https://www.unicef.org.uk/what-we-do/un-convention-child-rights/.

107. Hofstede, G. (1980), *Cultures Consequences: International Differences in Work-related Values*, Beverley Hills, CA: Sage Publications.

108. Klocker, N. (2007), 'An example of 'thin' agency: Child domestic workers in Tanzania', in R. Panelli, S. Punch and E. Robson (eds), *Global Perspectives on Rural Childhood and Youth: Young Rural Lives*, 83–94, New York: Routledge.

109. BenEzer, G. and Zetter, R. (2014), 'Searching for directions: Conceptual and methodological challenges in researching refugee journeys', *Journal of Refugee Studies*, 28 (3): 297–318, viewed 3 March 2023, https://www.academia.edu/44883562/Searching_for_Directions_Conceptual_and_Methodological_Challenges_in_Researching_Refugee_Journeys.

110. Veale and Dona (eds), *Child and Youth Migration: Mobility-in-Migration in an Era of Globalization*.

111. BenEzer and Zetter, 'Searching for Directions: Conceptual and Methodological Challenges in Researching Refugee Journeys'.

112. Veale and Andres, '"I Wish, I Wish…": Reflections on Mobility, Immobility and the Global "Imaginings" of Nigerian Transnational Children'.

113. Veale and Dona (eds), *Child and Youth Migration: Mobility-in-Migration in an Era of Globalization*.

114. Razy, E. (2014), 'Ways of being a child in a dispersed family: Multi-parenthood and migratory debt between France and Mali (Soninke Homeland)', in A. Veale and G. Donà (eds), *Children, Migration and Globalization*, 186–212, Basingstoke, UK and New York, USA: Palgrave Macmillan.

115. Suárez-Orozco, Todorova, and Louie, '"Making up for lost time": The experience of separation and reunification among immigrant families'.

116. Arnold, E. (1991), 'Issues of reunification of migrant West Indian children in the United Kingdom', in J.L. Roopnarine and J. Brown (eds), *Caribbean Families Diversity among Ethnic Groups*, 243–58, Greenwich, CT: Ablex Publishing.

117. Crawley, H. (2007), *When Is a Child Not a Child? Asylum Age Disputes and the Process of Age Assessment*, London: IPLA Report.

118. Sourander, A. (1998), 'Behaviour problems and traumatic events of unaccompanied refugee minors', *Child Abuse Negl.*, 22 (7): 719–27.

119. Suárez-Orozco, C. et al. (2011), '"I felt like my heart was staying behind": Psychological implications of family separations & reunifications for immigrant youth', *Journal of Adolescent Research*, 26: 222–57.

120. van Ijzendoorn, M.H. and Bakermans-Kranenburg, M.J. (2010), 'Invariance of adult attachment across gender, age, culture, and socioeconomic status?', *Journal of Social and Personal Relationships*, 27 (2): 200–8.

121. Bourdieu, P. (1986), 'The Forms of Capital', in John E. Richardson (ed.), *Handbook of Theory and Research for the Sociology of Education*, 241–58, Westport, CT: Greenwood Press.

122. Arnot, M. et al. (2014), *School Approaches to the Education of EAL Students: Language Development, Social Integration and Achievement*, Cambridge: The Bell Foundation.

123. Coard, B. (1971), *How the West Indian Child Is Made Educationally Sub-normal in the British School System*, London: New Beacon Books.

124. Back, L. (1996), *New Ethnicities and Urban Culture: Social Identity and Racism in the Lives of Young People*, Abingdon: Taylor and Francis.

125. Spicer, N. (2008), 'Places of exclusion and inclusion: Asylum-Seeker and refugee experiences of neighbourhoods in the UK', *Journal of Ethnic and Migration Studies*, 34 (3): 491–510.

126. Brickell, K. and Datta, A. (2011), *Translocal Geographies. Spaces, Places, Connections*, Farnham: Ashgate.

127. Sheringham, O. (2013), *Transnational Religious Spaces; Faith and the Brazilian Migration Experience*, Basingstoke, UK: Palgrave Macmillan.

128. Gilroy, P. (1987), '*There Ain't No Black in the Union Jack*': The Cultural Politics of Race and Nation, London: Hutchinson.

129. Crawley, '"Asexual, apolitical beings": The interpretation of children's identities and experiences in the UK asylum system', 1171–84.

130. Sedano, L.J. (2012), 'On the irrelevance of ethnicity in children's organisation of their social world', *Childhood*, 19: 375–88.

131. Katz, C. (2004), *Economic Restructuring and Children's Everyday Lives*, Minneapolis, US: University of Minnesota Press.

132. Klocker, 'An example of "thin" agency: Child domestic workers in Tanzania', 83–94.

133. Machel, G. (2001), *The Impact of War on Children: A Review of Progress since the 1996 United Nations Report on the Armed Conflict on Children*, London: C. Hurst and Co.

134. Smith, A., Lalonde, R.N., and Johnson, S. (2004), 'Serial migration and its implications for the parent-child relationship: A retrospective analysis of the experiences of the children of Caribbean immigrants', *Cultural Diversity and Ethnic Minority Psychology*, 10: 107–22.

135. Bhabha, *Child Migration & Human Rights in a Global Age*.

136. Wiese, E.B.P. (2010), 'Culture and migration: Psychological trauma in children and adolescents', *Traumatology*, 16 (4): 142–52.

137. Berry, J.W. (2005), 'Acculturation: Living successfully in two cultures', *International Journal of Intercultural Relations*, 29: 697–712.

138. Binder, S. and Tošić, J. (2005), 'Refugees as a particular form of transnational migrations and social transformations: Socioanthropological and gender aspects', *Current Sociology*, 53 (4): 607–24.

139. Bergmann, M.S. and Jucovy, M.E. (eds) (1982), *Generations of the Holocaust*, New York, US: Columbia University Press.

140. Dieterich-Hartwell, R. and Koch, S.C. (2017), 'Creative arts therapies as temporary home for refugees: Insights from literature and practice', *Behavioral Sciences*, 7 (4): 69, viewed 6 August 2022, https://www.ncbi.nlm.nih.gov/pmc/articles/PMC5746678/.

141. Blunt, A. and Dowling, R. (2022), 'Home, migration and diaspora', *Home*, London, UK and New York, US: Routledge.

Chapter 1

1. Baker, T.F.T. (1995), 'Hackney: Judaism', *A History of the County of Middlesex*, 10: 145–8, viewed 3 March 2023, https://www.british-history.ac.uk/vch/middx/vol10/pp145-148.

2. Cusack, Y. (2019), 'Inside Europe's biggest Hasidic community', *Hackney Magazine*, 28 April 2019, viewed 3 March 2023, http://www.hackneymagazine.com/jewish-communities-hackney/.

3. Ibid.

4. BBC (2016), 'Calais "Jungle": Demolition crews pull down migrant camp', *BBC News*, 25 October 2016, viewed 3 March 2023, https://www.bbc.co.uk/news/world-europe-37759032.

5. Woodruff, R. (2020), 'Scheme protecting unaccompanied refugee children ends in the UK', *Human Rights Pulse*, 28 July 2020, viewed 3 March 2023, https://www.humanrightspulse.com/mastercontentblog/scheme-protecting-unaccompanied-refugee-children-ends-in-the-uk.

6. Teen Action (2016), 'Oral history of Blanca Stern', *Hackney Museum*, June 2016, viewed 3 March 2023, https://museum-collection.hackney.gov.uk/object-2018-4.

7. US Holocaust Memorial Museum, 'Vienna', *Holocaust Encyclopaedia*, viewed 3 March 2023, https://encyclopedia.ushmm.org/content/en/article/vienna.

8. The National Holocaust Centre and Museum, *Rabbi Schonfeld*, viewed 3 March 2023, https://www.holocaust.org.uk/rabbi-schonfeld.

9. Fast, V. (2011), *Children's Exodus*, London, UK and New York, US: L.B. Tauris & Co.

10. Cohn, A.R. and Grunfeld, J. (2011), *Shefford*, Israel: Feldheim Publishers.

11. Kershaw, R. (2015), '"Collar the Lot": Britain's policy of internment during the Second World War', *The National Archives*, 2 July 2015, viewed 3 March 2023, https://blog.nationalarchives.gov.uk/collar-lot-britains-policy-internment-second-world-war/.

12. Grenville, A. (2018), *Encounters with Albion: Britain and the British in Texts by Jewish Refugees from Nazism*, Oxford: Modern Humanities Research Association.

13. Simmonds, L. (2014), 'Isle of Man Jewish Community', *Jewish Communities and Records*, 10 November 2014, viewed 3 March 2023, https://www.jewishgen.org/jcr-uk/Community/Iom/chistory.htm.

14. Parkin, S. (2022), '"I remember the feeling of insult": When Britain imprisoned its wartime refugees', *The Guardian*, 1 February 2022, viewed 3 March 2023, https://www.theguardian.com/world/2022/feb/01/when-britain-imprisoned-refugees-second-world-war-internment-camps.

15. The Warth Mills Project, *The Tragedy of the SS Arandora Star*, viewed 3 March 2023, https://www.warthmillsproject.com/stories/tragedy-of-the-arandora-star/.

16. Kempler, C. (2016), 'Imprisoned on the Isle of Man: Jewish Refugees Classified as "Enemy Aliens"', *B'nai B'rith International*, 19 September 2016, viewed 3 March 2023, https://www.bnaibrith.org/imprisoned-on-the-isle-of-man-jewish-refugees-classified-as-enemy-aliens-html/.

17. McDonald, C. (2018), '"We became British aliens": *Kindertransport* refugees narrating the discovery of their parents' fates', *Holocaust Studies*, 24 (4): 395–417, 31 January 2018, viewed 3 March 2023, https://www.tandfonline.com/doi/full/10.1080/17504902.2018.1428784.

18. US Holocaust Memorial Museum, *Death March from Auschwitz*, viewed 3 March 2023, https://www.ushmm.org/learn/timeline-of-events/1942-1945/death-march-from-auschwitz.

19. Kushner, T. (2012), 'Constructing (another) ideal journey: The *Kinder*, in *The Battle of Britishness: Migrant Journeys 1685 to the Present*, Manchester: Manchester University Press.

20. Ibid.

21. Ibid.

22. London, L. (2000), *Whitehall and the Jews, 1933–1948 British Immigration Policy, Jewish Refugees and the Holocaust*, Cambridge: Cambridge University Press.

23. Dubs, A. (2020), 'We simply can't turn our backs on refugee children', *The Guardian*, 10 January 2020, viewed 3 March 2023, https://www.theguardian.com/commentisfree/2020/jan/10/refugee-children-lone-reunite-rights-dublin-regulation.

24. Chance, C. (2020), *Brexit Delivered: The European Union (Withdrawal Agreement) Act 2020*, viewed 3 March 2023, https://www.cliffordchance.com/content/dam/cliffordchance/briefings/2020/01/brexit-delivered-the-european-union-withdrawal-agreement-act-2020.pdf.

25. The Law Society (2022), *Nationality and Borders Bill*, 28 April 2022, viewed 3 March 2023, https://www.lawsociety.org.uk/topics/immigration/nationality-and-borders-act.

Chapter 2

1. Jones, H. et al. (2017), *Go Home? The Politics of Immigration Controversies*, Manchester: Manchester University Press, viewed 3 March 2023, http://www.open-access.bcu.ac.uk/4687/1/Go%20Home%20The%20politics%20of%20immigration%20controversies%20-%20Open%20Access%20version.pdf.

2. Grayson, J. (2013), 'The shameful "Go Home" campaign', *Institute of Race Relations*, 22 August 2013, viewed 3 March 2023, https://irr.org.uk/article/the-shameful-go-home-campaign/.

3. Taylor, M. et al. (2013), '"Go Home" ad campaign targeting illegal immigrants faces court challenge', *The Guardian*, 26 July 2013, viewed 3 March 2023, https://www.theguardian.com/uk-news/2013/jul/26/go-home-ad-campaign-court-challenge.

4. Abdulrazaq, T. (2021), 'No, saying "Paki" is never "banter"', *TRTWORLD*, 19 November 2021, viewed 3 March 2023, https://www.trtworld.com/opinion/no-saying-paki-is-never-banter-51815.

5. Alpion, G. (2020), *Mother Teresa: The Saint and Her Nation*, India: Bloomsbury.

6. Blunt, A. (2002), 'Land of our mothers: Home, identity and nationality for Anglo-Indians in British India 1919–1947', *History Workshop Journal*, 54 (1): 49–72.

7. Younge, G. (2018), 'Ambalavaner Sivanandan obituary', *The Guardian*, 7 February 2018, viewed 3 March 2023, https://www.theguardian.com/world/2018/feb/07/ambalavaner-sivanandan.

8. Imperial War Museum, *Why Was the Suez Crisis So Important*, viewed 3 March 2023, https://www.iwm.org.uk/history/why-was-the-suez-crisis-so-important.

9. Hopley, C. (2022), 'Britain's favourite dish – let's go for a curry', *British Heritage Travel*, 4 May 2022, viewed 3 March 2023, https://britishheritage.com/food-drink/britains-favourite-dish-curry.

10. Anderson, D. (1999), *Shamiana: The Mughal Tent – illustrated edition*, London: V&A Publications.

11. Blunt, A., Bonnerjee, J., and Hysler-Rubin, N. (2012), 'Diasporic returns to the city: Anglo-Indian and Jewish visits to Calcutta', *South Asian Diaspora*, 4: 25–43.

12. Garwood, A. (2020), *Holocaust Trauma: Psychoanalytic Reflections of a Holocaust Survivor*, London: Routledge.

13. Jackson, A. (2021), 'How Rock against Racism Fought the Right', *JSTOR DAILY*, 27 January 2021, viewed 3 March 2023, https://daily.jstor.org/how-rock-against-racism-fought-the-right/.

Chapter 3

1. Garwood, A. (2002), 'The holocaust and the power of powerlessness: Survivor guilt an unhealed wound', in C. Covington, P. Williams, J. Knox and J. Arundale (eds), *Terrorism and War: Unconscious Dynamics of Political Violence*, London: Karnac Books.

2. Ker-Lindsay, J. (2011), *The Cyprus Problem What Everyone Needs to Know*, Oxford: Oxford University Press.

3. Varnava, A. (2017), *British Imperialism in Cyprus, 1878–1915: The Inconsequential Possession*, Manchester: Manchester University Press.

4. Çalişkan, M. (2012), 'The development of inter-communal fighting in Cyprus: 1948–1974', MA diss., Middle East Technical University, Ankara, Turkey, viewed 3 March 2023, https://www.academia.edu/2380949/THE_DEVELOPMENT_OF_INTER_COMMUNAL_FIGTHING_IN_CYPRUS_1948_1974.

5. Katsourides, Y. (2018), *The Greek Cypriot Nationalist Right in the Era of British Colonialism: Emergence, Mobilisation and Transformations of Right-Wing Party Politics*, Basel: Springer International Publishing.

6. Xypolia, I. (2019), *British Imperialism and Turkish Nationalism in Cyprus, 1923-1939: Divide, Define and Rule*, London: Routledge.

7. Parikiaki (2020), 'Tribute to the Cyprus regiment in World War Two', *Parikiaki*, 10 May 2020, viewed 3 March 2023, https://www.parikiaki.com/2020/05/tribute-to-the-cyprus-regiment-in-world-war-two/.

8. Richter, H. (2010), *A Concise History of Modern Cyprus 1878–2009*, Mainz, Germany: Rutzen.

9. Mallinson, W. (2005), *Cyprus a Modern History*, London and New York: I.B.Tauris/Bloomsbury.

10. Assir, S. (2015), 'Smartphones vital as Syrians head to Europe', *Daily Star, Lebanon*, 20 August 2015.

Notes

11. '*My Heart Belongs to*' – *100 Years of Turkish Cypriot Migration to the UK* (2017), [Film] Dir: Eithne Nightingale and Mitchell Harris commissioned by Council of Turkish Cypriot Associations, viewed 3 March 2023, https://www.youtube.com/watch?v=zkDXviGuE2U.

12. Nielson, M.B. et al. (2019), 'Risk of childhood psychiatric disorders in children of refugee parents with post-traumatic stress disorder: A nationwide, register-based, cohort study', *The Lancet*, 4: 53–359, viewed 3 March 2023, https://www.thelancet.com/action/showPdf?pii =S2468-2667%2819%2930077–5.

Chapter 4

1. Lammy, D. (2020), 'Two years after Windrush we're deporting people who've only known Britain as their home', *The Guardian*, 10 February 2020, viewed 3 March 2023, https://www. theguardian.com/commentisfree/2020/feb/10/windrush-deporting-people.

2. Olusoga, D. (2019), 'Windrush: archived documents show the long betrayal', *The Guardian*, 16 June 2019, viewed 3 March 2023, https://www.theguardian.com/uk-news/2019/jun/16/ windrush-scandal-the-long-betrayal-archived-documents-david-olusoga/.

3. Gentleman, A. (2019), *The Windrush Betrayal: Exposing the Hostile Environment*, London: Guardian Faber Publishing.

4. Gentleman, A. (2022), 'Windrush: only one in four applicants have received compensation', *The Guardian*, 22 June 2022, viewed 3 March 2023, https://www.theguardian.com/uk-news/2022/jun/22/windrush-one-in-four-applicants-received-compensation-home-office.

5. Ward, E.J. (2020), 'Home office deports around 20 "violent and persistent offenders" to Jamaica', *LBC*, 11 February 2020, viewed 3 March 2023, https://www.lbc.co.uk/news/uk/ government-appeals-deportation-flight-jamaica/.

6. Williams, W. (2020), 'Windrush lessons learned review', *Home Office, GOV.UK*, viewed 3 March 2023, https://www.gov.uk/government/publications/windrush-lessons-learned-review-progress-update/windrush-lessons-learned-review-progress-update-accessible.

7. Gentleman, A. *The Windrush Betrayal: Exposing the Hostile Environment,* 270–1.

8. Lammy, 'Two years after Windrush we're deporting people who've only known Britain as their home'.

9. View from the Mirror: A Cabbie's London (2018), *Lord Kitchener: The King of Calypso*, viewed 3 March 2023, https://blackcablondon.net/2018/06/22/lord-kitchener-the-king-of-calypso/.

10. Pennant, A. and Sigona, N. (2018), 'Black history is still largely ignored, 70 years after Empire Windrush reached Britain', *The Conversation*, 21 June 2018, viewed 3 March 2023, https://theconversation.com/black-history-is-still-largely-ignored-70-years-after-empire-windrush-reached-britain–98431.

11. Brinkhurst-Cuff, C. (2018), *Mother Country: Real Stories of the Windrush Children*, London: Headline.

12. Kofman, E. (2004), 'Family-related migration: A critical review of European studies', *Journal of Ethnic and Migration Studies*, 30: 243–62.

13. Coard, B. (1971), *How the West Indian Child Is Made Educationally Sub-normal in the British School System*, London: New Beacon Books.

14. Norwood, K.J. (2015), '"If you is white, you's alright … " stories about colorism in America', *Washington Studies Global Law Review* 14 (4), viewed 3 March 2023, https://openscholarship.wustl.edu/law_globalstudies/vol14/iss4/8.

15. Waters, R. (2019), *Thinking Black; Britain 1964–1985*, Oakland, California, US: University of California Press.

16. Gilroy, P. (1987), *There Ain't no Black in the Union Jack: The Cultural Politics of Race and Nation*, London: Hutchinson.

17. Maggs, J. (2019), *Fighting Sus: Then and Now*, London: Institute or Race Relations, viewed 3 March 2023, https://irr.org.uk/article/fighting-sus-then-and-now/.

18. Agnew-Pauley, W. and Akintoye, B. (2021), 'Stop and search disproportionately affects black communities – yet police powers are being extended', *The Conversation*, viewed 3 March 2023, https://theconversation.com/stop-and-search-disproportionately-affects-black-communities-yet-police-powers-are-being-extended-165477.

19. GOV.UK (2022), 'Ethnicity faces and figures: Stop and search', *Crime, Justice and the Law, GOV.UK*, 27 May 2022, viewed 3 March 2023, https://www.ethnicity-facts-figures.service.gov.uk/crime-justice-and-the-law/policing/stop-and-search/latest.

20. Travis, A. (2017), 'Young black people nine times more likely to be jailed than young white people – report', *The Guardian*, 1 September 2017, viewed 3 March 2023, https://www.theguardian.com/society/2017/sep/01/young-black-people-jailed-moj-report-david-lammy.

21. GOV.UK (2021), Ethnicity and the criminal justice system, 2020, *Ministry of Justice National Statistics, GOV.UK*, 2 December 2021, viewed 3 March 2023, https://www.gov.uk/government/statistics/ethnicity-and-the-criminal-justice-system-statistics-2020/ethnicity-and-the-criminal-justice-system–2020.

22. Williams, 'Windrush lessons learned review'.

23. Gentleman, A. *The Windrush Betrayal: Exposing the Hostile Environment*, 271.

24. Taylor, D. (2019), 'Revealed: five men killed in past year after being deported from UK to Jamaica', *The Guardian*, 9 May 2019, viewed 3 March 2023, https://www.theguardian.com/uk-news/2019/may/09/revealed-five-men-killed-since-being-deported-uk-jamaica-home-office.

25. Gentleman, 'Windrush: only one in four applicants have received compensation'.

Chapter 5

1. *Ugwumpiti* (2016), [Film] Eithne Nightingale, Maurice Nwokeji and Mitchell Harris: UK: Child Migrant Stories, viewed 3 March 2023, https://childmigrantstories.com/ugwumpiti/.

2. Rea, W. (2020), 'Legacies of Biafra', *African Arts*, 53 (1), viewed 3 March 2023, https://direct.mit.edu/afar/article/53/1/82/55150/Legacies-of-Biafra.

3. Nwaubani, A.T. (2020), 'Remembering Nigeria's Biafran war that many prefer to forget', *BBC News*, 15 January 2020, viewed 3 March 2023, https://www.bbc.co.uk/news/world-africa–51094093.

4. Migration Museum, London, viewed 3 March 2023, https://www.migrationmuseum.org.

5. Beyer, C. (2019), 'The beliefs and practices of Rastafari', *Learn Religions*, 25 June 2019, viewed 3 March 2023, https://www.learnreligions.com/rastafari–95695.

Notes

6. Curtis, M. (2020), 'How Britain's Labour Government facilitated the massacre of Biafrans in Nigeria – to protects its oil interests', *Declassified UK*, 5 May 2020, viewed 3 March 2023, http://markcurtis.info/2020/05/05/how-britains-labour-government-facilitated-the-massacre-of-biafrans-in-nigeria-to-protect-its-oil-interests/.

7. Hamilton, T. (1970), '5,000 Children evacuated from Biafra in civil war will be repatriated from Gabon and Ivory Coast', *New York Times*, 11 October 1970, viewed 3 March 2023, https://www.nytimes.com/1970/10/11/archives/5000-children-evacuated-from-biafra-in-civil-war-will-be.html.

8. Tims-Lewechi, C.P., *Women and Children Abuse in Border Communities during the Nigeria Civil War*, viewed 3 March 2023, https://www.academia.edu/7686496/WOMEN_AND_CHILDREN_ABUSE_IN_BORDER_COMMUNITIES_DURING_THE_NIGERIA.

9. Comment about *Ugwumpiti* on website childmigrantstories.com 2016 by Mary-Blossom Brown, Ph.D., Bolton, Lancashire.

10. Forsyth, F. (2020), 'Buried for 50 years: Britain's shameful role in the Biafran War', *The Guardian*, 21 January 2020, viewed 18 September 2022, https://www.theguardian.com/commentisfree/2020/jan/21/buried-50-years-britain-shameful-role-biafran-war-frederick-forsyth.

Chapter 6

1. Sparrow, A. and Rawlinson, K. (2019), 'Steve Baker declines role in Boris Johnson government as it happened', *The Guardian*, 25 July 2019, viewed 3 March 2023, https://www.theguardian.com/politics/live/2019/jul/25/boris-johnson-new-cabinet-prime-minister-chairs-first-cabinet-as-critics-say-party-now-fully-taken-over-by-hard-right-live-news?page=with:block-5d39b9b58f08d0b6ca537a93.

2. Azad Konor, A.K. (2018), *The Battle of Brick Lane*, London: Grosvenor House Publishing Ltd.

3. LBTH (2020), 'Altab Ali and the Battle of Brick Lane', *Altab Ali Foundation*, viewed 3 March 2023, https://www.youtube.com/watch?v=VHTijCA-mrU.

4. *The Battle for Brick Lane* (2018), [Film] BBC News World Service, Witness History, viewed 3 March 2023, https://www.bbc.co.uk/programmes/w3cswsnn.

5. Euston Town (2018), 'Did you know … the history of the Bengali Workers Association in Camden', *Euston Town News*, 26 July 2018, viewed 3 March 2023, https://medium.com/euston-town-news/did-you-know-the-history-of-the-bengali-workers-association-in-camden-d19b661fdf02.

6. BGSTC (1978), *Blood on the Streets: A Report by Bethnal Green and Stepney Trades Council on Racial Attacks in East London*, London: Bethnal Green and Stepney Trades Council.

7. Ullah, A.A. and Eversley, E. (2010), *Bengalis in London's East End*, London: Swadhinata Trust, 80–1.

8. Messy Nessy (2014), 'The Shoreditch Live Animal Market, 1946', *Messy Nessy, Cabinet of Chic Curiosities*, 6 November 2014, viewed 3 March 2023, https://www.messynessychic.com/2014/11/06/the-shoreditch-live-animal-market-1946.

9. Four Corners (2018), 'Oral history excerpt: Ruhul Amin', *Four Corners Archive*, recorded 8 May 2018, viewed 3 March 2023, https://www.fourcornersarchive.org/archive/view/0003779.

10. *A Kind of English* (1983), [Film] Dir: Ruhul Amin, UK: *Channel 4*, viewed 3 March 2023, https://www.youtube.com/watch?v=LkkrI8OdXSk.

11. Contrast Films Ltd. *Interview with Ruhul Amin: Hason Raja, a Galaxy Films Production*, viewed 3 March 2023, https://contrastfilms.tripod.com/id15.html.

12. Nightingale, E. (2020), 'Abdul Momen Obituary', *The Guardian*, 26 February 2020, viewed 3 March 2023, https://www.theguardian.com/uk-news/2020/feb/26/abdul-momen-obituary.

Chapter 7

1. Nightingale, E. and Swallow, D. (2003), 'The arts of the Sikh kingdoms: Collaborating with a community', in L. Peers and A. Brown (eds), *Museums and Source Communities*: *A Routledge Reader*, London: Routledge.

2. Tharoor, S. (2017), '"But what about the railways…?" The myth of Britain's gifts to India', *The Guardian*, 8 March 2017, viewed 3 March 2023, https://www.theguardian.com/world/2017/mar/08/india-britain-empire-railways-myths-gifts.

3. Dieterich-Hartwell, R. and Koch, S.C. (2017), 'Creative arts therapies as temporary home for refugees: Insights from literature and practice', *Behavioral Sciences*, 7 (4): 69, viewed 3 March 2023, https://www.ncbi.nlm.nih.gov/pmc/articles/PMC5746678/.

Chapter 8

1. Vu, K.T. and Puryear, C. (2016), *Catholic with Confucian Tendencies: The True Story of the Extreme Adventures of a Vietnamese Boat Person*, London: Self-published.

2. *Passing Tides* (2016), [Film} Dir: Eithne Nightingale, Linh Vu and Mitchell Harris, UK: Child Migrant Stories, viewed 3 March 2023, https://childmigrantstories.com/2016/06/09/passing-tides-story-of-a-young-girl-escaping-vietnam-with-her-father/.

3. Nghia, M.V. (2006), *The Vietnamese Boat People, 1954 and 1975–1992*, Jefferson, N.C., US: McFarland & Co.

4. Herring, G. (2001), *America's Longest War: The United States and Vietnam, 1950–1975*, New York, US: McGraw-Hill Education.

5. Vu and Puryear, *Catholic with Confucian Tendencies*.

6. Ibid:109–110.

7. Ibid:109.

8. Crangle, J. (2016), 'How not to resettle refugees – lessons from the struggles of the Vietnamese 'boat people', *The Conversation*, viewed 3 March 2023, https://theconversation.com/how-not-to-resettle-refugees-lessons-from-the-struggles-of-the-vietnamese-boat-people-63678.

9. Skaife, J. Le. (2011), 'A divided Vietnamese community in France and its political repercussions', *Newgeography,* 15 July 2011, viewed 3 March 2023, http://www.newgeography.com/content/002338-a-divided-vietnamese-community-france-and-its-political-repercussions.

Notes

Chapter 9

1. Heywood, F. (2010), 'The V&A through the eyes of refugees', *The Guardian*, viewed 20 September 2022, https://www.theguardian.com/society/2010/jun/09/victoria-and-albert-museum-refugee-tours.

2. Lindo-Fuentes, H. et al. (2007), *Remembering a Massacre in El Salvador: The Insurrection of 1932, Roque Dalton, and the Politics of Historical Memory*, Albuquerque, US: University of New Mexico Press.

3. Ching, E. (2016), *Stories of Civil War in El Salvador: A Battle over Memory*, Chapel Hill, US: University of North Carolina Press.

4. United States Institute of Peace (1993), *From Madness to Hope: The 12-Year War in El Salvador: Report of the Commission on the Truth for El Salvador*, viewed 3 March 2023, https://www.usip.org/sites/default/files/file/ElSalvador-Report.pdf.

5. *The House That Is Not There* (2018), [Film] Dir: Eithne Nightingale, Gabriela Bran and Mitchell Harris, UK: Child Migrant Stories, viewed 3 March 2023, https://childmigrantstories.com/the-house-that-is-not-there/.

Chapter 10

1. ECRI (2011), 'ECRI report on Turkey', *European Commission against Racism and Intolerance*, 8, viewed 3 March 2023, https://rm.coe.int/fourth-report-on-turkey/16808b5c7e.

2. Minority Rights Group International, 'Turkey: Alevis', *World Directory of Minorites and Indigenous People*, viewed 3 March 2023, https://minorityrights.org/minorities/alevis/.

Chapter 11

1. Hurrell, D. and Campbell, A. (2018), *Saving Jack: The Story of the Seamen's Mission of the Methodist Church, The Queen Victoria Seamen's Rest*, London: QVSR.

2. Abdullahi, S.B. and Wei, L. (2021), 'Living with diversity and change: Intergenerational differences in language and identity in the Somali community in Britain', *International Journal of the Sociology of Language*, 269: 15–45, viewed 3 March 2023, https://doi.org/10.1515/ijsl-2020-0007.

3. Griffiths, D. (1997), 'Somali refugees in Tower Hamlets: Clanship and new identities', *Journal of Ethnic and Migration Studies*, 23 (1): 5–24, viewed 3 March 2023, https://www.tandfonline.com/doi/abs/10.1080/1369183X.1997.9976572.

4. Abdullahi and Wei, (2021), 'Living with diversity and change', 15–45.

5. Lewis, J. (2021), *Women of the Somali Diaspora: Refugees, Resilience and Rebuilding after Conflict*, London: Hurst.

6. Open Society Foundations (2014), 'Somalis in London', *At Home in Europe, Education* 50–60, US: Pen Society Initiative for Europe, viewed 3 March 2023, https://www.opensocietyfoundations.org/uploads/cfbed57a-9d85-454f-9e8d-d65b3aeaf1b9/somalis-london-20141010.pdf.

7. Ibid.

8. Hemmings, J. (2010), *Understanding East London's Somali Community*, London: Options UK, 79–80, viewed 3 March 2023, http://karin-ha.org.uk/wp-content/uploads/2013/01/Understanding-East-Londons-Somali-Communities.pdf.

9. Richardson, H. (2019), 'Thousands of teenagers in care living without adults', *BBC News*, 13 March 2019, viewed 3 March 2023, https://www.bbc.co.uk/news/education-47539071. Solomon, E. (2020), 'Unregulated children: DFE must not forget about children who are not in care', *Children and Young People Now*, 12 June 2020, viewed 3 March 2023, https://www.cypnow.co.uk/blogs/article/unregulated-consultation-dfe-must-not-forget-about-children-who-are-not-in-care.

10. Hemmings, (2010), *Understanding East London's Somali Community*, 33–4.

11. Office for Students (2021), 'Consistency Needed: Care experienced students and higher education', *Insight*, 8 April 2021, viewed 3 March 2023, https://www.officeforstudents.org.uk/media/645a9c30-75db-4114-80b5-3352d4cf47a9/insight-8-april-2021-finalforweb.pdf.

12. Gutale, A. (2015), 'Life after losing remittances: Somalis share their stories', *The Guardian*, 18 June 2015, viewed 3 March 2023, https://www.theguardian.com/global-development-professionals-network/2015/jun/18/life-after-losing-remittances-somalis-share-their-stories-somalia.

13. Hemmings, (2010), *Understanding East London's Somali Community*, 85–7.

14. BBC (2018), 'Somalia profile – timeline', *BBC News*, 4 January 2018, viewed 3 March 2023, https://www.bbc.co.uk/news/world-africa-14094632.

Chapter 12

1. *Common English Bible*, I Kings 10.

2. Sanchez, F. (2021), 'Where did the Queen of Sheba rule – Arabia or Africa?', *National Geographic*, 7 June 2021, viewed 3 March 2023, https://www.nationalgeographic.co.uk/history-and-civilisation/2021/06/where-did-the-queen-of-sheba-rule-arabia-or-africa.

3. McLaughlin, D. (2007), *Yemen*, UK: Bradt.

4. United National Foundation, *Yemen – a Brief Background*, viewed 3 March 2023, https://unfoundation.org/what-we-do/issues/peace-human-rights-and-humanitarian-response/yemen-a-brief-background/.

5. Brehony, N. (2017), *Hadhramaut and Its Diaspora: Yemeni Politics, Identity and Migration*, London,UK and New York, US: I.B.Tauris.

6. Harb, T. (2019), 'Yemen – One of the worst places in the world to be a woman', *Amnesty International*, viewed 3 March 2023, https://www.amnesty.org/en/latest/campaigns/2019/12/yemen-one-of-the-worst-places-in-the-world-to-be-a-woman/.

7. Stark, F. (2010), *A Winter in Arabia: A Journey through Yemen* (reprint), UK: Tauris Parke Paperbacks.

8. Aljazeera (2018), 'Key facts about the war in Yemen', *Aljazeera*, 25 March 2018, viewed 3 March 2023, https://www.aljazeera.com/news/2018/3/25/key-facts-about-the-war-in-yemen.

9. BBC News (2017), 'Somaliland profile', *BBC News*, 14 December 2017, viewed 3 March 2023, https://www.bbc.co.uk/news/world-africa-14115069.

Notes

Chapter 13

1. United Nations (2016), 'Female genital mutilation on the rise', *United National Human Rights*, viewed 3 March 2023, https://www.ohchr.org/en/press-releases/2016/04/female-genital-mutilation-guinea-rise-zeid.

2. Ibid.

3. UNFPA-UNICEF (2018), 'Performance analysis for phase 11', *Joint Programme on Female Genital Mutilation: Accelerating Change*, 64, August 2018, viewed 3 March 2023, https://www.orchidproject.org/wp-content/uploads/2019/03/UNFPA-UNICEF-Phase2Performance_2018_web_0.pdf.

4. United Nations (2016), 'Female genital mutilation on the rise', *United National Human Rights*, viewed 3 March 2023, https://www.ohchr.org/en/press-releases/2016/04/female-genital-mutilation-guinea-rise-zeid.

5. Ibid.

6. Refugee Council (2022), *Identity Crisis: How the Age Dispute Crisis Puts Children at Risk*, September 2022, viewed 3 March 2023, https://media.refugeecouncil.org.uk/wp-content/uploads/2022/09/08125100/Identity-Crisis-September-2022.pdf.

7. Coram (2013), 'Happy birthday? Disputing the age of children in the immigration system', *Children's Legal Centre, Coram*, May 2013, viewed 3 March 2023, https://www.childrenslegalcentre.com/wp-content/uploads/2017/04/Happy_Birthday_Exec_Summary.pdf.

8. Solomon, 'Unregulated children'.

9. Devenney, K. (2020), 'Social work with unaccompanied asylum-seeking young people: Reframing social care professionals as "co-navigators"', *The British Journal of Social Work*, 50 (3): 926–43, viewed 3 March 2023, https://doi.org/10.1093/bjsw/bcz071.

10. *Child Migrants Welcome?* (2018), [Film] Dir: Eithne Nightingale and Mitchell Harris (UK): Child Migrant Stories, Gulwali Passarlay on age assessment 15.28–18.07, viewed 3 March 2023, https://childmigrantstories.com/films/child-migrants-welcome/.

11. Lambrechts, A. A. (2020), 'The super-disadvantaged in higher education: Barriers to access for refugee background students in England', *Higher Education* 80: 803–22, viewed 3 March 2023, https://doi.org/10.1007/s10734-020-00515-4.

Chapter 14

1. Hilton, R. (2017), 'Review: Dear Home Office 2: Still pending', *A Younger Theatre*, 16 September 2017, viewed 3 March 2023, https://www.ayoungertheatre.com/review-dear-home-office-2-still-pending/. Written by Dawn Harrison and directed by Dawn Harrison and Rosanna Jahangard.

2. Phosphoros Theatre, viewed 3 March 2023, https://www.phosphorostheatre.com.

Phosphoros Theatre was founded in 2015 and is an award-winning, industry-leading company focused on amplifying refugee voices and bringing them to the main stage. They collaborate with artists, audiences and community members with lived experience of forced migration, particularly current and former unaccompanied asylum-seeking children, inviting the public to listen, learn and advocate for change. As well as touring professional productions around the UK they have an extensive community engagement programme, including their women's only project 'Phosphoros Sisters'. They are a registered Charity and in 2019 became one of the first Theatre Companies of Sanctuary. The Artistic Directors are Kate Duffy-Syedi, Dawn Harrison and Juliet Styles, viewed 3 September 2022 https://www.phosphorostheatre.com.

3. MICLU, *Breaking the Chains*, viewed 3 March 2023, https://miclu.org/breaking-the-chains.

4. McKinney, C.J. (2019), 'Half of all immigration appeals now succeed', *Free Movement,* 13 June 2019, viewed 3 March 2023, https://freemovement.org.uk/half-of-all-immigration-appeals-now-succeed/.

5. Taylor, D. (2019), 'Eritrean refugee, 19, killed himself as he "feared he would be sent back"', *The Guardian*, 8 November 2019, viewed 3 March 2023, https://amp.theguardian.com/uk-news/2019/nov/08/eritrean-refugee-19-who-killed-himself-feared-he-would-be-sent-back.

6. Heit, L. (2019), 'Why are so many people fleeing Eritrea?' *Choose Love*, 27 February 2019, viewed 3 March 2023, https://chooselove.org/news/why-are-so-many-people-fleeing-eritrea/.

7. Taylor, A. (2015), 'The brutal dictatorship the world keeps ignoring', *Washington Post,* 12 June 2015, viewed 3 March 2023, https://www.washingtonpost.com/news/worldviews/wp/2015/06/12/the-brutal-dictatorship-the-world-keeps-ignoring/.

8. Human Rights Watch (2018), 'Human rights situation in Eritrea', *Submission to the African Commission on Human and People's Right*s, 27 April 2018, viewed 3 March 2023, https://www.hrw.org/news/2018/04/27/human-rights-situation-eritrea.

9. RMMS (2014), 'Going West: Contemporary mixed migration trends from the Horn of Africa to Libya & Europe', *The Regional Mixed Migration Secretariat,* June 2014, viewed 3 March 2023, https://mixedmigration.org/wp-content/uploads/2018/05/008_going-west.pdf.

10. Davies, T. and Isakjee, A. (2015), 'Geography, migration and abandonment in the Calais refugee camp', *Political Geography* 49: 93–5.

11. Dawn Harrison, Kate Duffy-Syedi's mother, has been a television writer for over twenty years: Kate has done a degree in Applied Theatre and has now begun her PhD on refugee theatre.

12. MvVeigh, K. (2016), 'Judges deem Eritrea unsafe for migrants' return as Home Office advice rebutted', *The Guardian*, 19 October 2016, viewed 3 March 2023, https://www.theguardian.com/global-development/2016/oct/19/judges-deem-eritrea-unsafe-for-migrants-return-home-office-advice-rebutted-inexcusable-delay.

Chapter 15

1. Abridged essay by Malek, Isle of Bute.

2. Wintour, P. and Watt, N. (2015), 'David Cameron says UK will fulfil moral responsibility over migration crisis', *The Guardian*, 3 September 2015, viewed 3 March 2023, https://www.theguardian.com/uk-news/2015/sep/03/david-cameron-says-uk-will-fulfil-moral-responsibility-over-migration-crisis.

3. BBC (2015), 'UK to accept 20,000 refugees from Syria by 2020', *BBC News*, 7 September 2015, viewed 3 March 2023, https://www.bbc.co.uk/news/uk–34171148.

Notes

4. Hamilton, J. (2015), 'Bute welcomes first of 15 refugee families from Syria', *The National*, 4 December 2015, viewed 3 March 2023, https://www.thenational.scot/news/14900781.bute-welcomes-first-of-15-refugee-families-from-syria/.

5. Reid, S. (2015), 'Senseless! Why are Syrian refugees being foisted on a remote Scottish island with high unemployment and poverty – then given perks some locals don't enjoy?', *Mail Online*, 8 December 2015, viewed 3 March 2023, https://www.dailymail.co.uk/news/article-3366575/Senseless-Syrian-refugees-foisted-remote-Scottish-island-high-unemployment-poverty-given-perks-locals-don-t-enjoy.html.

6. Briggs, B. (2016), 'One year on: From war in Syria to school on a small island in Scotland', *Theirworld*, 8 December 2016, viewed 3 March 2023, https://theirworld.org/news/one-year-on-syrian-refugee-children-at-school-on-scottish-island/.

7. De Block, L. and Buckingham, D. (2007), *Global Children, Global Media. Migration, Media and Childhood*, Basingstoke: Palgrave Macmillan.

8. Javid, S. (2019), 'New global resettlement scheme for the most vulnerable refugees announced', *Home Office, GOV.UK*, 17 June 2019, viewed 3 March 2023, https://www.gov.uk/government/news/new-global-resettlement-scheme-for-the-most-vulnerable-refugees-announced.

9. Patel, P. (2021), 'Refugee protection and integration, statement by the Secretary of State', *UK Parliament*, 18 March 2021, viewed 3 March 2023, https://questions-statements.parliament.uk/written-statements/detail/2021-03-18/hcws855.

Chapter 16

1. UNHCR (2022), *Operation Data Portal: Ukraine Refugee Situation*, viewed 3 March 2023, https://data.unhcr.org/en/situations/ukraine.

2. Save the Children (2022), *Ukraine Refugees*, viewed 3 March 2023, https://www.savethechildren.org/us/what-we-do/emergency-response/refugee-children-crisis/ukrainian-refugees.

3. GOV.UK (2022), '"Homes for Ukraine" scheme launches', *GOV.UK,* 14 March 2022, viewed 3 March 2023, https://www.gov.uk/government/news/homes-for-ukraine-scheme-launches.

4. Havana, O. (2022), 'Escaping War: What Ukrainian children carry with them', *Aljazeera*, 3 June 2022, viewed 3 March 2023, https://www.aljazeera.com/features/longform/2022/6/3/escaping-war.

5. Fortuna, G. (2022), 'EU relaxes paperwork for pets travelling with Ukrainian refugees', *EURACTVE.COM*, 27 February 2022, viewed 3 March 2023, https://www.euractiv.com/section/health-consumers/news/eu-relaxes-entry-paperwork-for-pets-travelling-with-ukrainian-refugees/.

6. Batha, E. (2022), 'Europe's schools show "huge solidarity" to welcome Ukraine's refugee children', *Global Citizen*, 24 March 2022, viewed 3 March 2023, https://www.globalcitizen.org/en/content/ukraine-refugee-children-schools-europe-education/?utm_source=paidsearch&utm_medium=ukgrant&utm_campaign=genericbrandname&gclid=CjwKCAjwt7SWBhAnEiwAx8ZLaiHMdephhi7g-0y93YIRec5cDbCFSObncQDEvNsjlEfDvkG7cMMyChoCS6AQAvD_BwE.

7. GOV.UK (2022), 'Apply for a UK family scheme visa', *UK Visas and Immigration and Home Office*, 4 March 2022, viewed 3 March 2023, https://www.gov.uk/guidance/apply-for-a-ukraine-family-scheme-visa.

8. Adams, C. (2022), 'Ukrainian refugees are now living in the UK – so how is it going?' *BBC News*, 28 May 2022, viewed 19 August 2022, https://www.bbc.com/news/uk-61548979.

9. Dugan, E. (2022), 'Hundreds of Ukrainian refugees left homeless in England, data shows', *The Guardian*, 16 June, 2022, viewed 3 March 2023, https://www.theguardian.com/world/2022/jun/16/hundreds-of-ukrainian-refugees-left-homeless-in-england-data-shows.

10. Vicol, D. and Sehic, A. (2022), 'Six months on: The UK's response to the humanitarian crisis in Ukraine, and how the government can better protect refugees', *Work Rights Centre*, 26 September 2022, viewed 3 March 2023, https://www.workrightscentre.org/media/1246/ukraine-report-six-months-on-ChapterConsistency-final.pdf.

11. BBC News (2022), 'Ukraine refugees: Calais visa scenes damaged UK – Mark Drakeford', *BBC News*, 8 March 2022, viewed 3 March 2023, https://www.bbc.com/news/uk-wales-politics-60664557.

12. Council of the EU (2022), 'Ukraine: Council unanimously introduces temporary protection for persons fleeing the war', *European Council of the European Union*, 4 March 2022, viewed 3 March 2023, https://www.consilium.europa.eu/en/press/press-releases/2022/03/04/ukraine-council-introduces-temporary-protection-for-persons-fleeing-the-war/.

13. UNHCR (2022), *Operation Data Portal: Ukraine Refugee Situation*, viewed 3 March 2023, https://data.unhcr.org/en/situations/ukraine.

14. Ibrahim (2022), 'Why did we have to freeze in the forest', *The New Humanitarian,* 15 March 2022, viewed 3 March 2023, https://www.thenewhumanitarian.org/first-person/2022/03/15/ukraine-poland-syria-refugee-welcome-forest.

15. Dugan, E. (2022), 'Government to change rules on letting Ukrainian children into UK', *The Guardian*, 21 June 2022, viewed 3 March 2023, https://www.theguardian.com/world/2022/jun/21/government-change-rules-unaccompanied-ukrainian-children-uk.

16. Adams, C. (2022), 'Ukrainian refugees are now living in the UK – so how is it going?', *BBC News*, 28 Mary 2022, viewed 3 March 2023, https://www.bbc.co.uk/news/uk–61548979.

17. Culbertson, A. (2022), 'Ukrainian MP reveals heartbreaking note left in child refugee's backpack by his mother', *Sky News*, 3 March 2023, viewed 19 August 2022, https://news.sky.com/story/ukrainian-mp-reveals-heartbreaking-note-left-in-child-refugees-backpack-by-his-mother-12623589.

18. GOV.UK. (2023), 'Transparency data: Ukraine Family Scheme, Ukraine Sponsorship Scheme (Homes for Ukraine) and Ukraine Extension Scheme visa data', *UK Home Office*, 1 June 2023, viewed 4 June 2023, https://www.gov.uk/government/publications/ukraine-family-scheme-application-data/ukraine-family-scheme-and-ukraine-sponsorship-scheme-homes-for-ukraine-visa-data--2#:~:text=9%2C400-,Total%20arrivals%20of%20Ukraine%20Scheme%20visa%2Dholders%20in%20the%20UK,via%20Ukraine%20Sponsorship%20Scheme%3A%20124%2C000.

19. Walsh, P.W. and Sumption, M. (2022), 'Migration and the Ukraine crisis', *The Migration Observatory, University of Oxford*, 14 March 2022, viewed 3 March 2023, https://migrationobservatory.ox.ac.uk/resources/briefings/migration-and-the-ukraine-crisis/.

Conclusion

1. Alÿs, F. (2021), 'Don't cross the bridge before you get to the river', *Galleries Now*, viewed 3 March 2023, https://www.galleriesnow.net/shows/francis-alys-dont-cross-the-bridge-before-you-get-to-the-river/.

2. UNHCR (1989), 'Convention on the rights of the child', *United Nations Human Rights: Office of the High Commissioner for Human Rights*, viewed 3 March 2023, http://www.ohchr.org/en/professionalinterest/pages/crc.aspx.

3. Ackers, L. and Stalford, H. (2004), *A Community for Children? Children, Citizenship and Internal Migration in the EU*, Aldershot: Ashgate.

4. Payne, S., Horb, S., and Relf, M. (1999), *Loss and Bereavement*, Philadelphia: Open University Press.

5. Suárez-Orozco, C., Todorova, I. and Louie, J. (2002), '"Making up for lost time": The experience of separation and reunification among immigrant families', *Family Process*, 41: 625–43.

6. Veale, A. and Dona, G. (eds) (2014), *Child and Youth Migration: Mobility-in-Migration in an Era of Globalization*, Basingstoke, UK and New York, USA: Palgrave Macmillan.

7. BenEzer, G. and Zetter, R. (2014), 'Searching for directions: Conceptual and methodological challenges in researching refugee journeys', *Journal of Refugee Studies*, 28 (3): 297–318, viewed 3 March 2023, https://www.semanticscholar.org/paper/Searching-for-Directions%3A-Conceptual-and-Challenges-Benezer-Zetter/4ab58e5fda0a2f93568179b05310ef10ceee44de.

8. Ansell, N. and van Blerk, L. (2006). 'Children's experiences of migration: Moving in the wake of aids', *Environment and Planning D: Society and Space*, 24 (3): 449–71.

9. Suárez-Orozco, C., Bang, H.J. and Kim, H.Y. (2011), '"I felt like my heart was staying behind": Psychological implications of family separations & reunifications for immigrant youth', *Journal of Adolescent Research*, 26: 222–57.

10. Arnold, E. (1991), 'Issues of reunification of migrant West Indian children in the United Kingdom', in J.L. Roopnarine and J. Brown (eds), *Caribbean Families Diversity among Ethnic Groups*, 243–58, Greenwich, CT.: Ablex Publishing.

11. Smith, A., Lalonde, R.N. and Johnson, S. (2004), 'Serial migration and its implications for the parent-child relationship: A retrospective analysis of the experiences of the children of Caribbean immigrants', *Cultural Diversity and Ethnic Minority Psychology*, 10: 107–22.

12. Miroff, N. (2020), 'Kids in cages': It's true that Obama built the cages at the border. But Trump's "zero tolerance" immigration policy had no precedent', *Washington Post*, October 23 2020, viewed 3 March 2023, https://www.washingtonpost.com/immigration/kids-in-cages-debate-trump-obama/2020/10/23/8ff96f3c-1532-11eb-82af-864652063d61_story.html.

13. Kushner, T. (2012), 'Constructing (another) ideal refugee journey: the *Kinder*', in T. Kushner (ed.), *The Battle of Britishness: Migrant Journeys 1685 to the Present*, 119–38, Manchester and New York: Manchester University Press.

14. Smith, Lalonde and Johnson, 'Serial migration and its implications for the parent-child relationship: A retrospective analysis of the experiences of the children of Caribbean immigrants'.

15. Bryceson, D. and Vuorela, U. (2002), 'The transnational families in the twenty-first century', in D. Bryceson and U. Vuorela (eds), *The Transnational Family: New European Frontiers and Global Networks*, 3–30, Oxford, UK: Berg.

16. Reliefweb (2016), 'CONNECTING REFUGEES – How internet and mobile connectivity can improve refugee well-being and transform humanitarian action', *UNHCR*, 21 July 2016, viewed 3 March 2023, https://reliefweb.int/report/world/connecting-refugees-how-internet-and-mobile-connectivity-can-improve-refugee-well-being?gclid=EAIaIQobChMI5_OfrWU-gIVlIODBx3I8QQpEAAYASAAEgJE9vD_BwE.

17. Davies, H. (2012), 'Affinities, seeing and feeling like family: Exploring why children value face-to-face contact', *Childhood*, 19 (1): 8–23.

18. Light, M. (2016), 'Do your parenting by Skype, UK Home Office tells father being deported to Jamaica', *OpenDemocracy website*, 6 September 2016, viewed 3 March 2023, https://www.opendemocracy.net/en/shine-a-light/do-your-parenting-by-skype-uk-tells-fathers-being-deported-to-jama/.

19. Dench, G., Gavron, K. and Young, M. (2006), *The New East End: Kinship, Race and Conflict*, London: Young Foundation.

20. Weale, S. (2018), 'Refugee children face long delays accessing education in the UK', *The Guardian*, 20 September 2018, viewed 3 March 2023, https://www.theguardian.com/education/2018/sep/20/refugee-children-face-long-delays-accessing-education-in-uk.

21. Spicer, N. (2008), 'Places of exclusion and inclusion: Asylum-seeker and refugee experiences of neighbourhoods in the UK', *Journal of Ethnic and Migration Studies*, 34 (3): 491–510.

22. Arnot, M. et al. (2014), *School Approaches to the Education of EAL Students: Language Development, Social Integration and Achievement*, Cambridge: The Bell Foundation.

23. Cummins, J. (2000), *Language, Power, and Pedagogy: Bilingual Children in the Crossfire*, Clevedon: Multilingual Matters.

24. Okolosie, L. (2014), 'How white, black and brown students learn the language of racist bullying', *The Guardian*, 10 January 2014, viewed 3 March 2023, https://www.theguardian.com/commentisfree/2014/jan/10/racist-bullying-children-media-white-black.

25. Sanghera, S. (2021), *Empireland: How Imperialism Has Shaped Modern Britain*, UK: Viking Books.

26. Virtual College (2021), 'What is the Children Act', *Virtual College website*, viewed 3 March 2023, https://www.virtual-college.co.uk/resources/what-is-the-children-act.

27. United Nations, 'Convention on the rights of the child'.

28. Giraud, M. (2009), 'Colonial racism, ethnicity. The lessons of migration experiences of French speaking Caribbean populations', in M. Cervantes-Rodriguez et al. (eds), *Caribbean Migration to Western Europe and the United States: Essays on Incorporation, Identity, and Citizenship*, 43–57, Philadelphia: Temple University Press.

29. Smith, F. and Barker, J. (2000), 'Contested spaces: Children's experiences of out-of-school care in England and Wales', *Childhood: A Global Journal of Child Research*, 7 (3): 315–33.

30. Sheringham, O. (2013), *Transnational Religious Spaces; Faith and the Brazilian Migration Experience*, Basingstoke, UK: Palgrave Macmillan.

31. Bagci, S.C., Kumashiro, M., Rutland, A., Smith, P.K. and Blumberg, H. (2014), 'Cross-ethnic friendships, psychology well-being, and academic outcomes: Study of South Asian and white children in the UK', *European Journal of Developmental Psychology*, 14 (2): 190–205.

32. Spicer, 'Places of exclusion and inclusion: Asylum-seeker and refugee experiences of neighbourhoods in the UK'.

33. Wells, K. (2009), *Childhood in a Global Perspective*, Cambridge, UK: Polity Press.

34. Maggs, J. (2019), 'Fighting Sus! then and now', *Institute of Race Relations*, 4 April 2019, viewed 3 March 2023, https://irr.org.uk/article/fighting-sus-then-and-now/.

35. Bourdieu, P. (1986), 'The Forms of Capital', in John E. Richardson (ed.), *Handbook of Theory and Research for the Sociology of Education*, 241–58. Westport, US: Greenwood Press.

36. Hodes, M. (2000), 'Pyschologically distressed refugee children in the United Kingdom', *Child Psychology and Psychiatry Review*, 5 (2): 57–68.

37. Blunt, A. et al. (2012), 'Diasporic returns to the city: Anglo-Indian and Jewish visits to Calcutta', *South Asian Diaspora*, 4: 25–43.

38. Zeitlyn, B. (2012), Maintaining transnational social fields, the role of visits to Bangladesh for British Bangladeshi children', *Journal of Ethnic and Migration Studies*, 38 (6): 953–68.

39. Tsuda, T. (ed.) (2009), *Diasporic Homecomings: Ethnic Return Migration in Comparative Perspective*, Stanford, US: Stanford University Press.

40. Burt, C. (1943), 'War Neurosis in British Children', *Nervous Child*, 2: 324.

41. Garwood, A. (2002), 'The Holocaust and the power of powerlessness', in C. Covington, P. Williams, J. Knox and J. Arundale (eds), *Terrorism and War: Unconscious Dynamics of Political Violence*, London: Karnac Books.

42. Wiese, E.B.P. (2010), 'Culture and migration: Psychological trauma in children and adolescents', *Traumatology*, 16 (4): 142–52.

43. Dieterich-Hartwell, R. and Koch, S.C. (2017), 'Creative arts therapies as temporary home for refugees: Insights from literature and practice', *Behavioral Sciences*, 7 (4): 69, viewed 3 March 2023, https://www.ncbi.nlm.nih.gov/pmc/articles/PMC5746678/.

44. Klein, H. (1984), 'The survivor's search for meaning and identity', *The Nazi Concentration Camps*, Proceedings of the fourth Yad Vashem International Historical Conference, pp. 543–52. Jerusalem: Yad Vashem.

45. Korfiati, I. (2016), 'Learning from child migrant stories: exploring the impact school sessions at the Hackney Museum have on Year 6 pupils' understanding of the refugee experience', MA diss., Institute of Education, University College London.

46. Greenblatt-Kimron, L. et al. (2021), 'Event centrality and secondary traumatization among Holocaust survivors' offspring and grandchildren: A three-generation study', *Journal of Anxiety Disorders*, 24 Apr 2021, viewed 3 March 2023, https://www.sciencedirect.com/science/article/abs/pii/S0887618521000487?via%3Dihub.

47. Ptsduk (2021), 'PTSD in refugees and asylum seekers', *ptsduk*, viewed 3 March 2023, https://www.ptsduk.org/what-is-ptsd/causes-of-ptsd/refugees/.

48. Vollans, C. (2021), 'Using art therapy to heal trauma', *Nursery World*, 1 September 2021, viewed 3 March 2023, https://www.nurseryworld.co.uk/features/article/using-art-therapy-to-heal-trauma.

49. *Child Migrants Welcome?* (2018), [Film] Dir: Eithne Nightingale and Mitchell Harris, UK: Child Migrant Stories, viewed 26 September 2022, https://childmigrantstories.com/films/child-migrants-welcome/.

50. UNHCR (2019), 'Teaching about refugees: Guidance on working with refugee children struggling with stress and trauma', *UNHCR*, viewed 3 March 2023, https://www.unhcr.org/uk/59d346de4.pdf.

51. Palanac, A. (2020), 'Towards a trauma-informed ELT pedagogy for refugees', *Language Issues*, 30 (2): 3–14, viewed 3 March 2023, https://www.researchgate.net/publication/341452361_Towards_a_trauma-informed_ELT_pedagogy_for_refugees.

52. *Child Migrants Welcome?* [Film] Dir: Eithne Nightingale and Mitchell Harris, UK: Child Migrant Stories.

53. Malik, K. (2021), 'Britain's offer to Afghan refugees is not 'generous'. It's blindly inhumane', *The Guardian*, 22 August, 2021, viewed 3 March 2023, https://www.theguardian.com/commentisfree/2021/aug/22/britains-offer-to-afghan-refugees-is-not-generous-but-blindly-inhumane.

54. Amnesty International et al. (2020), *The failure of French authorities to respect, protect and guarantee the rights of at-risk unaccompanied children (UAC) at France's internal land borders (French-Italian, French-Spanish and French-British)*, viewed 3 March 2023, https://refugee-rights.eu/wp-content/uploads/2021/05/Failure-Of-French-Authorities-To-Respect-Protect-Guarantee-Rights-Of-At-Risk-UAC.pdf.

55. Refugee Council (2021), *Thousands seeking asylum face cruel wait of years for asylum decision – fresh research shows*, July 2 2021, viewed 3 March 2023, https://www.refugeecouncil.org.uk/latest/news/thousands-seeking-asylum-face-cruel-wait-of-years-for-asylum-decision-fresh-research-shows/.

56. Refugee Council (2022), *New figures reveal scale of backlog crisis*, November 14 2022, viewed 3 March 2023, https://www.refugeecouncil.org.uk/latest/news/new-figures-reveal-scale-of-asylum-backlog-crisis/.

57. Scottish Government (2018), 'New Scots: Refugee Integration strategy 2018–2022', *Scottish Government*, viewed 3 March 2023, https://www.gov.scot/publications/new-scots-refugee-integration-strategy-2018-2022/.

58. Passarlay, G. (2015), *The Lightless Sky – An Afghan Refugee Boy's Journey to Escape to a New Life in Britain*, London: Atlantic Books.

59. Trilling, D. (2021), 'Cruel, Paranoid Failing inside the Home Office: Something is badly wrong at the heart of one of Britain's most important ministries. How did it become so broken?', *The Guardian*, 13 May 2021, viewed 3 March 2023, https://www.theguardian.com/politics/2021/may/13/cruel-paranoid-failing-priti-patel-inside-the-home-office.

60. Yeung, J. (2020), 'Climate crisis could displace 1.2 billion people by 2050, report warns', *CNN*, September 10 2020, viewed 3 March 2023, https://edition.cnn.com/2020/09/10/world/climate-global-displacement-report-intl-hnk-scli-scn/index.html.

61. GOV.UK (2021), 'Written evidence submitted by the UNHCR, the UN Refugee Agency (NBB34)', *UNHCR*, October 2021, viewed 3 March 2023, https://bills.parliament.uk/publications/43060/documents/788.

62. Ibid.

63. Ibid.

64. UNHCR, *Refugee Data Finder*, viewed 3 March 2023, https://www.unhcr.org/refugee-statistics/.

65. Hubbard, P. (2022), 'Suella Braverman's talk of an 'invasion' is a dangerous political gambit gone wrong', *Kings College London*, 3 November 2022, viewed 3 March 2023, https://www.kcl.ac.uk/suella-bravermans-talk-of-a-refugee-invasion-is-a-dangerous-political-gambit-gone-wrong.

66. GOV.UK (2022), 'National Statistics: How many people do we grant protection to?', *Home Office*, 24 November 2022, viewed 3 March 2023, https://www.gov.uk/government/statistics/immigration-statistics-year-ending-september-2022/how-many-people-do-we-grant-protection-to.

67. Refugee Council (2023), *Top facts from the latest statistics on refugees and people seeking asylum – for year ending 2022*, viewed 3 March 2023, https://www.refugeecouncil.org.uk/information/refugee-asylum-facts/top-10-facts-about-refugees-and-people-seeking-asylum/.

68. Patel, P. (2021), *Refugee protection and integration, statement made on 18 March 2021*, viewed 3 March 2023, https://questions-statements.parliament.uk/written-statements/detail/2021-03-18/hcws855.

69. Refugee Council, *Refugee Resettlement Facts,* viewed 3 March 2023, https://www.refugeecouncil.org.uk/information/refugee-asylum-facts/refugee-resettlement-facts/.

70. Bulman, M, and Kelly, N. (2022), 'Revealed: UK has failed to resettle Afghans facing torture and death despite promise', *The Guardian*, 3 December 2022, viewed 3 March 2023, https://www.theguardian.com/world/2022/dec/03/revealed-uk-has-failed-to-resettle-afghans-facing-torture-and-death-despite-promise.

71. GOV.UK, 'Written evidence submitted by the UNHCR, the UN Refugee Agency (NBB34)', *UNHCR*.

72. Blackall, M. (2022), 'More children crossing to UK since Brexit as official routes 'can't compete' with smugglers', *Inews*, 30 September 2022, viewed 3 March 2023, https://inews.co.uk/news/channel-migrants-children-crossing-uk-brexit-official-routes-smugglers–1871628.

73. Amnesty International et al. (2020), *The failure of French authorities*.

74. Brittle, R. (2021), 'Age assessment in the new plan: Something old, something new, something borrowed… something blue?', *Refugee Law Initiative, School of Oriental and African Studies*, viewed 3 March 2023, https://rli.blogs.sas.ac.uk/2021/05/21/age-assessment-in-the-new-plan-something-old-something-new-something-borrowed-something-blue/.

75. Refugee Council (2022), *Identity Crisis: How the age dispute crisis puts children at risk*, September, viewed 3 March 2023, https://media.refugeecouncil.org.uk/wp-content/uploads/2022/09/08125100/Identity-Crisis-September-2022.pdf.

76. Refugee and Migrant Children's Consortium (2022), *Briefing for debate on age disputes and removals to Rwanda*, viewed 3 March 2023, http://refugeechildrensconsortium.org.uk/wp-content/uploads/2022/07/RMCC-briefing-HoL-debate-Rwanda-age-disputes-Final_180722.pdf.

77. Weinstein, N. (2023), 'Sector's horror over reports of migrant children being trafficked from hotels', *Children & Young People Now*, 23 January 2023, viewed 3 March 2023, https://www.cypnow.co.uk/news/article/sector-s-horror-over-reports-of-migrant-children-being-trafficked-from-hotels.

78. GOV.UK. (2022), 'Nationality and Borders Bill: Children factsheet', *Home Office*, 22 February 2022, viewed 29 April 2023, https://www.gov.uk/government/publications/nationality-and-borders-bill-children-factsheet.

79. Pinter, I. (2022), 'Nationality and Borders Bill: Many of these proposals will negatively affect children, not just those concerning them directly', *LSE British Politics and Policy*, 2 January 2022, viewed 3 March 2023, https://blogs.lse.ac.uk/politicsandpolicy/nationality-borders-bill-children/.

80. Blackall, M., 'More children crossing to UK since Brexit as official routes "can't compete" with smugglers'.

81. Clarke, N. (2022), 'Terrified schoolboy scared his family will be deported to Rwanda while he's at school', *Birmingham Live*, 11 September 2022, viewed 3 March 2023, https://www.birminghammail.co.uk/black-country/terrified-schoolboy-scared-family-deported–24961409.

82. Taylor, D. (2022), 'Firm managing hotels for UK asylum seekers posts bumper profits', *The Guardian*, 31 October 2022, viewed 3 March 2023, https://www.theguardian.com/uk-news/2022/oct/31/firm-managing-hotels-for-uk-asylum-seekers-posts-bumper-profits.

83. appg (2021), *APPG on Immigration Detention. Inquiry into full detention - full report*, viewed 3 March 2023, https://appgdetention.org.uk/inquiry-into-quasi-detention-full-report-published/.

84. Crerar, P. (2023), 'Home Office to acquire fleet of ships to house asylum seekers', *The Guardian*, 1 May 2023, viewed 1 May 2023, https://www.theguardian.com/uk-news/2023/may/01/uk-planning-redundant-cruise-ships-house-asylum-seekers?CMP=Share_AndroidApp_Other.

85. GOV.UK (2022), 'Nationality and Borders Bill: Children factsheet', *Home Office*, 25 February 2022, viewed 29 April 2023, https://www.gov.uk/government/publications/nationality-and-borders-bill-children-factsheet/nationality-and-borders-bill-children-factsheet.

86. Refugee Council (2022), *Quarterly Immigration Statistics: August 2022*, viewed 3 March 2023, https://www.refugeecouncil.org.uk/wp-content/uploads/2022/09/Asylum-Statistics-September-2022.pdf.

87. Stroud, P. and Solomon, E. (2022), 'Braverman must reset Britain's refugee policy', *The Times*, 3 October 2022, viewed 3 October 2022, https://www.thetimes.co.uk/article/bca51ab0-426f-11ed-abc9-d0d53e948d21?shareToken=b4d6a50718e3178bfaddbbba04c0d7cc.

88. Stevens, A. et al. (2023), 'The UK Illegal and Immigration Bill: a child rights violation and safeguarding catastrophe', *The Lancet*, 26 April 2023, viewed 29 April 2023, https://t.co/szRkIJCWQl.

89. Solomon, E. (2023), 'Multiple government defeats are likely when the illegal immigration bill heads to the Lords', *The Guardian*, 27 April 2023, viewed 29 April 2023, https://www.theguardian.com/commentisfree/2023/apr/27/multiple-government-defeats-are-likely-when-the-immigration-bill-heads-to-the-lords/.

90. Children's Commissioner (2023), *Letter to the Home Secretary on the Illegal Migration Bill*, 13 March 2023, viewed 25 March 2023, https://www.childrenscommissioner.gov.uk/blog/letter-to-the-home-secretary-on-the-illegal-migration-bill/.

91. RCPG et al. Intercollegiate briefing paper: *Significant Harm – the effects of administrative detention on the health of children, young people and their families*, viewed 25 April 2023, https://www.bbc.co.uk/blogs/thereporters/markeaston/images/intercollegiate_statement_dec09.pdf.

92. Refugee Council (2023), *UK Government's new asylum bill threatens to lock up thousands of refugee children who come to the UK alone – Refugee Council and Barnardo's joint release*, viewed 25 April 2023, https://www.refugeecouncil.org.uk/latest/news/uk-governments-new-asylum-bill-threatens-to-lock-up-thousands-of-refugee-children-who-come-to-the-uk-alone-refugee-council-and-barnardos-joint-release/.

93. Children's Commissioner (2023), *Illegal Migration Bill – Unaccompanied Children Seeking Asylum*, 11 April 2023, viewed 25 April 2023, https://www.childrenscommissioner.gov.uk/blog/illegal-migration-bill-unaccompanied-children-seeking-asylum/.

94. Social Work Without Borders (2023), *Illegal Migration Bill: Warning to social workers!*, viewed 20 April, *2023* https://twitter.com/SocialWorkersWB/status/1648617444720689152

95. Ibid.

96. Refugee Council, *UK Government's new asylum bill threatens to lock up thousands of refugee children who come to the UK alone – Refugee Council and Barnardo's joint release*.

97. Children's Commissioner, *Illegal Migration Bill – Unaccompanied Children Seeking Asylum*.

98. Refugee and Migrant Children's Consortium (2023), *Illegal Migration Bill – Committee Stage Amendments to safeguard children*, viewed 8 June 2023, https://refugeechildrensconsortium.org.uk/wp-content/uploads/2023/03/RMCC-HOC-Committee-stage-briefing-Illegal-Migration-Bill-FINAL.pdf

99. Wheeler, C. (2023) 'Rishi Sunak faces rebellion over plans to lock up child migrants', *The Times*, 23 April 2023, viewed 25 April 2023, https://www.thetimes.co.uk/article/9c3d50f8-e116-11ed-9678-d2cf456d2b78?shareToken=6d7eea24b22aee113ee6e571b6b119a7.

100. Ibid.

101. Townsend, M. (2023), 'Home Office faces legal action against children missing from UK asylum hotels', *The Guardian*, 11 June 2023, viewed 14 June 2023.

102. May, T. (2023), 'Debate in UK parliament during the third reading of the Illegal Migration Bill', *BBC Parliament*, 26 April 2023.

103. GOV.UK (2023), *Assessing age for asylum applicants: caseworker guidance*, 31 March 2023, viewed 26 April 2023, https://www.gov.uk/government/publications/assessing-age-instruction.

104. Taylor, D. (2023), 'Hundreds of UK asylum seeker children wrongly treated as adults, report shows', *The Guardian*, 24 April 2023, viewed 26 April 2023, https://www.theguardian.com/uk-news/2023/apr/24/hundreds-of-uk-asylum-seeker-children-wrongly-treated-as-adults-report-shows.

105. Refugee and Migrant Children's Consortium (2023), *Illegal Migration Bill and Age Assessments, 24 April 2023.*

106. Taylor, D. (2023),' Data undermines Jenrick's claim about asylum seekers saying they are children', *The Guardian*,11 June 2023, viewed 14 June 2023 https://www.theguardian.com/uk-news/2023/jun/11/data-undermines-robert-jenrick-claim-about-asylum-seekers-saying-they-are-children.

107. Ibid.

108. Morrison, H. (2023), 'Death of asylum seeker Amir Safi sparks questions for Home Office', *The National*, I June 2023, viewed 14 June 2023, https://www.thenational.scot/news/23562358.death-asylum-seeker-amir-safi-sparks-questions-home-office/.

109. Ibid.

110. Refugee Council (2023), 'Refugee Council response and top facts from the Government's latest immigration statistics', *Refugee Council*, 3 June 2023, viewed 4 June 2023, https://www.refugeecouncil.org.uk/latest/news/refugee-council-response-and-top-facts-from-the-governments-latest-immigration-statistics/.

111. Lee, G. (2023), 'Asylum backlog more than ten times higher than in 2010', *Channel 4 News: FactCheck*, 7 March 2023, viewed 29 April 2023, https://www.channel4.com/news/factcheck/factcheck-asylum-backlog-more-than-ten-times-higher-than-in–2010.

112. Dathan, M. (2023), 'Small boats crisis; Just 13% of migrant asylum claims dealt with in five years', *The Times*, 19 April 2023, viewed 29 April 2023, https://www.thetimes.co.uk/article/small-boats-crisis-just-13-of-migrant-asylum-claims-dealt-with-in-five-years-3xnlsxxgt.

113. Ibid.

114. Ibid.

115. Ibid.

116. Cantor, D. (2023), 'Illegal Migration Bill: Helping force refugees into illegality and danger', *Free Movement*, 14 April 2023, viewed 27 April 2023, https://freemovement.org.uk/illegal-migration-bill-helping-force-refugees-into-illegality-and-danger/.

117. Matharu, H. (2021), 'History will judge this shabby government and its weaponisation of refugee lives' says Lord Dubs', *Byline Times*, 26 November 2021, viewed 27 April 2023, https://bylinetimes.com/2021/11/26/history-will-judge-this-shabby-government-and-its-weaponisation-of-refugee-lives-says-lord-alf-dubs/.

118. Ibid.

119. Syal, R. (2023), 'Braverman's comments on boat arrivals' values rejected by fellow Tories', *The Guardian*, 27 April 2023, viewed 29 April 2023, https://www.theguardian.com/politics/2023/apr/27/suella-braverman-comments-on-boat-arrivals-values-rejected-by-fellow-tories?CMP=Share_AndroidApp_Other

120. Ibid.

121. Ibid.

122. Dorling, D., Tomlinson, S. (2019), 'The spurious link between immigration and increased crime', *British Society of Criminology Blog*, 4 February 2019, viewed 29 April 2023, https://thebscblog.wordpress.com/2019/02/04/the-spurious-link-between-immigration-and-increased-crime/.

123. Crerar, 'Home Office to acquire fleet of ships to house asylum seekers'.

124. Stevens, 'The UK Illegal and Immigration Bill: A child rights violation and safeguarding catastrophe'.

125. Taylor, D. (2023), 'Judges urged to block Home Office plans to send refugees to Rwanda', *The Guardian*, 27 April 2023, viewed 29 April 2023, https://www.theguardian.com/uk-news/2023/apr/27/judges-urged-to-block-home-office-plans-to-send-refugees-to-rwanda.

126. Solomon, E. (2023), 'Refugee Council responds to the Court of Appeal ruling on Rwanda policy', *Refugee Council*, 29 June 2023, viewed 2 July 2023, https://www.refugeecouncil.org.uk/latest/news/refugee-council-responds-to-the-court-of-appeal-ruling-on-rwanda-policy/?utm_campaign=2324EMQ111&utm_source=rcmailchimp&utm_medium=email.

127. Taylor, D. (2023), 'Over 24,000 UK asylum seekers could be sent to Rwanda despite court ruling', *The Guardian*, 30 June 2023, viewed 2 July 2023, https://www.theguardian.com/uk-news/2023/jun/30/over-24000-uk-asylum-seekers-could-be-sent-to-rwanda-despite-court-ruling?CMP=Share_iOSApp_Other.

128. McDonald, A. (2023), 'Britain's plan to deport migrants to Rwanda will cost £169,000 per person', *Politico*, 27 June 2023, viewed 2 July 2023, https://www.politico.eu/article/uk-plan-to-deport-migrants-to-rwanda-will-cost-169000-per-person-migration-asylum/.

129. Donald, A., Grogan, J. (2023), 'The Illegal Migration Bill', *UK in a Changing Europe*, 25 April 2023, viewed 2 July 2023, https://ukandeu.ac.uk/explainers/the-illegal-migration-bill/#:~:text=The%20Bill%20will%20disqualify%20potential,an%20investigation%20or%20criminal%20proceedings.

130. BBC (2023), 'Interview of Andrew Gilmour, Assistant Secretary for Human Rights, UN, 2016–2019, by Faisal Islam, *BBC Newsnight*, 30 June 2023.

131. UK Parliament (2022), 'UK-Rwanda Migration and Economic Development Partnership', *House of Commons Library*, 20 December 2022, viewed 2 July 2023, https://commonslibrary.parliament.uk/research-briefings/cbp-9568/.

132. EIN (2023), 'Lords inflict multiple defeats on Illegal Migration Bill, including requiring it to be interpreted consistently with UK's international obligations', *electronic immigration network*, 28 June 2023, viewed 2 July 2023, https://www.ein.org.uk/news/lords-inflict-multiple-defeats-illegal-migration-bill-including-requiring-it-be-interpreted.

Notes

133. Singh, A. (2023), 'Suella Braverman's rhetoric is 'despicable' and peers will battle her over small boats law, Lord Dubs says', *iNews*, 27 April 2023, viewed 29 April 2023, https://inews.co.uk/news/politics/suella-braverman-rhetoric-despicable-peers-battle-small-boats-law-lord-dubs–2303090.

134. Picheta, R. et al. (2023), 'Britain sees record net migration levels, increasing pressure on government', *CNN*, 25 May 2023, viewed 14 June 2023, https://edition.cnn.com/2023/05/25/uk/uk-net-migration-figures-gbr-intl/index.html

135. Taylor, D. (2023), 'Data undermines Jenrick's claim about asylum seekers saying they are children', *The Guardian*, 11 June 2023, viewed 14 June 2023, https://www.theguardian.com/uk-news/2023/jun/11/data-undermines-robert-jenrick-claim-about-asylum-seekers-saying-they-are-children.

136. Jenrick, R. (2023), 'Illegal Migration Update', *UK Parliament*, June 2023, viewed 14 June 2023, https://questions-statements.parliament.uk/written-statements/detail/2023-06-08/hcws837.

137. BBC (2023), 'Interview of Stephen Kinnock, shadow minister of immigration, by Victoria Derbyshire', *BBC Newsnight*, 26 April 2023.

138. Solomon, 'Multiple government defeats are likely when the illegal immigration bill heads to the Lords'.

139. Williams, W. (2020), 'Windrush lessons learned review', *Home Office, GOV.UK*, viewed 3 March 2023, https://www.gov.uk/government/publications/windrush-lessons-learned-review-progress-update/windrush-lessons-learned-review-progress-update-accessible.

140. Braverman, S. (2023), 'Update on the Windrush Lessons Learned Review Recommendations', *UK Parliament*, 23 January 2023, viewed 3 March 2023, https://questions-statements.parliament.uk/written-statements/detail/2023-01-26/hcws523.

141. Gentleman, A. and Syal, R. (2023), 'Windrush inquiry head disappointed as Braverman drops 'crucial' measures', *The Guardian*, 26 January 2023, viewed 3 March 2023, https://www.theguardian.com/uk-news/2023/jan/26/windrush-inquiry-head-wendy-williams-disappointed-suella-braverman-drops-crucial-measures.

142. Arnold, E. (2012), *Working with Families of African Caribbean Origin: Understanding Issues around Immigration and Attachment*, London and Philadelphia: Jessica Kingsley Publishers.

143. Mudlark121 (2016), 'Today in London's radical history: Fascist rally in Ridley Road market, smashed by Jewish 43 Group, 1947', *past tense, London radical histories and possibilities*, viewed 3 March 2023, https://pasttenseblog.wordpress.com/2016/06/01/today-in-londons-radical-history-fascist-rally-in-ridley-road-market-smashed-by-jewish-43-group–1947/.

144. BBC (2023), 'Any questions', *BBC Radio 4*, 29 April 2023.

145. Rogers, A. (2023), 'Illegal Migration Bill suffers 20 defeats in the House of Lords in fresh blow for Rishi Sunak', *Sky News*, 5 July 2023, viewed 11 July 2023, https://news.sky.com/story/illegal-migration-bill-suffers-20-defeats-in-house-of-lords-in-fresh-blow-for-rishi-sunak-12915729.

146. Singh, A. (2023), 'Home Office has painted over Mickey Mouse murals at asylum centre for lone children', *iNews*, 6 July 2023, viewed 11 July 2023, https://inews.co.uk/news/politics/home-office-painted-mickey-mouse-murals-children-asylum-centre-2461147.

147. Mandela, N. (1995), 'Nelson Mandela quotes about children', *Nelson Mandela's Children's Fund website*, 12 August 2015, viewed 3 March 2023, https://www.nelsonmandelachildrensfund.com/news/nelson-mandela-quotes-about-children.

INDEX

Abbott, Diane 29
Across Seven Seas and Thirteen Rivers (Adams) 6
Adams, Caroline 6
adult life 13–15, 179–80
affectional/emotional bonds 3, 11–12, 131
Afghanistan 19, 114, 152, 155, 184, 186, 192
Afwerki, Isaias 153–4
age assessment 185, 187
Ahmed Ali 15–16, 125–30, 132, 139, 152, 176–7, 192
Akbar, Shireen 36
Akikur 84
Akuma 64, 67
Albania 151
Al-Huda mosque 128, 130, 132, 137, 192
Ali 159, 161–2, 164. *See also* Ahmed Ali; Altab Ali
Ali El Faki, Zainab 182
Ali, Waris 75
All-Party Parliamentary Group on Immigration Detention 185
Altab Ali 73
Alÿs, Francis 175–6
Amin. *See* Ruhul Amin
Anglo-Indian 30–3
Ansar Ahmed Ullah 7
Anschluss 18–9
An Viet 97, 102–4
Anya 167–8, 170, 172, 174
Arab Spring 138, 154
Arandora Star 23
Argun Imamzade 15, 39–49, 141, 176–7, 180, 192
Argun Printers and Stationers 39
Argyll and Bute Council 159, 162–3
Arnold, Elaine 191
arrival 12–13, 177
Arts of the Sikh Kingdoms (exhibition) 89
Ashford 100
Association of Directors of Social Services 186
asylum backlog 188
Aydin 43, 46
Auschwitz concentration camp 19, 24
Ayub 75–6, 80–3, 86, 179

Bangladesh 15, 73–7, 79, 82–85
Bangladeshi 73–5, 81, 84, 87, 178–9, 191
Bangladeshi settlement in east London 4–5
Bangladeshi Youth Organisations 82, 83

Bangladesh Liberation War 84
Bangladesh Youth Movement 73, 84
Banglatown 4, 191
Barnett. *See* Lisa Barnett
Barnardo's 186
Baroness Uddin of Bethnal Green. *See* Pola Uddin
Battle of Brick Lane 5, 73, 190–1
Bengali 73–4, 82, 83–5, 127–8, 141
Bengali Workers Action Group 74
Bethnal Green 1, 75, 80, 84, 121, 125, 130, 139–40
Biafra (civil war) 15, 63–6, 69, 71–2, 180
Biên Hòa 98–9
Bilqis 16, 135–8, 176
Binboga. *See* Eylem Binboga
Black and British: A Forgotten History (Olusoga) 4
Black Lives Matter 190–1
Blanca Stern 19–25, 180, 192
Bow 57
Bran. *See* Gabriela Bran
Bran. *See* Henry Bran
Braverman, Suella 184, 186, 188–9, 192
Bressey, Caroline 4
Brew for Two 117–18, 192
Brick Lane 7, 9, 73, 75, 77, 78, 82, 191
British citizen/citizenship 61, 104, 131–2, 149–50, 164, 172, 176, 193
British East India Company 30, 90
British Empire 2, 4, 15, 40, 48, 52, 64, 90, 135, 176
British National Party 122
BSIX Sixth Form College in Hackney 147
Bucha 173
Burao 125–6, 129, 139–41

Calais 19, 98, 114, 152–5, 173, 182–3
Calcutta 15, 30, 32–3, 35, 37–8, 180–1
Camden Committee for Community Relations 60, 74
Cameron, David 37, 158, 186
Catholic 30–1, 37, 59, 98, 102, 107–8
Catholic with Confucian Tendencies (Vu) 97
Cazenove Road 18, 22, 58, 60
Chanukah 20–2
Charedi community 18
Chelsea Hospital 127
Child Migrant Stories (films) 10, 180, 191
Child Migrant Stories: Voices Past and Present (film) 113–14

Index

child migration schemes 3
Child Migrants Welcome? (film) 7, 17, 153, 163, 182, 192
child migration
    past and present 2–3
    research 7–10
child soldiers 66, 109, 113–14
Children Act (1989) 186–7
Christian 32, 98, 107, 113, 142, 149
Christmas 35, 98, 101–2
Clapton School 24, 54, 137
class 54–5, 70, 82, 91, 179
Clissold Park 21
colourism 59
Conakry 143, 147
Council of Turkish Cypriot Associations (CTCA) 48
COVID-19 87, 130, 150, 163, 178
creativity 180–1
criminality 188
Cyprus 39–40, 43, 45–6, 48, 180

Dachau concentration camp 20
Dalston 59, 103, 120–1, 191–2
Damascus 157–8, 162
D'Aubuisson, Roberto 108–9
Dear Home Office: Still Pending 151, 155–6
departures 11–12, 175–6
de Souza, Dame Rachel 186–7
Diwali 89
Djibouti 126, 153
Don't Cross the Bridge before You Get to the River (Alÿs) 175
drawings 9
Dublin 111 26, 184
Dubs, Lord Alf/Alfred 17, 19, 25, 188, 192
Duffy-Syedi. *See* Kate Duffy-Syedi
Duncan Ross 15, 29–38, 39, 180, 192

Eastbourne 150
East End of London 4–5
Easter 98, 105, 168
Edinburgh Festival 151, 155
education 13, 178
Egypt 160
Eid 120, 137–8, 149
El Salvador 107–15
Empire Windrush 51, 53
English as an Additional Language (EAL) 158, 169
English for Speakers of Other Languages (ESOL) 140–1
EOKA 40
Epping Forest College 122
Eritrea 16, 151–6
Errol 57, 59, 61

Ethiopia 151, 153
ethnicity 179
European Commission Against Racism and Intolerance 120
European Court of Human Rights (ECHR) 189
EU Withdrawal Bill 26
extended family 3, 11–14, 26, 53–4, 59, 64, 89, 140, 176–7, 191
Eylem Binboga 15, 117–24, 129, 176, 178–9, 181, 192

family households 12–13
family migration 3, 11–12
Farabundo Martí National Liberation Front (FMLN) 108–9, 111
Farage, Nigel 15, 30, 37
Farah, Sir Mo 2, 132, 141
Fedaa 161–2, 164–5
Federation of Bangladeshi Youth Organisations 83
feelings of home 4, 8, 14, 37, 179–80
Feldman. *See* Rayah Feldman
female genital mutilation (FGM) 144–5, 176
Flame in My Heart (film) 82
foreign national offenders (FNOs) 52, 61, 190
Forsyth, Frederick 71–2
foster care/carer, 13, 127, 153, 155, 182–3, 191
Four Aces 59
Fryer, Peter 4
Fuerza Armada de El Salvador (FAES) 108

Gabon 65–6
Gabriela Bran 114
Galyna 171–4
Gardiner-Smith, Beth 184
gender 139, 179
Gentleman, Amelia 52, 61
George Green School 140–1
Germany 21–2, 40, 118, 173
Glasgow 71, 91–5, 158, 163–5, 178, 192
Glasgow airport 160
Glasgow School of Art 89, 92
Global North 12, 175–6
Global South 12, 176
Gluck. *See* Necha Gluck
Gluck, Rabbi Herschel 17–9, 24–5
'GO HOME' vans 29
Greek Cypriots 40, 43, 45–6
Green Line 46
Green Street Market 192
Group 1 refugee status 183
Group 2 refugee status 183–5
Grunfeld, Judith 22
guardianship programme 182
Guinea 16, 143–5, 148–9
Guru-Murthy, Krishnan 29

Habib, Shekiba 182
Hackney 5, 7–8, 17–19, 25, 39–40, 46, 53, 60, 63–4,
        64, 70–1, 97, 102–3, 105, 113, 120–1, 137
Hackney Community College 131
Hackney Downs Grammar School 34, 192
Hackney Social Services 147
Hadhramaut 135–8
Hare Duke, Teresa 7
Hargeisa 154
Harris. *See* Mitch/Mitchell Harris
Harrow 151–2, 155
Heavens, Simon 82
Helen Bamber Foundation 187
Helmi's bakery 165
Henry Bran 7, 15, 107–15, 176, 180
Hindus 32–3
Hinrichsen, Klaus 23
Holi 32
Holmes, Colin 3, 97, 104–5
Holocaust 6, 18, 24–5
home. *See* feelings of home
Home (film) 25
Home Office 13, 23, 29, 37, 51–2, 56, 61, 74, 86,
        121, 131, 146–8, 151–2, 155–6, 173, 177,
        182–3, 186–8
Homerton Hospital 54, 56, 113
Homes for Ukraine scheme 167, 172–3, 183
Horsham 167, 169–70
hostile environment 29, 51, 180
The House That Is Not There (film) 114
Humans for Rights Network 187
human rights 2, 11, 153–4, 183, 189, 193
Hurmus Imamzade 39–40, 45–7, 192

Igbo 63–4, 68, 180
Illegal Migration Bill/Act 2023 189, 188–90, 192
Imamzade. *See* Argun Imamzade
Imamzade. *See* Hurmus Imamzade
Immigration Act 1971 51
Immigration Act 2016 19
impact on adult life 8, 14–15, 179–80
India 30, 32–4, 37, 89–90, 180
insider status 6
intercommunal violence 40
İşçi Birliği 121–2
Isle of Man 22–3
Isle of Bute 7–8, 16, 71, 158, 163, 165, 179–80, 183,
        191–2
Italy 153–4

Jalal Rajonuddin 73–6, 83–6, 179
Jama. *See* Nimo Jama
Jama 7, 125, 127–8, 130–2
Jamaica 52–4, 56–61
Jana 161–2, 164–5

Javid, Sajid 52, 163
Jenrick, Robert 187, 193, 220 n.106, 222 n.135
Jewish 1, 15, 17–20, 22–6, 34, 44, 46, 55, 57–8, 69,
        79, 143, 191–2
John Bull's Island: Immigration to Britain 1871–1971
        (Holmes) 3–4
Johnson, Samuel 5
Johnson, Boris 73, 163–4
Jones, Dan 1
Jordan 158, 160
journeys 12, 176–7
'Jungle' (Calais) 19, 152, 155

Karachi 89–90, 94
Kate Duffy-Syedi 151, 155
Kayseri 117
Kindertransport 2–3, 5, 15, 17–20, 24–6, 176–7, 192
A Kind of English (film) 82
Kingston (Jamaica) 54, 57
Kinnock, Stephen 190
Kristallnacht 20
Kurdi, Aylan 10
Kurdish Alevis 15, 119–20, 122
Kurdish language 120
Kushner, Tony 5
Kyiv 167–8, 170–1

Labour Party 75, 83, 110
Lammy, David 51–2, 60–1
Lebanon 160
Legacies of Biafra exhibition 63
leper 32
Libya 154
Life Is a Destiny (film) 47–8
*The Lightless Sky – An Afghan Refugee Boy's Journey
        to Escape to a New Life in Britain* (Passarlay)
        183
Linh Vu 7, 15, 97–106, 176, 179
Lisa Barnett 174
Local Government Association 186
London, Louise 26
Lorna Morss 159–62, 165
Lue. *See* Richard Lue

Malek 157–65, 178–80
Malik, Kenan 182
Malkie 20, 24
Mandela, Nelson 193
Manuhar 9, 73, 75–6, 81
Mariam 16, 143–50, 152, 176, 178, 182–3, 187
Marie 1, 7, 10, 193
Mariia 16, 167–72, 174
Mariupol 173
Martinez, Hernandez 108
Matthews, Lisa 182–3

Index

Maureen Shaw 159–61, 163, 165
Maurice Nwokeji 15, 63–72, 177, 180, 192
May, Theresa 29, 163–4, 187
McIntrye, Renford 52
Médecins Sans Frontières 184
medicine 76, 129, 165
Meisler, Frank 17, 21, 25
mental health 14, 54, 146, 152, 171, 180
Mid-Autumn Festival (Chinese/Vietnamese) 98
migrants
    oral history with 5–6
    testimonies 5–6
Migration Museum 63
migration to Britain 3–5
Mile End 29–30, 36, 105, 128, 181
Mitch/Mitchell Harris 10, 18, 39, 47, 48, 68–9, 71,
    97, 105, 113, 153, 158–9, 163
mixed heritage 94
mobile phones 48
modern slavery 2, 187
Mogadishu 16, 130–3
Momen, Abdul 74, 86–7
Montefiore Centre 81
Morss. See Lorna Morss
Moseley, Clare 184
motherland 15, 31, 33, 54, 171
Mount Stuart 162–3
Museo de Arte Contemporáneo de Buenos Aires
    (MACBA) 175
Muslim and/or Muslims 18, 29, 32–3, 37–9, 43, 79,
    84, 85, 89, 93–4, 120, 142–3, 149
My Heart Belongs to … (film) 49
My V&A tours 7, 107

National Front 5, 8, 15, 38, 73–5
Nationality and Borders Act 2022 183–90, 192
Nazis 20, 22, 24–5
Necha Gluck 26
Newbigin, John 80
Newham College 140
Nigeria 63–4, 180
Nimo Jama 138–42, 177–8
North Yemen 135–6
Nwokeji. See Maurice Nwokeji

Olusoga, David 4
open-ended approach 6, 8
Operation Vaken 29
oral history 5–6, 8–10
Ottoman Empire 40, 135
outsider status 6
Oxford Migration Observatory 188

Pakistan 73, 76–8, 81, 86, 89–95
Palanac, Aleks 181

Paphos 39, 40, 42–3, 45
Paris 44, 104, 119, 191
partition (India) 32–3, 89, 95, 180
Passarlay, Gulwali 183, 187, 193
Passing Tides (film) 97, 105, 192
Patel, Priti 163–4, 184, 186
Pat Till 158–9
People's Democratic Republic of Yemen (South
    Yemen) 135
Pho Mile 191
Phosphoros Theatre 151–2, 155, 210 n.2
photographs 9
Plashet Park 76
Poland 168, 171, 173
Pola Uddin 75–77, 84–6, 90, 159, 176–9
political activism 8, 14, 75, 78, 81, 154, 190
post-partition (India) 33, 180
Progressive Youth Organisation 73, 75, 81
PTSD study 181
Purbo London (film) 80–2

Queen Mary University of London 2, 10, 135
Quran 90, 93, 130, 136, 139, 145

Rabia 161, 164–5
racism 3, 6, 8, 13–14, 34, 38, 56, 59, 61, 74, 77, 81,
    91, 94, 178–9, 183, 188, 190–1
Rajonuddin. See Jalal Rajonuddin
Rajshahi 76–7
Rastafarianism 15, 64
Rayah Feldman 143, 147, 149
Red Cross 65, 154
Refugee and Migrant Children's Consortium 186
Refugee Council 146–7, 181, 185–6, 190
Refugee Week 107, 163
refugees
    Jewish 22–3
    oral history with 5–6
    Syrian 158–60, 163
    Ukrainian 167, 173–4
reggae 59, 63–4
remittances 128
Republic of Yemen 135
returns 85, 179
Richard Lue 53, 57–62, 177, 179–180
Ridley Road Market 69, 103, 192
Right to Remain 51–2, 182
Roberta 53–7, 59–61, 177–9
Rock Against Racism 38, 190
Romero, Oscar 108
Ross. See Duncan Ross
Rothesay 158–9, 163
Rothesay Joint Campus 158, 163, 191
Royal College of Art 89, 92
Rudd, Amber 52

Ruhul Amin 74–6, 78–82, 177–8
Rutnam, Philip 188
Rwanda 2, 10, 185, 188–90, 193

Sabbath 21–3
Safa 161, 164
safe and legal routes 164, 184, 186, 190, 192
Safe Passage 26, 184–5
Sahara 154, 176
Said 16, 130–3
Saigon 98–9, 104
Salam 9, 73–76, 80, 81, 86
Saleh, Ali Abdullah 138
San Miguel 107–8, 110–112, 114
Schonfeld, Rabbi 17, 20–1, 23, 192
School of Oriental and African Studies (SOAS) 63, 102
Scotland 91, 94, 158–9, 161, 182–3, 192
Second World War 2, 17, 19, 41, 51, 53, 103, 125, 153, 167, 170, 174, 183
Seeking Sanctuary on a Scottish Island (film) 71, 163
Separation and Reunion Forum UK 191
Shamiana, the Mughal Tent exhibition 36
Shaw. *See* Maureen Shaw
shebeen 59–60
Shefford 22–3
Shushik 167–72, 174
Sierra Leone 144–5, 149
Singapore 100
Sivanandan, Ambalavaner 2, 33
Solomon, Enver 127, 190
Somalia 5, 16, 126, 128–9, 135, 138–9, 151
Somalia (civil war) 130–3
Somaliland 16, 125, 128–31, 138–9
Sopley 100–1
South Bank 63, 149, 152
South China Sea 97, 100, 106
South Yemen 135
Spain 54, 80, 124, 184
Spitalfields 4, 73, 80, 83, 180
Stamford Hill 18, 21, 24, 192
Stark, Freya 136
Staying Power: The History of Black People in Britain (Fryer) 4
Stepney Green School 81, 114, 127–8, 131
stepping out 13–14, 178–9
Stern. *See* Blanca Stern
Stoke Newington 17–18, 24, 58, 60, 191
Stop and Search 60
St Paul's 29, 35–6, 127
Sudan 152–4, 186, 192–3
super-diverse city 4, 178
Surma 7
sus laws 60, 190
Sutton House 192

Swadhinata Trust 7
Swallow, Deborah 36, 77
Sylhet 4, 6, 73, 75–80, 83, 177
Sylhet Town 78, 81
Syrian Pie restaurant 164–5
Syria/Syrian/Syrians 16, 19, 71, 85, 114, 158–65, 173, 176, 179–81, 183

Temple-Smith, Sarah 181–2, 190
Temporary Protection Directive (TPD) 173
Thanh Vu, MBE 7, 97–8, 106
Thompson, Paul 5
Thorney Island 97–8, 100, 105
Tilbury Dock 34
Till. *See* Pat Till
TMT 40
Tottenham 51, 54–5, 80
Tower Hamlets 6, 76, 81, 83–5, 127–8, 140, 141, 191
Tower Hamlets Arts Committee 80
Tower Hamlets College 110, 128, 132, 140–1
Tower Hamlets Council 83, 128
Tower Hamlets Social Services 127
Tower Hamlets Training Forum 7, 75, 77, 81–2, 86
trauma 3, 6–9, 12, 14–15, 19, 37, 63, 71, 113, 168, 171, 176, 180–1, 185
Trump, Donald 87
trust building 8
Turkey 15, 39–40, 46, 48, 117, 119
Turkish Cypriot 40, 43, 46, 48

Uddin. *See* Pola Uddin
Ugwumpiti (film) 63, 65, 71
the UK 2, 8, 27, 31, 33, 38, 44, 59, 62–3, 70–1, 90, 141, 153, 155, 167, 175–6, 185, 194–6, 201, 206–10, 212–17
Ukraine 2, 16, 167–74, 176, 183, 192–3
Ukraine Family Scheme 172–3
UK Resettlement Scheme 163, 184
Ullah. *See* Ansar Ahmed Ullah
Ultra-Orthodox Jewish 17–18
unaccompanied (child migrants) 12–13, 26, 173, 184–8
UNHCR 181, 183–4
United Kingdom Independence Party (UKIP) 30, 37
United Nations Convention on the Rights of the Child (UNCRC) 11, 12, 176
the United States 5, 55, 61, 107, 111, 169
University of Brighton 122
University of Dundee 178
University of Westminster 148
UN 1951 Refugee Convention 183
UN Security Council 46
Urdu 91, 93–4

Index

V&A 1, 8, 36, 89, 94–5
V&A Museum of Childhood 1–2, 7–8, 36, 49, 89, 94–5, 114, 130, 135, 193
Vanriel, Vernon 52
Vietnam 97–105, 191–2
Vietnam War 99, 101
Vietnamese New Year 101–2
The Voice of the Past (Thompson) 5
Vu. *See* Linh Vu
Vu. *See* Thanh Vu, MBE
Vulnerable Persons Resettlement Scheme (VPRS) 16, 158, 163
vyshyvankas (shirts) 170

walking interviews 9
Walthamstow School for Girls 121
War of Liberation 86

Warsi, Sayeeda 188
Whitechapel 77, 81, 130, 191–2
Wilson, Paulette 52
Windrush Compensation Scheme 62
Windrush Lessons Learned report 52, 61, 190
Windrush Lessons Learned Review 52, 61, 190
Windrush scandal 51, 61, 183
Winton, Nicholas 25
Woodberry Down Estate 103
World in the East End gallery 1–2, 7

Yemen 18, 135–8
Yemenis 137
Yosef 16, 151–4, 176, 182–3

Zohra 15, 89–95, 104, 178–9